THE
ASTROLOGY BIBLE

♈ ♉ ♊ ♋ ♌ ♍ ♎ ♏ ♐ ♑ ♒ ♓

THE
ASTROLOGY BIBLE
THE DEFINITIVE GUIDE TO THE ZODIAC

Judy Hall

 A GODSFIELD BOOK
www.godsfieldpress.com

First published in Great Britain in 2005
by Godsfield Press, a division of
Octopus Publishing Group Ltd
2–4 Heron Quays
Docklands
London E14 4JP

10 9 8 7 6 5 4 3 2 1

Printed and bound in China

ISBN 1 84181 245 5
EAN 9781841812458

CONTENTS

Introduction

A highly versatile tool, astrology gives you the ability to know yourself fully. The map of the heavens at the moment of your birth, known as your natal or birthchart, is a reflection of your unique personality, it can advise on your love life, point you towards a suitable career, even help you be a better parent. But astrology is much more than this. One of the best means available to understand other people, once you know how to combine the different factors in a birthchart, you can look behind the face someone presents to the world and discover who that person really is.

For thousands of years, astrologers have been studying the effects of planetary activity and its correspondence with human behaviour, personality, health, karma and much else besides. This 'bible' contains everything you need to know about astrology. The more you understand of this profound art, the greater insight you will gain into your life and the lives of the people around you. If you already have astrological skills, this book will deepen and expand your knowledge of zodiac lore.

TREASURE TROVE

To the ancients, the planets were living breathing beings who ruled precise areas of life that were described by the signs of the zodiac. Each sign and planet had its own physiological correspondences and associated herbs which could be used for healing. Each sign and planet also had its own metal, gems, colours and animals. All this knowledge was charted over the millennia and became a treasure trove of astrological lore. This book contains everything you need to know about the astrological correspondences and how to apply them. The more you understand about astrology, the greater the insight you gain into your life and that of everyone around you.

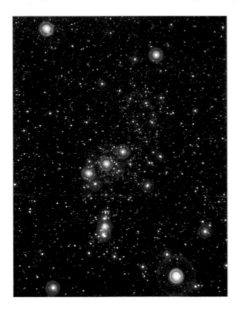

The zodiac

In the first section of this book you will explore the signs of the zodiac and their quintessential personalities, gaining insights into what they are like as parents and children, discovering their strengths and weaknesses,

Ancient man looked at the sky and saw pictures.

and delving deep into their emotions and minds. This section brings to light shadow qualities and karma, likes and dislikes, and attitudes towards money. Here you will also discover which careers and leisure activities the different signs are best suited.

The planets and their surroundings

In the sections that follow you will find everything you need to understand the planets and the effect of the geometric relationships they form with each other; the elements and qualities to which signs belong and which subtly alter the way planetary energy flows; and the structure of the chart, the theatre in which the planets play out the dance of life.

Synthesis

The art of astrology lies in bringing together the different components of the birthchart into a coherent whole. Piecing it All Together (see pages 288–97) shows you how to synthesize the various parts, weighing strengths and weaknesses to see how the energies will manifest as personality and potential.

Using astrology in your life

However, there is more to astrology than reading character from the natal chart. Astrology can help you with your relationships and your health. It also assists you, by understanding the significance of planetary movement from day to day, with the timing of events and aligning to the unfolding future.

A comprehensive glossary at the back of this book (see pages 390–93) defines astrological terms.

PAST AND PRESENT

Astrology in ancient times

Humans have looked to the heavens for guidance since time began.
Some 35,000 years ago, one of our ancestors scratched a lunar
calendar on to a piece of bone to record the phases of the Moon.
Worshipped for its life-giving powers, the waxing and waning of this
mystical body told early communities when to plant and harvest, and
guided the hunter. Stonehenge, dated 20,000 years later, was built as
an elaborate lunar and solar calculator, mapping out complex
astronomical phenomena in stone. Similar sites and devices have been
discovered all over the ancient world.

In these earliest times, no division was made between astrology –
divining meaning from close observation of the skies – and astronomy,
the strictly scientific study of the celestial bodies. In Babylon, Arabia,
India, China and Egypt, maps of
the sky enabled the astronomer-
priests to calculate propitious
timings for affairs of state and
royal marriages. Their observations
were far from primitive. As the
sky maps in ancient Egyptian
temples show, early astrologers
were aware of events in deep space

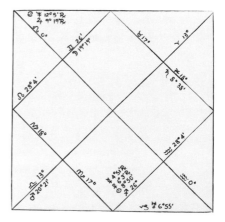

*Medieval and ancient charts were
drawn within a square format.*

far beyond the scope of all but the most modern telescope.

The recent past

In medieval Europe, and in early America, astrology pervaded all aspects of life. Medical practice was based on astrology: herbs were grown, harvested and prescribed according to astrological principles. The moment an illness struck, a chart was drawn up for the sufferer, who would be given a herbal mixture based on its interpretation.

Many medieval manuscripts have wonderful zodiacal illustrations.

Astrologers of the Middle Ages also refined the art of prediction. Nostradamus is perhaps the best known of these medieval astrologers, although his projections had to be disguised in obscure 'quartets' to avoid the attention of the Inquisition.

Astrology today

In its contemporary form, astrology is used in all walks of life, by anyone who seeks greater understanding. Astrology is used regularly as a psychological and counselling tool, to inform business decisions and in career guidance. As a practical tool for enhancing personal wellbeing, it can identify areas of compatibility and conflict, indicate the perfect timing for an important event, and point the way forward when all paths seem blocked.

ASTROLOGICAL DISCIPLINES

Natal astrology

Natal astrology is concerned with the natal, or birth, chart as it describes life unfolding, from birth to old age (see also page 22). You can use it to arrive at a better understanding of self: to confirm your personality type, identify your emotional needs and to explore your inner thought processes. A birthchart reveals innate potential. By recognizing your strengths and weaknesses, you can take advantage of opportunities for growth as they arise. Natal astrology is also used to advise people in specific areas of life, such as relationships and careers.

Astrologers have always seen a correlation between events in the heavens and those on earth.

Predictive astrology

Astrology has been used for millennia to predict the future. Whilst the planets do not actually make things happen, astrologers have long observed correlations between particular planetary activity and earthbound events taking place at that moment. Accidents are more likely to happen, for example, when the explosive planet Uranus crosses paths with the fiery, headstrong Mars.

By observing the day-to-day movement of the planets and calculating how that movement will affect your sun-sign or natal chart, a predictive astrologer can foresee events, recognize the possibility of change and identify opportunities or blockages in your path. Nothing is static: by understanding the progression of the planets, you can learn how to harness changes in your favour.

Counselling astrology

People tend to consult an astrologer when they reach a crisis point in life. They may seek understanding or reassurance or a way to deal with change. For this reason, many astrologers combine their astrological understanding with qualification as a therapist or counsellor. In this capacity, they can help identify 'lifescripts' – inbuilt, unconscious expectations passed on from parents that limit life experience. By learning how to respond to events and people in a new way, you can regain control and reach your full potential.

Synastry (relationship analysis)

Synastry is the branch of astrology that looks at relationships. It is used to identify areas of compatibility, to overcome innate difficulties in a relationship and to find new ways to increase intimacy. Simply comparing Sun and Moon signs with a partner can lead to a better understanding of the other person and the dynamics at play within a relationship. To gain deep insight into someone's personality and emotional needs, you need study his or her birthchart (see also pages 354–57 and 364–7).

Medical astrology

The first task of a medical astrologer is to ascertain when the illness first struck. A chart is then prepared for that moment that will uncover the underlying cause, often revealing stresses and strains, depleted energies and subtle imbalances and deficiencies. As part of a holistic course of treatment, a medical astrologer usually prescribes appropriate herbs or homeopathic remedies (see also Astrology and health, page 368).

Karmic (past-life) astrology

A karmic astrologer seeks the answers to the problems of the present in past lives. As such, a karmic astrological chart pinpoints the credits, deficits and in-built patterns of emotional expectation an individual carries from life to life. This branch of astrology is used to help people understand relationships, vocations, family life and to bring an end to recurring patterns of negative behaviour.

Horary astrology

Horary astrologers deal in specific questions, such as 'Should I buy this house?' or 'Will I marry this person?', to which they can give unequivocal answers. A chart is prepared for the exact time the question was initiated, and a set of 'rules' is then applied to arrive at the answer.

Electional astrology

Electional astrology is concerned with identifying propitious moments. If a budding entrepreneur wants to find out the best time to set up a new business, an electional astrologer can draw up charts for several possible dates and pinpoint the most favourable.

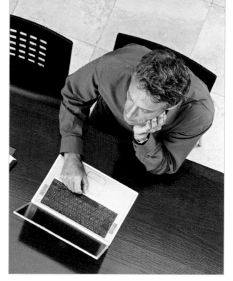

Many businesses benefit from astrological expertise.

Mundane astrology

Encompassing the specialized fields of financial and political astrology, mundane astrology is concerned with world events and socioeconomic trends. Specialist astrologers can predict the movement of stocks and shares with reliable accuracy and many businesses take advantage of this skill.

Business astrology

Business astrology is a rapidly expanding field. Many businesses actually employ their own astrologer, in much the same way ancient kings did. An in-house astrologer may be tasked with building personality profiles on prospective employees, predicting financial and marketing trends or giving advice on the best time to buy and sell assets.

ASTRODATA

The geocentric framework

Astrology is geocentric, meaning it places earth at the centre of our universe. Although we know that the earth actually rotates around the Sun, astrologers draw their charts as though the Sun, Moon and the planets move around the earth. They do this because this is what *appears* to be the case when you view the heavens from earth. Astrological charts are presented as wheels because they also show the hidden part of the sky below the horizon.

Astrological circles

The drawing of astrological charts has its basis in a series of intersecting circles. Although these circles are invisible, they can be plotted mathematically. The circular path taken by the Sun each year is called the ecliptic. The imaginary circle that girdles the earth and marks its centre is the equator. The name given to the lateral extension of the terrestrial equator into space is the celestial equator.

A fourth circle is formed by the great wheel of stars, grouped into constellations, that appear to lie in the path of the Sun as it makes its annual journey around the earth. This vast circle, which is divided into 12 equal areas, is the zodiac.

The Great Year

Because the gravitational pull exerted by the Sun and the Moon is unequal, the earth does not rotate uniformly. Like a spinning top, it turns with a wide, swinging motion, executing a slow precession. An imaginary white dot marked on the very top of the earth would therefore appear to move around in a circle. The time taken by the poles of the earth to complete an entire rotation around this circle is known as the Great Year – a period of approximately 25,800 years as we normally understand them.

The precession of the equinoxes

When the Sun, viewed from our perspective, makes its annual journey around the earth, it appears to cross over the equator twice – south-north into the northern hemisphere and north-south into the southern

THE SOLSTICES AND EQUINOXES

June 21 · Summer solstice
(Sun overhead at Tropic of Cancer)

September 21 · Autumn equinox
(Sun overhead at equator)

Sun's path

Terrestrial equator

Ecliptic

March 21 · Spring equinox
(Sun overhead at equator)

December 21 · Winter solstice
(Sun overhead at Tropic of Capricorn)

THE AGE OF AQUARIUS

For the last 2,000 years, the Sun has been rising in the constellation of Pisces. In keeping with the distinctive characteristics of that sign, the Age of Pisces on earth has been characterized by religion and the establishment of societies that share a belief system. Astrologers believe that the age that is dawning now, the Age of Aquarius, will be a humanitarian age in which men and women will strive to live freely and equally in peace and brotherhood.

hemisphere. These biennial crossing points are what astronomers call the equinoxes.

Over the course of each Great Year, as the earth makes its slow rotation, the crossing points of the Sun move slightly with respect to the background stars, so that the Sun appears to edge towards the neighbouring constellation. This phenomenon is known as the 'precession of the equinoxes'.

Astrologically speaking, the Great Year is divided into 12 'months' or ages, each approximately 2,000 years long. With each new age, the Sun appears to rise in a new constellation, or sign of the zodiac, at the vernal (spring) equinox. Over the course of one entire Great Year, the vernal equinox will therefore travel through all the signs of the zodiac.

The symbolic zodiac

Astrologers recognize that the universe is not static and that the skies above us are constantly shifting. However, rather than redraw the zodiac, they prefer to use the zodiac as it was drawn up when astrology was first practised. According to this original zodiac, the vernal equinox *always* takes place at what astrologers call 0° Aries.

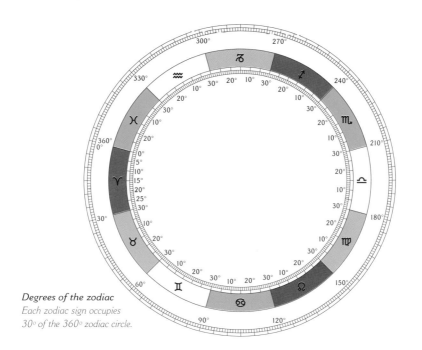

Degrees of the zodiac
Each zodiac sign occupies
30° of the 360° zodiac circle.

The symbolic, astrological Sun then continues on its journey, moving counter-clockwise through the constellations, to finish the year in the sign of Pisces.

The Nodes

The Nodes are abstract points in space, based on the points at which the planets cross the ecliptic, the annual path of the Sun. Although every planet has Nodes, most astrologers only utilize the Nodes of the Moon, potent points in the Moon's monthly orbit around the Earth and site of eclipses (see also pages 220–27).

ASTROLOGICAL TIME

Greenwich Mean Time

Astrologers base their calculations according to Greenwich Mean Time (GMT). You need to make adjustment to work out planetary position at the time of your birth if you were born in a time zone other than GMT. For countries east of London, add the time difference to the time of your birth to find GMT; subtract the difference for countries west of London. You may also need to make adjustment to allow for Daylight Saving, since this would also put the official time of your birth outside GMT.

Planetary placements

Astrologers use tables of planetary movements to ascertain where the planets are at any given time. A table such as this, known as an ephemeris, also shows the phases of the Moon and eclipses.

TIME ZONES

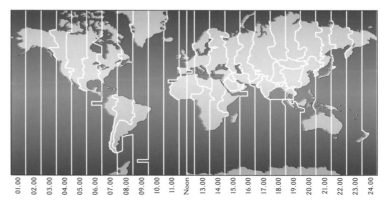

01.00 02.00 03.00 04.00 05.00 06.00 07.00 08.00 09.00 10.00 11.00 Noon 13.00 14.00 15.00 16.00 17.00 18.00 19.00 20.00 21.00 22.00 23.00 24.00

To ascertain the position of a planet, turn to the relevant month in the ephemeris, then read down the left-hand column to find the date and day. Place a ruler across the page to read off the position of the planets. (Nowadays computers make the calculation and adjustment for time differences for you.)

An ephemeris gives positions at noon, so adjustments are needed to calculate planetary positions at other times. To do this, note how far the planet has moved since noon the previous day, divide the answer by 24 to give hourly movement, then add or subtract the hourly movement, multiplied by the time difference between noon and the time being calculated, for example multiply by 4 for 4 pm.

HOW TO READ AN EPHEMERIS

NOVEMBER 2003 **LONGITUDE**

Day	Sid. Time	☉	0 hr ☽	Noon ☽	True ☊	☿	♀	♂	♃	♄	♅	♆	♇
1 Sa	14 41 27	8♏38 44	5♒ 50 23	12♒ 33 39	20♉ 31.9	13♏ 6.8	28♏15.2	7♓29.9	13♍ 9.7	13♋ 9.7	28♒55.0	10♒25.5	18♐ 18.3
2 Su	14 45 24	9 38 47	19 11 35	25 44 27	20R 31.4	14 42.6	29 29.8	7 53.0	13 19.5	13R 11.2	28R 54.6	10 25.9	18 20.1
3 M	14 49 20	10 38 50	2♓ 12 33	8♓ 36 13	20 30.5	16 17.9	0♐ 44.4	8 16.6	13 29.1	13 10.3	28 54.3	10 26.2	18 22.0
4 Tu	14 53 17	11 38 55	14 55 47	21 11 35	20 29.3	17 52.7	1 59.0	8 40.6	13 38.6	13 9.3	28 54.1	10 26.6	18 23.9
5 W	14 57 13	12 39 2	27 23 58	3♈ 33 14	20 28.1	19 27.2	3 13.6	9 5.0	13 48.1	13 8.2	28 53.9	10 27.1	18 25.9
6 Th	15 1 10	13 39 10	9♈ 39 43	15 43 43	20 27.1	21 1.2	4 28.2	9 29.8	13 57.4	13 7.0	28 53.8	10 27.6	18 27.8
7 F	15 5 6	14 39 20	21 45 31	20 45 23	20 26.4	22 34.9	5 42.8	9 55.0	14 6.6	13 5.7	28 53.7	10 28.1	18 29.8
8 Sa	15 9 3	15 39 32	3♉ 43 35	9♉ 40 24	20 26.0	24 8.1	6 57.4	10 20.6	14 15.7	13 4.2	28D 53.7	10 28.6	18 31.7
9 Su	15 13 0	16 39 46	15 36 3	21 30 49	20D 25.9	25 41.1	8 12.0	10 46.5	14 24.7	13 2.7	28 53.7	10 29.2	18 33.7
10 M	15 16 56	17 40 1	27 24 57	3♊ 18 44	20 26.0	27 13.7	9 26.5	11 12.8	14 33.5	13 1.0	28 53.8	10 29.8	18 35.7
11 Tu	15 20 53	18 40 19	9♊ 12 27	15 6 24	20 26.2	28 45.9	10 41.1	11 39.5	14 42.3	12 59.2	28 53.9	10 30.4	18 37.8
12 W	15 24 49	19 40 38	21 0 55	26 56 21	20 26.3	0♐ 17.8	11 55.7	12 6.5	14 50.9	12 57.4	28 54.1	10 31.1	18 39.8
13 Th	15 28 46	20 40 59	2♋ 53 4	8♋ 51 28	20R 26.4	1 49.4	13 10.3	12 33.8	14 59.5	12 55.4	28 54.3	10 31.8	18 41.9
14 F	15 32 42	21 41 21	14 51 59	20 55 3	20 26.3	3 20.7	14 24.8	13 1.5	15 7.9	12 53.3	28 54.6	10 32.6	18 43.9
15 Sa	15 36 39	22 41 46	27 1 10	3♌ 10 47	20 26.1	4 51.7	15 39.4	13 29.4	15 16.1	12 51.2	28 55.0	10 33.3	18 46.0
16 Su	15 40 35	23 42 13	9♌ 24 25	15 42 34	20 26.0	6 22.4	16 53.9	13 57.7	15 24.3	12 48.9	28 55.3	10 34.1	18 48.1
17 M	15 44 32	24 42 41	22 5 42	28 34 16	20D 25.9	7 52.7	18 8.5	14 26.3	15 32.3	12 46.5	28 55.8	10 35.0	18 50.2
18 Tu	15 48 29	25 43 11	5♍ 8 43	11♍ 49 22	20 26.1	9 22.8	19 23.0	14 55.2	15 40.2	12 44.0	28 56.3	10 35.9	18 52.4
19 W	15 52 25	26 43 43	18 36 32	25 30 23	20 26.6	10 52.5	20 37.6	15 24.3	15 48.0	12 41.4	28 56.8	10 36.8	18 54.5
20 Th	15 56 22	27 44 17	2♎ 30 58	9♎ 38 11	20 27.2	12 21.8	21 52.1	15 53.8	15 55.6	12 38.7	28 57.4	10 37.7	18 56.7
21 F	16 0 18	28 44 52	16 51 49	24 11 25	20 27.9	13 50.8	23 6.6	16 23.5	16 3.1	12 36.0	28 58.0	10 38.7	18 58.8
22 Sa	16 4 15	29 45 30	1♏ 36 24	9♏ 5 58	20 28.4	15 19.3	24 21.1	16 53.5	16 10.5	12 33.1	28 58.7	10 39.7	19 1.0
23 Su	16 8 11	0♐ 46 9	16 39 10	24 14 56	20R 28.6	16 47.4	25 35.7	17 23.7	16 17.7	12 30.1	28 59.4	10 40.7	19 3.2
24 M	16 12 8	1 46 49	1♐ 52 3	9♐ 29 18	20 28.1	18 15.0	26 50.2	17 54.3	16 24.8	12 27.1	29 0.2	10 41.8	19 5.4
25 Tu	16 16 4	2 47 31	17 5 24	24 39 7	20 27.1	19 42.1	28 4.7	18 25.0	16 31.7	12 23.9	29 1.1	10 42.9	19 7.6
26 W	16 20 1	3 48 14	2♑ 9 20	9♑ 35 1	20 25.5	21 8.5	29 19.2	18 56.1	16 38.5	12 20.7	29 2.0	10 44.0	19 9.8
27 Th	16 23 58	4 48 58	16 55 19	24 9 35	20 23.7	22 34.2	0♑ 33.7	19 27.3	16 45.2	12 17.3	29 2.9	10 45.1	19 12.0
28 F	16 27 54	5 49 44	1♒ 17 18	8♒ 18 11	20 21.9	23 59.2	1 48.2	19 58.8	16 51.7	12 13.9	29 3.9	10 46.3	19 14.2
29 Sa	16 31 51	6 50 30	15 12 7	21 59 8	20 20.6	25 23.2	3 2.7	20 30.5	16 58.0	12 10.4	29 5.0	10 47.6	19 16.5
30 Su	16 35 47	7 51 17	28 39 24	5♓ 13 12	20D 20.0	26 46.2	4 17.1	21 2.5	17 4.2	12 6.9	29 6.0	10 48.8	19 18.7

Ephemeris for November 2003 *As you can see from this ephemeris, at noon on 23 November 2003 Venus ♀ was positioned at 25°, 35.7 (within the constellation of) Sagittarius. By noon the next day, Venus had moved to 26°, 50.2 Sagittarius. So by 11 pm on 23 November, as plotted on the natal chart on pages 22–3, Venus would have moved roughly half a degree.*

THE NATAL CHART

The natal chart takes a moment in time and freezes it. It is a map of
what you would have seen at your birth had you opened your eyes and
gazed into the heavens, together with what was hidden from sight
below the horizon. From your perspective on earth, the planets appear
to move around you, so you are placed at the centre of your birthchart.

COMPONENTS OF THE NATAL CHART

• The zodiac signs (see pages 24–123)   • The angles (see pages 228–39)

• The elements (see pages 124–35)   • The houses (see pages 240–63)

• The qualities (see page 136–47)   • The aspects (see pages 264–87)

• The planets and their placement
  (see pages 148–227)

The qualities and the elements usually appear in boxes towards the bottom of the
chart. The planetary placements, house cusps and aspects appear both on the
chart wheel and in the boxes beneath.

COMPUTER-GENERATED CHARTS

Although it is entirely possible to draw up your own birthchart, these days most
people take advantage of modern technology by getting a computer to do it for
them. There are many companies that offer this service, many of which advertise
in astrological magazines and on the Internet. To obtain a copy of your unique
chart, all you need to supply is the date, time and place of your birth.

HOW TO READ A NATAL CHART

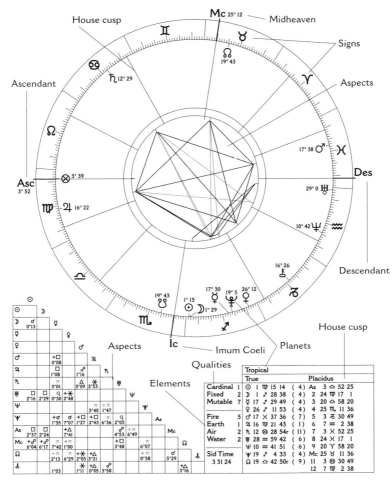

Natal chart for 11:22 pm, 23 November 2003 On this day the new Moon was eclipsed in 1º Sagittarius. The Ascendant is in Virgo and the Midheaven in Taurus.

The zodiac

The zodiac is the path the sun *apparently* takes through the heavens. It is divided into twelve signs that represent the whole of human experience, each sign describing a distinct, basic personality type linked to the position of the Sun at birth.

Each sign has its constructive, positive side, and its destructive, negative side. Aries, for example, is an impulsive, courageous sign with a strongly assertive nature. This is its constructive aspect. When used destructively, that assertive nature turns aggressive and Aries becomes the bully.

The hidden qualities of a sign reside in its 'shadow'. These shadow attributes reflect the negative aspects of a sign, or the dark side of the sign that lies opposite to it on the zodiac. Taurus and Scorpio, for example, share a jealous, resentful shadow who has a very long memory, whilst Gemini's tendency to skip over the truth is the dishonest shadow of Sagittarius.

By attuning to the more positive and constructive side of a chart, personal evolution and soul growth become possible.

THE ZODIAC JOURNEY

The zodiac is not simply the celestial path of the Sun – it is a voyage through human experience. It represents the journey of the soul (the Sun) from its conception through childhood to old age.

In Aries, at the journey's outset, the soul comes into incarnation and takes on an ego. This is where 'I' begins – the awareness of self. In Taurus, the soul takes on substance, becoming a physical body. Gemini is the point at which the soul seeks to communicate with others and express itself. In the fourth sign, Cancer, the overriding instinct is to nurture others, whereas in Leo, the fifth sign and the natural leader of the zodiac, the soul strives to shine and be recognized. Virgo encapsulates the urge we have to be of service to our fellow human beings and our daily routine.

Halfway around the zodiac, in Libra, the soul is ready to enter into a relationship, to meet itself in another. This is where the soul learns to compromise and adapt. In Scorpio, the soul comes to recognize its creative and regenerative power. By the time it reaches Sagittarius, the soul is on a quest for meaning. In Capricorn, the drive is toward an ordered and stable society and, in humanitarian Aquarius, the urge is for the good of the whole. When the soul reaches Pisces, the soul's desire is to merge with the oneness from which it started – or to escape from the eternal round.

THE SOLAR YEAR

It takes the Sun approximately a year to travel around the zodiac, spending about 30 days in each sign. The exact dates of ingress and egress differ from year to year due to the cyclic adjustment that creates leap years.

The Sun's progression around the zodiac affects the structure of a chart. The Sun always rises over the horizon at dawn, but the sign in which it appears to do so depends on the time of year. This explains why the Ascendant – the sign that was 'rising' over the horizon at the time of someone's birth – is different in spring and summer even if the time of day is the same.

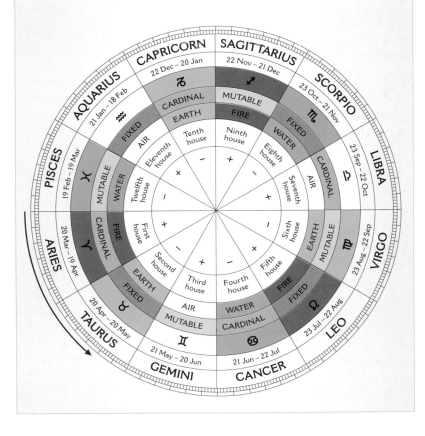

ARIES
The ram

Glyph	The Aries glyph, or symbol, has its basis in the ram's horns, symbolizing the assertive, thrusting nature of the sign and its associated ability to meet challenges head-on.
Dates	20 March–19 April
Ruler	Mars
Natural house	First
Quality	Cardinal
Element	Fire
Polarity	Positive
Exaltation	Sun
Fall	Saturn
Detriment	Venus
Keywords	Self-expression, assertion, forcefulness, urgency, initiative, courage, aggression, impulse, enterprise, passion, selfishness, leadership, egotism, combustible, foolhardy, survival instinct

Appearance

Lean and active, Aries radiates energy and self-assurance. The face is often ruddy and the hair may also be tinged with red. One of the most striking features of an Arien face is the bold 'ram's horn' eyebrows, which grow to meet in the middle of a characteristically strong forehead. Dress sense is usually smart-casual or sporty.

Impetuous Aries' love of risk may lead to a love of gambling.

Personality

It is impossible to ignore Aries. This is an assertive, idealistic personality driven by a powerful ego. Subtlety doesn't play a part in it. What you see – and hear – is what there is, and Aries always speaks out. Headstrong and dynamic, the ram charges through life. The aim is to win, no matter the competition, which is what makes it all so exciting.

A natural leader, Aries truly believes that he is always right. Combine this with an independent nature and you have a personality that prefers to tackle things unaided. This is not a team player. If things go wrong – always a risk when you rush headlong – Aries simply draws from the well of eternal optimism and moves on.

Mind

Aries has a quick-witted mind that thrives on challenge. A serial innovator, Aries has the ability to give total attention to the moment. Impulsive rather than rational, there's a tendency towards snap decisions, which are generally astute. Detail goes by the wayside, as something with which others can concern themselves. This is a restless mind that is easily bored and likes to move on quickly.

Aries has a good sense of humour, which finds expression in satirical wit. Rarely at a loss for words, Aries is not beyond cruel sarcasm and sadistic wordplay, either. Anyone found lacking is dealt with swiftly when an Aries is present.

Emotions

Although prone neither to introspection nor moodiness, Aries has a childlike naivety that makes him or her surprisingly vulnerable. When fired up, the ram's temper flashes spectacularly, without warning and then disappears in a moment. Tending towards self-centredness, Aries rarely shows empathy. But when made aware of a situation, Aries will fight wholeheartedly for the underdog or underprivileged.

Strengths

Aries is a courageous, enterprising pioneer who values freedom and frank discussion. This is a generous, enthusiastic person who

makes things happen. Passionate Aries throws everything into work and play. Problems are faced head-on with a view to finding innovative solutions.

Sandy hills are ruled by Aries' sign but Aries is unlikely to be found walking them – this sign prefers more active pastimes.

Weaknesses

Aries can be manipulative and less than truthful. Eternally restless, this sign lacks perseverance, wanting everything *now*. Projects and people may be abandoned halfway through. The Arien personality can be exceedingly selfish. If the risk-taking gets obsessive, Aries has no compunction about jeopardizing the security of others.

Aries is a romantic at heart, given to impulsive gestures such as buying a single red rose.

Shadow

The Aries shadow incorporates the vacillating tendencies of its opposite sign, Libra, leading to procrastination. Like Libra, the shadow has difficulty saying no. There is an 'anything for a quiet life' attitude that promises much but delivers little.

Karma

Arien karma arises from past selfishness and egocentricity. A failure to consider the needs of others, and an insensitivity to their feelings, creates the present-life karmic challenges of leadership without oppression and self-awareness without self-absorption.

Likes

Noise, excitement, danger, sex, satire.

Dislikes

Peace and quiet, monotony, hypocrisy, injustice.

Money

Aries spends freely and often on impulse. With a penchant for risk-taking, safeguards like insurance and savings don't hold much temptation. Aries people enjoy the thrill of gambling. If they speculate on the stock or commodities markets, it's only because there's an opportunity to make a lot of money quickly.

Fiery chilli peppers personify Aries' hot nature.

As a parent

Young at heart, Aries positively enjoys child play, especially if the child in question has an adventurous nature. It's a companionable style of parenting rather than a strict one. This type of parent has most difficulty with children who are introspective and seek solitude.

As a child

Young Aries is energetic, pushy, loud, excitable, ebullient – and accident-prone. Fearless, this child can take heart-stopping risks. Injuries to the head are common.

An Aries child hates to play alone. This is a child who requires constant stimulation. Happiest in an active educational environment, Aries learns by doing and by competition. When unhappy, bored or not the centre of attention, an Arien child expresses outrage in the form of temper tantrums.

Careers

Aries relishes any opportunity to build on strong leadership and entrepreneurial skills. Suitable careers include army officer, butcher, metal worker, surgeon, satirist, entrepreneur, racing driver, test pilot, fire-fighter, salesperson, wheeler-dealer, insurance assessor, surveyor, electrician, psychologist, explorer, herbalist or naturopath, designer and actor. Self-employment suits the sign's independent nature. If employed, Aries prefers to be the boss.

Leisure activities

Shunning all notions of rest and recuperation, Aries is happiest when active, usually in short, exhausting bursts. Cycling and running are good tests of Arien stamina, while mountain climbing provides sought-after danger. Motorcycling, rally driving, dangerous sports, martial arts and paintball are also appropriate. Not a natural team player, Aries nevertheless enjoys hockey, rugby and boxing. Going to parties is also a favourite pastime. The sign's affinity with anything sharp makes wood-carving or metalwork likely activities for quieter times.

Suitable gift ideas

A performance car or some top-of-the-range accessories will flatter the Arien ego, while a subscription to a health club or a weekend adventure break suggest a pleasing level of activity. Aries people also like power tools, designer clothes, red roses, sportswear and personalized gifts of all kinds.

Behind the wheel of a powerful car,
Aries is a speed-demon. Watch out!

TRADITIONAL CORRESPONDENCES

Season	Spring
Day	Tuesday
Number	9
Physiology	Head and face, adrenal and suprarenal glands
Birthstones	Ruby, diamond
Crystals	Amethyst, aquamarine, aventurine, bloodstone, carnelian, citrine, fire agate, garnet, iron pyrite, jadeite, jasper, kunzite, magnetite, pink tourmaline, orange spinel, spinel, topaz
Associations	Electricity, sharp things, metals, anger, satire
Metal	Iron
Colours	Red, white
Animals	Dragons, sheep, tigers
Foods	Hot, spicy and strong-tasting foods, anything red, garlic, onions, capers, mustard, cayenne
Herbs	Milk thistle, hops, nettles, burdock root, gentian, cayenne, broom, honeysuckle, red clover, gotu kola, fo ti, sassafras, yellow dock, St John's Wort, yarrow, garlic, rosemary
Trees	Hawthorn, holly, chestnut, witch hazel, spruce, thorny trees and shrubs
Plants	Nettle, geranium, thistle, honeysuckle, dock, fern, mustard, viper's bugloss, anemone, bryony
Places	England; Germany; Israel; France, especially Burgundy; Italy, especially Florence, Naples and Padua; Poland, especially Krakow; North America, especially Las Vegas and Brunswick; all capital cities; places with sporting facilities; places formerly occupied by sheep, cattle, deer, thieves, limekilns or brickworks; newly cultivated land; sandy or hilly ground; buildings with high ceilings and elaborate plasterwork; stables

TAURUS
The bull

Glyph	☉	The horns and head of the bull form the Taurus glyph, signifying the strength and determination of the sign.
Dates		20 April–20 May
Ruler		Venus
Natural house		Second
Quality		Fixed
Element		Mutable
Polarity		Negative
Exaltation		Moon
Fall		Uranus
Detriment		Mars/Pluto
Keywords		Endurance, materialism, steadfastness, productivity, practicality, thoroughness, security, fixity, sensuality, stubbornness, possessive, routine, patient, slow, hedonistic, patient, self-indulgent

Appearance

Taurus is characterized by a large head, short neck and strong shoulders atop a stocky body which tapers towards feet planted firmly on the ground. The eyes are large and striking, set below a broad forehead, and hair tends to be coarse and dark. Lips may be thick and fleshy. A Taurean dresses comfortably but sensually.

As an earth sign, Taurus gains enormous pleasure from gardening or being out in nature.

Personality

Determination is a key feature of the Taurean personality, as are inflexibility and risk-aversion. Routine and security are essential, meaning Taurus often gets stuck in a rut. Extremely reliable, devotion to duty and loyalty are the personal qualities that Taurus values the highest, making her or him an excellent team member. This is a tenacious personality that approaches even the most mundane of tasks with diligence and patience.

Such a stoic, conformist character is unlikely to cause upset. Taurus can show incredible stamina under pressure, while adhering outwardly to convention. But there is a much lighter side to this personality. A love of music, the arts and the good things of life is typically Taurean. This self-indulgent personality is a pleasure seeker who enjoys his or her sensuality to the full.

Mind

Taurus has a slow, deliberate, but not unintelligent mind, and thinks problems through, paying close attention to detail, arriving at solutions that are always practical and often creative. With imagination kept on a tight rein, a Taurean relies heavily on data received through the senses and rejects 'illogical' or 'irrational' intuitions. Once a decision has been reached, Taurus rarely reconsiders.

For someone with such firmly held opinions, although often unexpressed, Taurus can be surprisingly fearful of being judged, especially in the intellectual arena. It is difficult for Taurus to see the world from anyone's perspective but his or her own, which often translates as intolerance.

Emotions

Stemming from an overwhelming need for security, the emotions that resonate most with a Taurean are possessiveness and jealousy. This sign does not let go easily. Not just material goods, it wants to own people too. A furious temper lurks behind a typically calm exterior, ready to erupt if the bull's sense of ownership is threatened. Slow to start, it's a fury that takes a long time to subside. Resentment runs deep in the Taurus psyche.

Strengths

Dependable Taurus has tremendous personal resilience and integrity. With common sense in abundance, this industrious sign is excellent at planning and organization. Taurus can be relied upon to carry things through no matter what obstacles lay in the path. Complementing this practical aspect is an earthy creativity and artistic ability.

Weaknesses

Unable to appreciate different points of view, Taurus often builds up entrenched opinions. The bull refuses to take risks or to try anything new. Taurus can be excessively possessive with people and belongings. This personality can also exhibit self-indulgence and ostentatious behaviour in pursuit of the good life.

Shadow

The Taurean shadow incorporates the unpleasant side of Scorpio. Venomous ill-humour, envy, jealousy and resentment fuel an underlying, smouldering rage. The archetypal grudge-bearer, Taurus never forgets and finds it impossible to forgive.

Retail therapy is a popular Taurean pastime, but quality is all-important.

Karma

Taurean karma arises from an overwhelming attachment to material possessions and a tendency to find security in external things. The karmic challenge is to learn to let go in pursuit of an inner security that is eternal and indestructible.

Likes

Comfort of any kind, including good food, good company, sex, luxury, and high-quality retail therapy.

Dislikes

Change, uncertainty; being hurried; feeling cold, hungry or uncomfortable.

Money

In the interest of security, Taurus amasses money in the bank, but also spends on good-quality, luxury items. This character puts money into bricks and mortar and has everything insured. Never fooled by get-rich-quick schemes, Taurus only invests after careful research.

Foxglove is associated with Taurus and was used to treat heart problems caused by over-eating.

As a parent

Taurus is a conscientious parent, favouring discipline and routine. Children of a Taurean enjoy a highly structured environment. There's little room for spontaneity but practical creativity is encouraged.

Opulent and expensive, emerald is Taurus's birthstone.

As a child

The typical Taurean child needs a predictable daily routine and a practical education that utilizes both the body and the senses. Most have a 'security blanket' or a treasured item that makes them feel safe. Often fearful of venturing into the world, this child benefits from gentle encouragement. Head-to-head confrontation is best avoided as it usually leads to a temper tantrum or obstinate refusal to move.

Careers

An abiding interest in good food makes Taurus an excellent restaurant critic or restaurateur. The sign's deep connection with the land often finds expression in work as a landscape gardener, horticulturist, organic farmer, surveyor, builder, architect or estate agent. Taurus is also suited to work as a singer or musician, art or antique dealer, body artist, jeweller or craft-worker. Reliable Taurus makes an excellent government employee, administrator, financier, banker, investment broker, pensions administrator or office manager.

Leisure activities

Wining and dining are a favourite Taurean pastime. Given the strong earth connection, landscape gardening, building renovation, carpentry and sculpture are also popular outlets, as is painting. Love of the home

manifests itself in cookery, collecting art and antiques, interior decoration, dressmaking and upholstery. If exercise is on the agenda at all, yoga, dance, wrestling, judo, football and walking are all appropriately Taurean choices.

Suitable gift ideas

Ostentatious Taurus appreciates a gold watch, a gourmet meal or designer accessories. High-quality chocolates, expensive scented oils and lotions, silk lingerie and satin pyjamas also go down well with this sensual sign. External appearance means a great deal so gifts should be wrapped attractively.

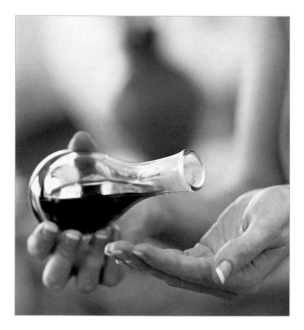

Expensive, sensually perfumed oils delight a Taurean heart, especially if used for massage.

TRADITIONAL CORRESPONDENCES

Season	Late spring
Day	Friday
Number	6
Physiology	Throat, neck, thyroid gland, vocal cords and ears
Birthstones	Emerald
Crystals	Topaz, aquamarine, azurite, black spinel, boji stone, diamond, emerald, kyanite, kunzite, lapis lazuli, malachite, rose quartz, rhodonite, sapphire, selenite, tiger's eye, tourmaline, variscite
Associations	Nature, singing, wealth and possessions
Metal	Copper
Colours	Green, pink, pale blue, white with lemon
Animals	Cows, elephants
Foods	Apples, spinach, beetroot, wheat and other cereals, grapes, pears, asparagus, artichokes, plantains
Herbs	Sage, thyme, tansy, silverweed, licorice, slippery elm, goldenrod, bearberry, fenugreek, mint, lovage
Trees	Fig, almond, plum, ash, cypress, apple, myrtle
Plants	Rose, poppy, violet, foxglove, vine, lily, daisy, moss, dandelion, narcissus, lily-of-the-valley, larkspur, flax
Places	Cyprus; Iran; the Greek Islands; Switzerland; Turkey; Ireland, especially Dublin; Germany, especially Leipzig; Italy, especially Mantua, Parma and Palermo; North America, especially St Louis; luxury hotels; anywhere warm, comfortable and luxurious with excellent food; gently rolling countryside; stables; cellars and low rooms; furniture shops or markets

GEMINI
The twins

Glyph	♊	The Roman numeral II represents the duality of the Gemini nature.
Dates		21 May–20 June
Ruler		Mercury
Natural house		Third
Quality		Mutable
Element		Air
Polarity		Positive
Exaltation		North Node
Fall		South Node
Detriment		Jupiter
Keywords		Communicative, multi-faceted, adaptability, duality, duplicity, versatility, inquisitiveness, sociability, superficiality, cunning, wit, two-faced, capricious, restless, fickle, symmetry

Green tourmaline, one of Gemini's birthstones, calms the nerves.

Appearance

Youthful-looking, Gemini is wiry and energetic, with long, slender arms and legs that are never still. Piercing, bird-like eyes are set under tapering brows in a narrow face with thin, fairish hair. The Gemini head is often cocked to one side in enquiry. Gemini's dress sense is quirkily fashionable, with the male of the species often favouring a professorial look.

Personality

Gemini is the original dual personality. Bright, communicative and charming at one moment, this person can be sullen or acerbic the next. It's an essentially sociable personality and the most talkative of all the signs. Gemini has a touch of the child about his or her character, positively refusing to grow old. Gemini delights in tricks and puzzles, and is an inveterate practical joker.

Always busy, Gemini often holds down two or more jobs. This sign switches opinions daily, while never admitting to being wrong. There's a lack of focus in Gemini that hampers any hope of a consistent lifestyle. Gemini is always looking for a new stimulus. The ideas are quick in coming, but Gemini doesn't always possess the stamina to see them through.

Gemini's mind is rarely still; this sign seeks constant stimulation.

Mind

Gemini insists on commenting on the world as it is experienced. Using highly developed verbal skills, this mind flits like a butterfly, instantly processing information from many sources and leaping to conclusions that are communicated to anyone who will listen. Gemini knows a little about everything, but lacks the concentration to focus on any one thing for long.

Silver-tongued Gemini has no qualms about bending the truth to get the right result. This mind manipulates and persuades, and can convince someone that black is white if necessary. Determined to win in a verbal battle, this sign's usual quick wit and love of puns can degenerate into sarcasm.

The darting flight of the butterfly symbolizes the Geminian mind.

Emotions

Gemini is not comfortable with emotion and lacks emotional resilience. This cerebral sign prefers to dissect other people's feelings, but has little empathy or sensitivity. Neatly rationalizing his or her own emotions out of existence, Gemini uses talking as a way of hiding genuine feeling. Emotional burn-out can lead to deep depression.

Strengths

A versatile mind is Gemini's greatest asset. The ideas flow thick and fast and multi-tasking comes naturally.

Weaknesses

Gemini has problems knowing exactly what the truth is and regularly changes stories without even noticing. Inconvenient facts tend to get discarded, especially when there's an opportunity to manipulate. Two-faced Gemini loves to gossip but finds it impossible to hold a secret.

Shadow

The untrustworthiness of the Gemini shadow appears quite openly from time to time. This is the trickster fixer, the con artist who persuades you it's actually a good deal. The motivation is often boredom, a reaction to stupidity or a sense of being snubbed.

Karma

Karma in the realm of Gemini usually centres around untruths or nefarious schemes. Past negativity may involve gossip, slander, betrayal or misinformation and deliberate deception. The present-life karmic challenge is to identify the truth and stick by it.

Likes

Anything to do with words: books, theatre, journalism, the Internet; puzzles and games.

Gemini enjoys the quirky eccentricity of old-fashioned writing tools.

Dislikes

Peace and quiet, feeling bored or lonely, people who don't listen or whose opinions are rigid.

Money

Money in the bank is not important. This resourceful sign is always able to raise cash when required, even if by questionable means. Gemini invented the get-rich-quick scheme and the financial con. This personality shows no hesitation in borrowing from friends or in lending money in return, and doesn't worry about running up enormous debts on a credit card. A natural gambler and shrewd investor, Gemini has a flutter – and wins.

As a parent

Although happy to play, Gemini parents treat their children like small adults. They expect to be able to reason as a means of discipline. A withdrawn or introverted child leaves Gemini floundering.

As a child

Inquisitive and communicative, the Gemini child benefits from an intellectually stimulating environment, right from birth. Gemini simply has to know. Young Gemini will take something apart completely to see how it works, read every book in the library,

Lavender is excellent for helping insomniac Gemini to sleep.

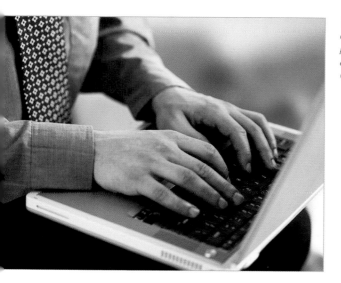

The lap-top computer was most probably first envisaged by a busy Gemini on the run.

suitable or not, surf the Internet without being taught and have the music on full when doing homework.

While Gemini is happy as an only child, friends are extremely important. If no one is to hand, an invisible playmate will do. The biggest problem this child has is sitting still and listening. A bored Gemini will quickly resort to destructive behaviour.

Careers

Gemini is eminently suited to anything involving multi-tasking and communication, such as journalism, commentating, broadcasting or teaching. Gemini also makes an excellent navigator, civil engineer, personal assistant or bookseller. As possessor of a silver tongue, sales representative, advertising or travel agent, demonstrator, spin doctor or communication expert are all suitable occupations.

Yoga is an excellent way for Gemini to unwind and still the butterfly mind.

Leisure activities

The preference is for activities that involve other people and party invitations are always well received. If Gemini has to sit still, it's to watch a film or mend a clock. Top choices of physical activity are t'ai chi, yoga and racquet sports. Playing keyboard or woodwind instruments in a group are also popular Gemini pastimes, while writing, languages and computers keep this agile mind occupied. Gemini may be a shopaholic.

Suitable gift ideas

Gemini likes gadgets, especially the latest communication devices. Jewellery is also bound to please, as are theatre tickets and books.

Jewellery always makes an acceptable present for Gemini, especially if it is unusual.

TRADITIONAL CORRESPONDENCES

Season	Early summer
Day	Wednesday
Number	5
Physiology	Nervous and respiratory systems, hands and arms, thymus
Birthstones	Tourmaline, agate
Crystals	Apatite, apophyllite, aquamarine, blue spinel, calcite, chrysocolla, chrysoprase, citrine, dendritic agate, green obsidian, green tourmaline, sapphire, serpentine, tourmalinated and rutilated quartz, tiger's eye, topaz, variscite, ulexite, zoisite
Associations	Writing instruments
Metal	Mercury
Colours	Yellow, black, white with red spots
Animals	Magpie, small birds, parrots, monkeys, butterflies
Foods	Nuts, seeds, vegetables grown above ground, except cabbage
Herbs	Coltsfoot, mullein, horehound, yerba santa, hyssop, elecampane, lemon balm, skullcap, parsley, meadowsweet, caraway, marjoram, aniseed
Trees	Nut-bearing trees, especially hazel
Plants	Lily-of-the-valley, lavender, lobelia, fern, yarrow, woodbine, tansy, dog-grass, madder, flax
Places	Armenia; Sardinia; Belgium; North America, especially New York and San Francisco; England, especially London; Italy, especially Lombardy; Spain, especially Cordoba; Germany, especially Nuremberg; city centres; hills, mountains and barren places; barns and storehouses; coffers, trunks and chests; playhouses; dining rooms; educational establishments

CANCER
The crab

Glyph	♋	The crab's claws symbolize the clinging nature of this sign, but the glyph also suggests the nurturing quality of the breast.
Dates		21 June–22 July
Ruler		Moon
Natural house		Fourth
Quality		Cardinal
Element		Water
Polarity		Negative
Exaltation		Jupiter
Fall		Mars
Detriment		Saturn
Keywords		Nurture, emotionality, defensiveness, sympathy, vulnerability, clinging, tenacity, ambition, moody, protective, touchy, clannish, shrewd, insecure, nostalgia, sentimental, manipulative

Cancer always finds great solace in being by water.

Appearance

A typical Cancerian has a pale moon-face and light brown hair. The body tends to be short and stocky with, in women, a generous bosom. Pale and watery eyes peep shyly sideways under lowered lids. The characteristic stance is protective, with hands crossed over the midriff. Cancer chooses clothes that are comfortable and familiar. This sign wears a favourite outfit until it literally falls to pieces.

Personality

The great nurturer of the zodiac, Cancer is never upfront or showy, making this personality easy to overlook. What lies beneath the crab's shell is well hidden and hard to fathom. Closely aligned to the phases of the Moon, Cancer swings between kind, caring and compassionate, and tough, prickly and full of self-pity. There is a distinct clash between the ambitious and outgoing part of the sign and the soft, sensitive aspect that desperately yearns for approval. Cancer wants to belong, to be part of family and community, but also craves success and is quite prepared to alienate people to achieve it.

Home is of vital importance to Cancer. Any disruption at home causes an emotional angst that affects every other part of life. Moving house is a major trauma. Sentimental and nostalgic, Cancer treasures everything from the past. What others see as clutter, Cancer clings on to as absolutely essential to his or her feelings of security.

Mind

Cancer rarely goes directly to the point and frequently finds him or herself overwhelmed by emotion, so that thought processes can be irrational and security-orientated. Events and relationships of the past also play an enormous part in intellectual decisions. While the typical Cancerian mind works best when intuition is allowed free rein, any decisions made this way benefit from logical assessment at a later point, as they may have been influenced by emotional needs or other people's feelings.

Emotions

Cancer puts all else aside in a desire to protect and nurture. Being so tuned into other people's feelings and needs, it can be difficult for this personality to draw back from others and define his or her own position. It's a sign that often feels put upon and is prone to mood swings. Misunderstandings and resentments arise all too easily in a prickly emotional landscape where everything is assessed in the light of previous experience. When self is threatened, which it often is, this secretive, vulnerable personality withdraws into a womb-like environment where emotions can be processed and understood.

Strengths

Highly intuitive of other people's needs, Cancer is extremely caring and fiercely protective. There are times when this solicitous sign seems to be the social worker for the rest of the zodiac. In the professional sphere, the shrewdness of the Cancerian mind, coupled with an excellent memory, often translates as business acumen.

The beautiful waterlily symbolizes Cancer's receptive nature.

Weaknesses

Weaknesses arise out of emotional sensitivity. When vulnerable, Cancer becomes jealous and possessive, grabbing at whatever represents security.

Shadow

The shadow side of Cancer arises from the strong emotional hold this sign would like to have over things – and people. It's a slippery shadow, born of personal insecurity.

Karma

The Cancer character is almost always burdened by situations or relationships of the past that Cancer refuses to let go. There may be issues of co-dependence and 'smother love' that need attention. Positive karma often takes the form of the nurturing Cancer has given. The

Moonstone is the Cancerian birthstone.

challenge for this sign is to find a way to nurture self rather than to rely on emotional support from others.

Likes

Home, anything to do with water, items of sentimental value, good food.

Dislikes

The limelight, emotional independence in others.

Money

This security-orientated sign feels broke without a substantial nest egg. Cancer is often accused of meanness but is generous with loved ones. As this personality type has a flair for business and rarely trusts others, financial affairs are usually self-managed. Investments are considered carefully.

Motherhood and parenting are always close to the Cancerian heart.

As a parent

Flowing with maternal feeling, Cancer is a caring and solicitous parent who provides a loving home environment. At the extreme of the sign, the love can be possessive so hindering the development of self-sufficiency. A Cancerian parent stands by heart in mouth if a child is the least adventurous, and will become ferocious if that child is threatened by danger, real or imagined.

As a child

The emerging Cancerian needs a stable, protective environment in which to learn and the constant reassurance of parental love. This is an affectionate child who wants to remain close to his or her parents. A great deal of encouragement is necessary to help young Cancers spread their wings.

Careers

Nurturing Cancer makes an excellent social worker, nursery nurse, nanny, midwife, home or care-worker, human resources director, housing officer, nursery teacher or nurse. The connection with food is borne out in careers such as hotelier, caterer or chef; and with the home in property-related work, interior or textile design. As this sign is happy on or near water, a career as a boat-builder, fisherman or sailor would be appropriate. Other suitable occupations are antique dealer, museum curator, business person or historian.

Leisure activities

With a firm emphasis on homemaking, activities such as needlework, knitting, DIY, collecting antiques, visiting flea markets and dinner parties are all typical of the sign. Cancer's strong affinity with water shows itself in sailing, fishing and swimming. Silversmithing is a suitable hobby, as is photography. A favourite sport is wrestling. This kindhearted sign also finds time for charity work.

Suitable gift ideas

Cancer values anything from the past, so antiques or a night out to see an old film are both excellent ideas. Silver or pearl jewellery or sweet-smelling white flowers are appreciated, as is a photograph of the family.

Sailing is an excellent pastime for this watery sign –
who can be surprisingly competitive.

TRADITIONAL CORRESPONDENCES

Season	Midsummer
Day	Monday
Number	2
Physiology	Breasts, nipples, lymphatic system, female reproductive organs, alimentary canal
Birthstones	Moonstone, pearl
Crystals	Amber, beryl, brown spinel, carnelian, calcite, chalcedony, chrysoprase, emerald, moonstone, opal, pink tourmaline, rhodonite, ruby, moss agate, fire agate, dendritic agate
Associations	The past, the home
Metal	Silver, copper
Colours	White, smoky greys, green, russet, iridescence
Animals	Crabs, frogs
Foods	Shellfish, lettuce, mushrooms, cucumber, squashes, melon, fig, milk, foods with high water content, cabbage, papaya, lettuce
Herbs	Peppermint, spearmint, verbena, tarragon, hyssop
Trees	Alder, willow, acanthus, trees rich in sap
Plants	Convolvulus, white rose, lotus, water lily, rushes, wild flowers, sundew, marigold, bogbean, chickweed, honeysuckle, dog's tooth violet
Places	Canada; Scotland; Mauritius; the Netherlands, especially Amsterdam; Italy, especially Venice; Turkey, especially Istanbul; New York City; anywhere peaceful near or on water; all navigable waters, especially large rivers and the sea; houses near water; lakes, wells, ditches, springs or marshy ground; cellars and laundries

LEO
The lion

Glyph	♌	The symbol for Leo is the lion's mane. The King of Beasts symbolizes the regal nature of the sign.
Dates		23 July–22 August
Ruler		Sun
Natural house		Fifth
Quality		Fixed
Element		Fire
Polarity		Positive
Exaltation		Neptune
Fall		None
Detriment		Uranus
Keywords		Endurance, regal, pride, enthusiasm, self-assurance, generosity, opinionated playfulness, boisterous, conceit, drama, benevolent, overbearing, dignified, pompous, patronizing

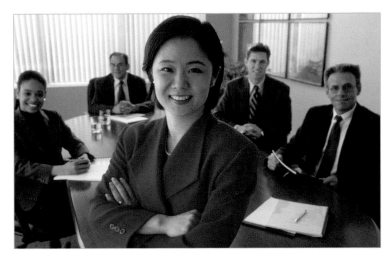

Appearance

Leo is impossible to overlook. This is a dramatic personality who likes to make

A female Leo is more than likely to be the chairman of the board or team leader.

an impact. Above average height, the body is generous and shapely. The stance is commanding and authoritative, or playful and kittenish depending on mood. Leo's eyes are bold and inviting. Hair is styled to make an impression and clothes are expensive and elegant.

Personality

The lion is a great poseur. Possessing magnanimity of spirit and an infectious love of life, Leo belongs centre stage and demands adulation as of right. This sign is a natural ruler, put on earth to rule over everyone else, whether they like it or not. Fortunately, Leo has such a charming nature that most people forgive this intrusion into their lives. Megalomaniac or benevolent despot, there is something

Hot sandy places are ruled by Leo, who revels in the heat.

exuberant and childlike about Leo, even when bossy and domineering.

Leo believes him or herself to be special and will go to great lengths to obtain special treatment. There is enormous pride at play in this personality type. Others will often kowtow to Leo without thinking. This isn't someone people want to offend. When Leo is rankled, the temperature plummets, the looks are withering and it can be difficult to coax the lion back into the arena.

Mind

It is virtually impossible to get Leo to change his or her mind over anything. Often bombastic, this sign thinks in straight lines. The opinions Leo formulated during youth remain into old age. Thought processes are slow and deliberate – and sometimes pompous. The lion may claim to have given matters careful consideration, and yet details are often overlooked and conclusions tend to be based on intuition rather than fact. What will make Leo look good and afford the greatest power are undoubted influences.

Emotions

Pride is the strongest of Leo's emotions. This sign's external face never shows anything less than confidence and *joie de vivre*. The situation may be different on the inside. When a Leo has strong self-belief, amazing things can happen, but if that belief is knocked, Leo takes a long time to recover.

Naïve and trusting, Leo is sometimes taken advantage of by others, mostly because Leo assumes that everyone has the same high standards of integrity and loyalty. Surrounded by the right team, Leo is powerful and creative.

Leo, the natural ruler of the creative fifth house, often has strong artistic leanings.

Strengths

Leo's warm benevolence and good nature can bring sunshine into other people's lives. This is a highly creative spirit.

Weaknesses

The lion is prone to lording it over others. Wanting to look good makes the sign vulnerable to false praise. Snobbery, pride and arrogance undermine this sign, as does a penchant for good living.

Shadow

This sign's tendency to organize other people can become a compulsive urge to control. The shadow side of the Leo character seeks to exploit other people's weaknesses.

Karma

Autocratic and unbending, Leo needs to recognize the responsibility of holding power. The karmic challenge is to become personally empowered rather than to enjoy power over others.

Likes

Applause, shopping, good food, wine, the arts, the opera, anything with passion and verve.

Dislikes

Put downs, being laughed at, 'mousey' people, attempts at budgetary control.

Many Leos are connoisseurs of fine wine.

Money

Leo is a spender and often lives well above his or her means. Money simply falls through these golden fingers. Not that Leo minds, since this sign has an innate ability to generate more and others always give support. Even when broke, this sign is generous and maintains an ostentatious lifestyle.

Rare and beautiful, Cat's eye is one of Leo's birthstones.

As a parent

Leo is a warm, playful and creative parent. This parental type prides him or herself on providing well for the children, who are encouraged to explore the world creatively. Children are expected to do exceptionally well, following the Leonian model.

As a child

This is the golden child who stands out from the crowd. Leo as a child always has a court of devoted admirers, which can lead to problems with spoiling. This child needs a school environment in which he or she can shine, with opportunities for dance and drama. Discipline is also important in order to keep Leo's developing ego in check. A Leo child soon turns into a drama-queen if thwarted.

Career

Leo is a natural actor, dancer, television producer or presenter, fashion model, rock star, sportsperson or fashion designer. This sign also makes an excellent window dresser, heating engineer, goldsmith or gold dealer. Leo is happy exercising authority as a judge, youth worker, teacher, politician, president, managing director, lawyer, fundraiser or bond dealer. With the sign's strong connection with play and leisure, careers as a play-therapist or leisure centre manager are also appropriate; and given the link to the heart, many Leos become cardiologists or cardiac surgeons.

Dance gives Leo the opportunity to shine.

Leisure activities

Leo combines indolence with energy, disliking sports that work up a sweat, but enjoying being seen at a fashionable gym. Aerobics keep Leo looking good, as does dance. Gentle team sports are acceptable, provided Leo is the captain.

There is nothing Leo enjoys more than sun-worshipping at the beach.

A natural actor, Leo excels at amateur dramatics, debating and anything that involves performance. Eating out is always a pleasure. The lion's creative side shows itself in artistic hobbies, and working for a good cause warms Leo's heart. A sign that is surprisingly interested in strategy, Leo often prefers board games to computers.

Suitable gift ideas

Leo adores anything flashy and ostentatious, and preferably expensive. A box at the opera is good idea, or a suite in a hotel. Cashmere and gold also score highly, as would a picture of Leo in an ornate frame.

TRADITIONAL CORRESPONDENCES

Season	Late summer
Day	Sunday
Number	1
Physiology	Heart, spine, lower back
Birthstones	Cat's eye, ruby
Crystals	Tiger's eye, amber, boji stone, carnelian, chrysocolla, citrine, danburite, emerald, fire agate, garnet, golden beryl, green and pink tourmaline, kunzite, larimar, muscovite, onyx, orange calcite, petalite, pyrolusite, quartz, red obsidian, rhodochrosite, topaz, turquoise, yellow spinel
Associations	Wine
Metal	Gold
Colours	Orange, golden yellow, red, green
Animals	Lions, domestic cats, lynxes
Foods	Parsley, rich foods, meat, walnuts, honey, spinach, kale, watercress
Herbs	Eyebright, fennel, St John's Wort, borage, motherwort, saffron, rosemary, rue, anise, camomile,
Trees	Citrus trees, cedar, bay, palm, laurel, walnut
Plants	Passionflower, celandine, sunflower, marigold, daffodil, lavender, yellow lily, poppy, mistletoe,
Places	Italy, especially Rome; France, especially the Riviera; Czech Republic, especially Prague; Turkey; southern Iraq; Lebanon; Bohemia; India, especially Mumbai; Rome; North America, especially Chicago or Philadelphia; exclusive resorts; jungles; woods and forests; deserts and inaccessible places; anywhere near a fire or furnace; castles

VIRGO
The maiden

Glyph	♍	The glyph for Virgo represents a maiden holding an ear of wheat, symbolizing the productive nature of the sign.
Dates		23 August–22 September
Ruler		Mercury
Natural house		Sixth
Quality		Mutable
Element		Earth
Polarity		Negative
Exaltation		Mercury
Fall		Venus/Neptune
Detriment		Jupiter/Neptune
Keywords		Service, discrimination, analysis, efficiency, perfectionism, conscientious, purity, fruitfulness, fastidious, submissive, modest, efficient, nit-picking, pedantic, narrow-minded

Appearance

Virgo is almost always well groomed, radiating efficiency. The body is slender, gestures are economical and the hairstyle orderly. The stance is attentive, ready to serve. Many Virgos wear uniforms of one kind or another. When not in uniform, Virgo opts for stylish, functional clothes that won't date. Colours are matched and coordinated.

Meticulous note-taking is Virgo's forte.

Personality

Quiet and self-contained, the Virgo personality is an extremely efficient one. Virgo always has matters under control. The fact that all the other signs rely on this can make Virgo something of a workaholic. Selfless and imbued with an instinct to serve, it's hard not to comply. Virgo likes things to be just right and this has a price. This sign can be a critical personality and failure is not tolerated. Excessive worry can result in nervous exhaustion.

Virgo embodies a strong conflict between the natural sensuality of a fruitful earth sign and an innate desire for purity. Part of the Virgo personality is always kept untouched and virginal. The maiden's other aspect is voluptuous and fecund. When inhibitions are lowered, this personality reveals a fondness for pleasures of the flesh that can lead to a crisis of conscience later.

Mind

Ruled by the planet Mercury, Virgo is an intellectual sign. It's a personality that tends towards specialist knowledge, exercising a clarity of mind few other signs can match. But there's a narrow-minded pedantry about this sign, too. Virgo plays safe, preferring to categorize, analyze and organize than show breadth of vision. Confronted with a problem, Virgo's instinct is to break it down into tiny chunks, often at the expense of the bigger picture. A chronic worrier, this sign can exhibit considerable nervous tension, which disturbs concentration levels and creates 'dis-ease' in the body.

Emotions

Emotions are unpleasantly messy, as far as Virgo is concerned. When the goal is to be perfect and failure is your deepest fear, you don't want to risk seeing imperfections on the inside. Emotions for Virgo can also be seriously confused, especially when the sign's powerful sex drive comes into conflict with its innate fastidiousness. Virgo's only escape is to analyze the feelings out of existence.

Strengths

Virgo's efficiency is legendary. This sign is graced with integrity, practical creativity, common sense, reliability and an eye for detail. Although quiet and reserved, this sign is always there for others.

The humble buttercup is one of Virgo's flowers.

Weaknesses

At the extreme of the sign, an obsession with detail renders Virgo pedantic and blinkered. The tendency to be critical and self-righteous, combined with unattainable goals, means that this personality can never quite meet the standards of perfection that would raise self-esteem and ameliorate self-doubt.

Small, brightly coloured flowers are ruled by Virgo.

Shadow

Virgo's prudish shadow shies away from anything 'unwholesome' and yet can be deeply attracted to voyeurism or pornography. This repressed, meddling persona has a sneaking suspicion that he or she knows better than anyone else.

Karma

Taken too far, the Virgo personality can easily fall into servility. This sign needs to learn to serve from the heart with true humility, seeking neither recognition nor reward. The karmic challenge is to exercise judgment and discernment without becoming critical or pedantic.

Likes

Making lists, neatness and order, arts and crafts.

Peridot is one of Virgo's birthstones.

Dislikes

Mess, dirt, disorganization, immodest behaviour in others, noise.

Money

Thrifty Virgo budgets carefully and rarely spends money on frivolous things, preferring to shop around and seek out bargains. By living modestly and spending below income, Virgo always has money in the bank. This sign knows exactly where the money goes. Bills are paid on time and debt is abhorred. Financial planning is important for this cautious sign and investments are chosen that grow slowly but steadily in value.

Chess is a suitably challenging game for this sign's love of strategy and organization.

As a parent

Supportive Virgo parents care greatly for their children and plan carefully for their future. They set high standards and take any failure to meet those standards seriously – but only because they have the child's best interests at heart.

As a child

Tidy and organized even when very young, Virgo always knows exactly where to find his or her belongings. This child appreciates

practical experience and carefully staged learning.
Not normally one to get dirty, this child is likely
to find personal nourishment from being in
touch with the soil. Gardening is a
favourite activity, as are handicrafts.

Careers

Drawing on a strong connection with
health and hygiene, Virgo is often
employed as a health professional, dental
hygienist, hygiene operative, pharmacist,
nurse, dietician or nutritionist. The sign's
inherent efficiency makes for an excellent
personal assistant, scientist, inspector,
analyst, writer, critic, research worker,
librarian, data processor, market researcher,
proof-reader, bookkeeper, management
trainer or statistician. Virgo may also find
satisfaction as a craftsperson, gardener, shop
assistant, teacher, linguist, consultant or
yoga teacher.

Leisure activities

Team games appeal to Virgo, as does
the health club, yoga, walking and
cycling. Many Virgos are excellent
craftspeople, taking up hobbies such
as carpentry, woodcarving, needlepoint

*Virgo's need to serve often takes
this sign into the caring professions.*

and model-making. Repairing electrical goods is also a popular pastime. To exercise an active mind, Virgo often studies for pleasure or takes up charity work. The sign's precise and efficient approach to life is mirrored in chess and computers.

Suitable gift ideas

A year's subscription to a health club or magazine is a suitably practical present. Aids to relaxation and luxury bath oils are also a good choice, or something pertaining to a favourite pastime.

Virgo has a very strong association with health and fitness and, as a sensual earth sign, enjoys being pampered.

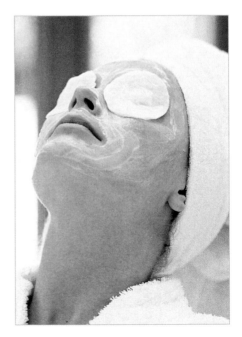

TRADITIONAL CORRESPONDENCES

Season	Early autumn
Day	Wednesday
Number	5
Physiology	Abdomen, intestines, spleen, central nervous system
Birthstones	Peridot, sardonyx
Crystals	Amazonite, amber, blue topaz, dioptase, carnelian, chrysocolla, citrine, garnet, magnetite, moonstone, moss agate, opal, purple obsidian, rubellite, rutilated quartz, sapphire, sodalite, sugilite, smithsonite, okenite
Associations	Harvest
Metal	Mercury, copper
Colours	Navy blue, dark grey, brown, green, black, anything speckled and spotted
Animals	Mice, insects, cats, bees
Foods	Endive, millet, corn, wheat, barley, oats, rye, rice, potatoes, carrots, turnips, swedes, plantain, all vegetables that grow under the earth, nuts, blackberries, fennel
Herbs	Skullcap, dill, fennel, valerian
Trees	Nut-bearing trees, elder, horse chestnut
Plants	Small brightly coloured flowers, buttercup, lavender, skullcap, forget-me-knot, aster, morning glory, mimosa, flax
Places	Switzerland; the eastern Mediterranean; France, especially Paris and Lyon; Greece, especially Crete; Turkey; Germany, especially Heidelburg; North America, especially Boston; libraries; closets; health farms; dairies; cornfields; granaries and malthouses; hayricks and barns; anywhere ploughed or cultivated

LIBRA
The scales

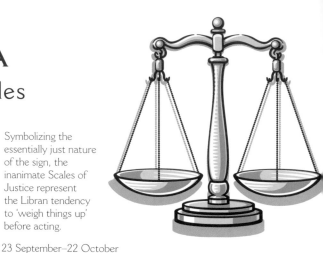

Glyph	Symbolizing the essentially just nature of the sign, the inanimate Scales of Justice represent the Libran tendency to 'weigh things up' before acting.
Dates	23 September–22 October
Ruler	Venus
Natural house	Seventh
Quality	Cardinal
Element	Air
Polarity	Negative
Exaltation	Saturn
Fall	Sun
Detriment	Mars
Keywords	Relationship, harmony, partnership, cooperation, diplomatic, conciliation, perfectionist, indecisive, compromise, insincerity, judgment, adjustment, adaptation, vacillating, frivolous, peaceable, congenial, aesthetic, determined

Appearance

Laidback Libra always looks good – but checks in every mirror just to be sure. It's an attractive face, with good bone structure and a clear gaze. Libran hair is typically long and wavy, whereas the curvy body is more likely to be short. This sign opts for luxurious fabrics, keeping an eye on colour coordination. But if Libra wore sackcloth, the effect would still be pleasing.

Personality

Often cited as the most balanced sign of the zodiac, this isn't necessarily the case. Libra is a vacillating personality that can swing wildly between extremes or sit on the fence. As such, this outwardly charming and sociable character may be a people-pleaser who prefers harmony to truth, and who is not above lying and manipulating to keep life the way this sign wants it. Libra may adapt, adjust and compromise to keep everyone happy, but underneath this character is tough.

A relationship is crucial to Libra, who feels incomplete when alone. This personality does everything possible to attract a partner.

Loving relationships are vital to Libra's happiness.

Music of all kinds appeals to Libra's artistic nature.

Mind

Libra has an agile mind that is capable of abstract thought and discerning judgment. Librans show great flair for planning strategy. This mind also enjoys the cut and thrust of debate – perhaps because it releases pent-up aggression.

Libra's mental weakness is vacillation born of a tendency to see all sides of a picture – and to sit on the fence. Any pressure to make a decision is therefore experienced as stress. Libra wants to get it right – and to be fair. In an effort to please everyone, this sign will perform mental gymnastics, adding in a few white lies to avoid hurt feelings. But when the lies start snowballing and the deceit becomes too complex, Libra soon wearies of the game and comes clean.

Emotions

Ideally, this sign would stand back from emotions altogether, except when it comes to romantic love. Libra's deep desire for partnership can lead to intense emotions. Generally speaking, this sign does not suffer from jealousy, but any threat to an emotional partnership can arouse insecurity and feelings of inadequacy.

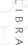

Strengths

This sign possesses excellent powers of negotiation and mediation. A tactful and diplomatic personality, Libra smoothes matters down and finds the middle ground. Libra also has innate good taste and an ability to create a harmonious atmosphere, no matter the surroundings.

Weaknesses

In pursuit of perfection, Libra paradoxically overlooks inadequacies and glosses over problems.

Libra finds enormous pleasure in nature – the one place she or he is happy to be alone.

The need to be in a relationship can be so acute that too many compromises are made, leading ultimately to dissatisfaction. Indecision and a tendency to laziness means that, ultimately, Libra can fail to deliver.

Shadow

For such a peaceable sign, Libra has a surprisingly selfish shadow, incorporating the more obnoxious traits of Aries. Self-absorbed and obstinate, it is as though all the concern for the welfare of others that Libra normally exhibits is inverted. This shadow figure lies and cheats in pursuit of its own selfish ends.

Karma

Karma for Libran personalities centres around relationships and a tendency to adapt to the detriment of self. Indecisiveness and a relaxed relationship with the truth are other areas worthy of examination. The karmic challenge for Libra is to be open and truthful in future relationships, so that the needs of both parties are met equally.

Likes

Peace and harmony, a pleasing environment, the arts.

Dislikes

Hassle, arguments, differences of opinion.

The dove, symbol of peace, is traditionally associated with Libra.

Money

Although Libra makes meticulous financial plans, he or she may still be deep in debt on account of a love of good living. Fortunately, Libra has the ability to earn enough to pay off the debts.

Libran investments are carefully researched and designed to achieve long-term security – when Libra can be bothered. Always generous and willing to spend on luxury and quality, Libra loves window-shopping and can't resist a bargain.

As a parent

A Libran parent enjoys playing with his or her children, provided the games don't involve confrontation. This is a parent who disciplines through kindness rather than strict rules. Nevertheless, the Libran desire for perfection can result in exacting standards, especially where academic work is concerned.

As a child

Libra as a child quickly learns to please people and mediate in disputes. This winsome individual needs to be steered gently through life. People-orientated, this child learns best in a sociable environment where the emphasis is on cooperation rather than competition, and where a love of learning and the arts is encouraged.

Strawberries are the Libran food of love.

Careers

Libra's excellent taste and love of aesthetics point towards a career as an interior or set designer, graphic artist, image consultant, beautician, dress designer, personal shopping consultant, art dealer or anything in the music business. Looking so good, Libra may be a model. A reputation for diplomacy and fairness suggests judge or lawyer, diplomat, welfare worker, conciliator, management consultant, dating

Sapphires symbolize Libra's commitment to love.

agency employee, property valuer or negotiator. Libra may also find professional satisfaction as a veterinarian, hairdresser, sex therapist or airline steward.

Leisure activities

Libra is into pair-orientated sports such as racquet games or dancing. T'ai chi, swimming and membership of a health club also appeal. Libra enjoys designing and making beautiful clothes and enhancing home and garden. Quiet activities such as painting, photography, reading and listening to music are appropriate, and attending art exhibitions, shopping, going to the cinema, concerts and nightclubs all offer this sociable sign an outlet.

Suitable gift ideas

Having exquisite taste, Libra is repelled by cheap or tasteless gifts. With such exacting standards to meet, the safest present may be a gift voucher from somewhere truly exclusive.

TRADITIONAL CORRESPONDENCES

Season	Mid-autumn
Day	Friday
Number	6
Physiology	Kidneys, lumbar region, endocrine system
Birthstones	Sapphire, opal
Crystals	Ametrine, apophyllite, aquamarine, aventurine, bloodstone, chiastolite, chrysolite, green spinel, green tourmaline, jade, kunzite, lapis lazuli, lepidolite, mahogany obsidian, moonstone, peridot, prehnite, sunstone, topaz
Associations	Wine, music
Metal	Copper
Colours	Pale blue, pink, black, dark crimson, amber, lemon yellow
Animals	All small animals, doves, swans, lizards and small reptiles
Foods	Watercress, strawberries, milk, honey, fruit, wheat, artichokes, asparagus, spices
Herbs	Cleavers, pennyroyal, thyme, feverfew, catmint, silverweed, archangel, bearberry, burdock, corn silk, parsley, prince's pine, uva ursi, buchu leaves
Trees	Ash, white sycamore, fig, poplar, lilac, juniper
Plants	All blue flowers, mallow, opulent roses, vine, balm, violets, lemon, pansy, primrose, dahlia, daisy, cabbage rose
Places	Argentina; Burma; China; Tibet; Vienna and the alpine region of Austria; Portugal, especially Lisbon; France, especially Arles; large cruise liners; barns, windmills, outhouses and sawpits; the side of hills, tops of mountains and anywhere with pure, clear air; barren, sandy or gravelly fields where hawking was formerly practised; inner chambers; attics

SCORPIO
The scorpion

Glyph	♏	The sting in Scorpio's tail is implied by the barbed glyph. The arrow also suggests the transcendant nature of the sign.
Dates		23 October–21 November
Ruler		Mars and Pluto
Natural house		Eighth
Quality		Fixed
Element		Water
Polarity		Negative
Exaltation		Uranus
Fall		Moon
Detriment		Venus
Keywords		Transformation, intensity, mastery, magnetism, penetration, power, sexuality, secrets, destruction, mysterious, suspicious, covert, trauma, self-destruction, vindictive, resentment, controlling

Appearance

Inscrutable Scorpio has dark, brooding eyes and an intense gaze. The body is strong, subtly magnetic and the gaze gives nothing away. Hair and complexion are often dark. A sleek, power wardrobe puts the gloss on a generally impressive effect.

Personality

Charismatic Scorpio is difficult to get to know and prefers it that way. The fact that Scorpio maintains an air of secrecy only adds to the scorpion's dangerous charm. This is a highly intuitive personality that understands other people very well, instinctively picking up on any feelings they try to hide.

With a desire for power paramount, Scorpio does not hesitate to use knowledge gained through insight to manipulate people for his or her own ends. This sign goes where other signs fears to tread,

Scorpio is traditionally the most sexual and the most intense sign of the zodiac.

Traditionally, Scorpio has a correspondence with almonds.

breaking all the taboos. It is nevertheless a change-resistant personality. Scorpio has refined passive resistance to an art form. This person rarely says an outright no, even when it would be in his or her best interest. In the same vein, when the proverbial sting in the tail does its damage, it can be self-destructive. Scorpio rarely understands why he or she has behaved in this way.

Mind

Scorpio has an astute mind that goes straight to the core of a problem. Combining logic with intuition, the scorpion is an excellent strategist who can virtually hypnotize other people into doing what it wants. Thinking patterns and opinions tend to be rigid and unchanging. Not many have managed to change a Scorpio's mind.

Scorpio can be ruthlessly self-critical, especially when trying to understand motivation. This is a suspicious personality that dwells on past hurts and allows vengeful thoughts to develop. Everything is judged in the light of past pain, especially at an emotional level. Slow to trust, if Scorpio is betrayed, this sign never forgives and forgets.

Emotions

Scorpio's emotions are kept firmly under wraps, but are all the more intense for that. This personality type experiences incredibly powerful emotions, many of which centre around love and jealousy. When Scorpio is in the grip of these, reason goes out the window.

Scorpio can suffer from feelings of inadequacy, which will be masked with an arrogant manner. Always suspecting betrayal and abandonment, this sign's insensitive behaviour often elicits exactly that response through his or her behaviour and power ploys.

Strengths
Tenacious Scorpio has enormous resilience and staying power. This perspicacious sign can penetrate into the depths of another person.

Weaknesses
Compulsive and obsessive, Scorpio is a touchy soul who seeks total control over other people. The Scorpio sting is lethal and Scorpio can be intensely masochistic.

Dark red roses symbolize the passion – and the glamour – of Scorpio.

Shadow

The Scorpio shadow is venomous and full of spite. It comprises all the grudges the sign has ever held, and combines them with the mulish obstinacy it shares with its opposite sign, Taurus. Drawn strongly towards self-destruction, this shadow falls easily into masochistic and sadistic practices.

Karma

This personality has issues relating to the use, abuse and misuse of power. The karmic challenge for Scorpio is to uncover the treasure hidden in the traumatic events of the past. The fact of Scorpio's survival is part of that treasure, as is the strength of personality that has developed as a result of challenge.

Likes

Anything mysterious, clandestine or taboo; the erotic and the exotic; dangerous sports; planning revenge.

Dislikes

Personal exposure, change.

Money

Scorpio is always in control and has a 'what's mine is mine' attitude when it comes to money, although this person isn't necessarily mean.

Scorpio likes both dangerous sports and the underworld.

The sign's instinct for self-preservation shows itself in well-ordered finances aimed at conserving wealth. At the same time, Scorpio is a lavish spender and enjoys making risky investments that Scorpio knows intuitively are a good bet.

As a parent

Scorpio takes parental responsibility seriously, with the early establishment of an orderly routine. This parent is a disciplinarian with fixed ideas on child-rearing. Scorpio also takes time to promote an interest in the wonders of the natural world, encouraging risk-taking while exploring the environment.

As a child

Quiet and intense, this secretive child often resides in an inner world of fantasy. This is a sensitive character, easily hurt and intensely jealous. Under pressure, young Scorpio can sting without apparent provocation. This child also has a cruel streak, which may manifest in activities such as pulling the legs off flies. The stimulus of an intellectually challenging environment, in which Scorpio can delve deep into the workings of the universe, will do much to reduce the damage.

Careers

With links to everything hidden and covert, Scorpio is often employed as a doctor, scientist, detective, surveillance operator or private investigator, pathologist, hospice worker, psychiatrist, research worker, psychologist, hypnotherapist, undertaker, insurance agent or investigator. The sign's links to sex and medicine take Scorpio into gynaecology, midwifery and sex therapy. Scorpio's profile is also suited

As a water sign, Scorpio is drawn to any water-based activity but especially swimming.

to nuclear weapons design, or work as a submariner, diver, law enforcement officer, complementary medicine practitioner, butcher, business person or sewage worker.

Leisure activities

Scorpio is particularly attracted to the occult, metaphysics and mysteries and magic of all kinds. This Mars-ruled sign also enjoys martial arts, working out and jogging. The danger that the sign craves can be found in motor racing, pot-holing, or reading thrillers. Barhopping or night clubbing are popular evening entertainments. Water is a strong attraction, and diving or snorkelling are both appropriate. This intense personality is also into self-improvement and studies for pleasure. This sign can be obsessive about computers.

Suitable gift ideas

Scorpio would make an excellent detective, so a murder mystery weekend could be the answer. A book on occult conundrums is also a good idea. Exotic underwear or leather is appreciated by both sexes.

Turquoise is one of Scorpio's birthstones.

TRADITIONAL CORRESPONDENCES

Season	Mid-autumn
Day	Tuesday
Number	9
Physiology	Genitals, reproductive organs, bladder, urethra, rectum
Birthstones	Topaz, turquoise
Crystals	Malachite, apache tear, aquamarine, beryl, boji stone, charoite, dioptase, emerald, garnet, green tourmaline, herkimer diamond, kunzite, moonstone, obsidian, red spinel, rhodochrosite, ruby, hiddenite, variscite
Associations	Sex, death, birth and rebirth
Metal	Iron, plutonium
Colours	Deep red, maroon, black, brown
Animals	Scorpions, eagles, snakes, lizards, invertebrates
Foods	Beans, onions, leeks, meat, spicy, pungent and strong-tasting foods
Herbs	Horehound, blackberry leaves, milk thistle, horse radish, toadflax, wormwood, sarsaparilla, black cohosh, blue cohosh, aloe vera, cascara sagrada, cramp bark, dong quai, ginseng, pennyroyal, raspberry leaf, senna, saw palmetto, squaw vine, false unicorn
Trees	Bushy trees, blackthorn, bramble, rhododendron, birch, thorn apple
Plants	Dark red flowers, amaryllis, lilies, aconite, chrysanthemum, carnation, rhododendron, honeysuckle, gentian, heather, charlock
Places	Tibet; Norway; South Africa; Morocco; Uruguay; Syria; North America, especially Cincinnati and Washington, DC; desert islands; anywhere near water, including stinking pools, muddy swamps, quagmires and marshes; caves; moors; gardens, orchards and vineyards; kitchens, larders, washhouses; battlefields; places where vermin and reptiles breed or rubbish is stored.

SAGITTARIUS
The archer

Glyph	The arrow flying into the air symbolizes the quest that drives this sign; the centaur suggests a dual nature that fuses instinct with intellect.
Dates	22 November–21 December
Ruler	Jupiter
Natural house	Ninth
Quality	Mutable
Element	Fire
Polarity	Positive
Exaltation	South Node
Fall	North Node
Detriment	Mercury
Keywords	Seeker, quest, questioning, adventure, spontaneity, optimism, tactlessness, philosophy, freedom, careless, idealistic, extravagant, jovial, freedom-loving, exaggeration, restlessness

Topaz is one of Sagittarius' birthstones.

Appearance

Sagittarius fairly bounces with enthusiasm. Hair is typically chestnut brown, the face long and horsy, the complexion healthy and perhaps ruddy. It's a rangy, athletic body type, at least until middle age sets in. The look is unplanned. Many Sagittarians simply throw on whatever clothes come to hand.

Personality

Jovial and boisterous, this is a sociable personality that needs the stimulation of friends, new faces and places. Freedom-loving Sagittarius

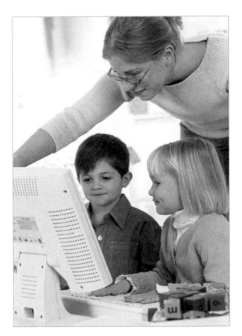

hoards maps and travel brochures 'just in case'. This sign is always poised for the off, but isn't one for booking ahead. Sagittarius prefers a last-minute approach. In distant shores, optimistic Sagittarius hopes for answers and fulfilment, revealing this sign's tendency to live in what might be rather than what is.

Sagittarians are natural teachers as they love learning.

Blunt and often tactless, Sagittarius has an unfortunate habit of telling others how to live their lives whilst seldom living by the same principles. This is a blisteringly honest personality that doesn't deal in nuance. Sagittarius acts impulsively, often releasing the arrow without any clear target. As far as the archer is concerned, any action is better than none and this sign will think about it later.

Mind

The Sagittarian mind is philosophical and impractical, preferring ideas to applications. Not that Sagittarius doesn't enjoy working through problems and coming up with an unconventional solution that works. This is the eternal student, who asks all the big questions and seeks out the meaning of life. There is nothing this inventive mind likes better than an in-depth debate.

Sagittarius is basically an honest sign, but can exaggerate or be creative with the truth if reality isn't deemed exciting enough. When bored, badly treated or overlooked, Sagittarius uses language as a weapon. This character can be at his or her most hurtful when lashing out with the harsh truth.

Borage is associated with Sagittarius.

Emotions

All things considered, Sagittarius would prefer not to think about emotions and certainly not to feel them. Sagittarian emotions tend to be shallow. Optimism and enthusiasm are constantly at the fore. Sagittarius has no desire to explore any sense of inadequacy or self-doubt that may lie beneath.

Strengths

Sagittarius brings enormous enthusiasm to projects and is highly creative. This sign is excellent at initiating and seizing opportunities, drawing on a highly developed imagination and sense of adventure. Sensing someone in trouble, Sagittarius will always fight for the underdog.

Adventurous Sagittarius always has a bag packed 'just in case'.

Weaknesses

The quest for freedom that drives this personality can make Sagittarius an untrustworthy and unreliable sign. Moving on in a hurry, Sagittarius can overlook duties and responsibilities, leaving 'detail' to fall by the wayside. This is a tactless sign that often offends.

Shadow

The Sagittarian shadow shares Gemini's ability to dissemble. An accomplished liar, this character promises many things, and then simply forgets about it in the pursuit of yet more experience. The insincerity permeates every aspect of life. Boastful and rebellious, the Sagittarian shadow wants to be noticed – and to be liked. When pushed, the natural tactlessness of the sign takes on a cutting, spiteful aspect.

Karma

Sagittarius has explored many belief systems during his or her lifelong quest for meaning. The karmic challenge is to distinguish what is truth and to live according to that.

Likes

Travel, freedom, wide-open spaces, the company of good friends.

Dislikes

Being tied down, routine.

Money

Extravagant Sagittarius enjoys money when there is some and runs up huge debts if there isn't. Somehow, something always turns up. Problems often arise because Sagittarius never looks at bank statements and can be naively trusting when asked for a loan. A gambler by nature, Sagittarius tends to leave financial planning to chance and, totally trusting, is easily drawn into get-rich-quick schemes.

As a parent

This adventurous parent likes to take children travelling as part of their education, encouraging risk-taking and exploration. More of a friend and co-conspirator than a parent, discipline tends to be haphazard and routine is seen as something to be avoided.

As a child

The Sagittarian child is born asking questions. Jolly and enthusiastic, this child needs to be active and rarely sits still. Usually honest, if

discovered up to mischief, young Sagittarius invents a different version of the truth. This adventurous child is happiest in an educational environment that promotes self-expression. Pet ownership will help encourage a sense of responsibility that may not develop otherwise.

The freedom of the wide open range is craved by adventurous Sagittarius.

Careers

Sagittarius is happiest in a career that offers a degree of freedom and intellectual stimulation. Travel guide, pilot, philosopher, tutor, lecturer, teacher, lawyer, psychotherapist, interpreter, public relations consultant, bookseller, writer or publisher all suit this sign, as does guru, priest or feng shui consultant. Sporty Sagittarians may enjoy running a sports centre or work as a personal trainer. More adventurous types may do well as a croupier.

Leisure activities

A typical Sagittarian enjoys sport, so hiking, camping, snow boarding, surfing, archery, volleyball, basketball, mountain biking and horse riding are likely activities. Outside of sport, Sagittarius may find satisfaction in studying languages, religions, philosophy, sociology or anthropology. Reading, writing and also partying suit every aspect of the sign.

Suitable gift ideas

Anything connected with travel makes Sagittarius happy. Shares in a racehorse would also satisfy the gambler at the heart of this sign.

Archery is the traditional sport associated with Sagittarius, although the arrows may fly skyward.

Tomato is associated with the sign of Sagittarius but that doesn't mean that Sagittarians enjoy them.

TRADITIONAL CORRESPONDENCES

Season	Winter
Day	Thursday
Number	3
Physiology	Sciatic nerve, hips and thighs, pituitary gland
Birthstones	Topaz, turquoise
Crystals	Azurite, blue lace agate, chalcedony, charoite, dark blue spinel, dioptase, garnet, gold sheen obsidian, labradorite, lapis lazuli, malachite, snowflake obsidian, pink tourmaline, ruby, smoky quartz, spinel, sodalite, sugilite, wulfenite, okenite
Associations	Horses, archery, travel, books
Metal	Tin
Colours	Purple, dark royal blue, yellow, green
Animals	Horses, stags and all hoofed or hunted animals
Foods	Asparagus, tomatoes, ethnic foods, currants, sultanas, mulberries, bilberries, grapefruit, chicory, vegetables with bulbs
Herbs	Dandelion, mandrake, wild yam, agrimony, red clover, burdock, feverfew, borage
Trees	Lime, mulberry, ash, oak, birch, chestnut
Plants	Pinks, wood betony, mallow, narcissus, goldenrod, carnation, horsetail
Places	China; India; Spain; Australia; Spain; South Africa; Arabia; Madagascar; Australia, especially Sidney; Germany, especially Stuttgart; Italy, especially Tuscany; Toronto; anywhere foreign; stables; great houses; fields, hills and high places; upper rooms with fireplaces

CAPRICORN
The goat

Glyph	♑	Capricorn symbolizes stability and conformity, as embodied by the mythical sea goat who rose from the waters of the unconscious to bring civilization to humanity.
Dates		22 December–20 January
Ruler		Saturn
Natural house		Tenth
Quality		Cardinal
Element		Earth
Polarity		Negative
Exaltation		Mars
Fall		Jupiter
Detriment		Moon
Keywords		Consolidation, authority, authoritarianism, discipline, conservation, caution, responsibility, duty, consistency, scapegoat, society, pessimism, prudent, patient, conventional, narrow-minded, callous

Appearance

A mountain goat at heart, Capricorn finds strength in the hills.

A typical Capricorn is long and lean in body, face, hands and feet – which may be bony. The dignified stance is authoritative. Colouring tends towards grey or black, the complexion is often sallow and the facial expression may be severe. Choosing dark and conservative colours, Capricorn likes to look stylish even when casual.

Personality

Capricorn is a traditionalist who devotes tremendous energy to resisting change. This personality type reflects the conflict that this active, Saturn-ruled sign has in also having negative, essentially passive, polarity. The Saturnine qualities of discipline, strength, resilience and ambition collide with the receptivity of a negative sign. As such, Capricorn loses spontaneity and joy from life, taking up instead the heavy mantle of duty and responsibility.

Maturity is, generally, a much happier time than youth for Capricorn. It is only when this personality has proved him or herself in the material world, by achieving success and status, that the softer

Poppies are traditionally associated with Capricorn – and with death.

intuitive qualities of Capricorn can emerge. Capricorn may then experience a strong desire to explore the spiritual realm or help society.

Mind

Capricorn has a shrewd mind that can formulate long-term strategies. Goal-orientated and controlling, this mind has mapped out a rigid path into the future. Although wise and practical, Capricorn rarely thinks outside the box. A certain narrow-mindedness is inevitable when convention is followed with such determination. The status quo definitely rules in this sphere of the zodiac.

Emotions

It isn't that this personality does not feel emotions, more that the ability to express them is blocked by the energies of Saturn. Underneath a façade of self-confidence, Capricorn often feels lonely and cut off, unable to break out by expressing warmth and affection. A stern judge and critic, this sign permits only what ought to be felt rather than what is.

Capricorn rates success according to achievements in the material world rather than in terms of personal development. As such, this character may have deep feelings of inadequacy, hidden beneath a drive to succeed and prove worth.

Strengths

Blessed with infinite patience, Capricorn excels at handling difficult tasks. This sign also has a flair for organization, incorporating wisdom, an eye for detail and an ability to see things through. A tendency to take life too seriously is mitigated by a sardonic sense of humour.

Weaknesses

Capricorn is a control freak and often judges people according to the position they hold or what they can do to assist Capricorn climb the social or business ladder. This controlling personality sees the world in excessively rigid terms, imposing endless 'oughts and shoulds' rules on themselves and others.

Shadow

Criticalness, narrow-mindedness, pessimism and rigidity define the Capricorn shadow. Inner dissatisfaction creates a driving need for validation and success in the outside world.

Karma

Capricorn maintains a blinkered adherence to the mores of religion or society. The karmic challenge for this individual is to find his or her inner voice and to

Garnet is one of the traditional birthstones of Capricorn.

allow that to direct life; and to integrate the spiritual into everyday, material reality.

Likes
Certainty, order, rules and regulations.

Dislikes
Muddle, inefficiency, rebels.

Money
Capricorn possesses an innate respect for money and never spends frivolously. Purchases are of excellent quality, designed to last. This cautious sign plans the financial future carefully: savings, insurance and pension plans are in place early in life. Investments are made after careful consideration and consultation with an expert. Capricorn never takes a risk.

Capricorn always has money in the bank and takes finances very seriously indeed.

As a parent
Capricorn takes the responsibility of parenthood seriously and lays down strict rules. Children are expected to conform and to follow the Capricorn code of behaviour: act responsibly and sensibly at all times. This authoritarian parent, who has difficulty showing affection, may seem cold to a child, particularly because that child will be valued mostly in terms of what the child achieves.

As a child

This child is old beyond his or her years. Many children born under this sign feel as though they carry a burden or that they have a duty of some kind early in life. An orderly, conventional educational environment is appropriate for this sign, with a degree of competitiveness and challenge.

Careers

Capricorn is ambitious and closely associated with bureaucracy and government, so employment as a chief executive officer (CEO), civil servant or other government employee, pensions administrator, politician, administrator or law enforcement officer suits this personality, as does entrepreneur, bank manager, teacher or planner. With this sign's link to the skeletal system, chiropractor, orthopaedic surgeon, osteopath or dentist are other possibilities. Given Capricorn's liking for structure, a career as an architect, surveyor, builder, mathematician, engineer, biographer or geologist would be appropriate. Post-retirement, Capricorns often take on a role as a magistrate, counsellor or voluntary support worker.

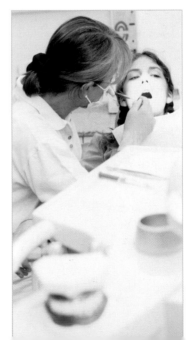

Given Capricorn's link to teeth and bones, dentistry often appeals.

Leisure activities

Hill walking or climbing are excellent leisure pursuits for Capricorn, who feels at home in this environment. The enduring nature of the sign is reflected in marathon running, whereas a fondness for structure is shown in dance, yoga and golf. Hobbies include genealogy, local history, gardening, pottery, sculpture and DIY. Capricorn tends to enjoy reading, especially biographies and historical non-fiction. Visiting museums or community service are also likely pastimes, as is eating out. Many Capricorns are wine buffs.

Suitable gift ideas

Capricorn values presents that combine usefulness with quality. Executive toys, a beautiful leather briefcase or a case of

Capricorn is associated with evergreens, such as pine, that keep their colour in winter.

port would please a male of the species, while a female Capricorn is likely to appreciate antique jewellery or classic fragrances.

TRADITIONAL CORRESPONDENCES

Season	Winter
Day	Saturday
Number	8
Physiology	Knees, skin and skeleton
Birthstones	Jet, garnet
Crystals	Turquoise, onyx, amber, azurite, carnelian, fluorite, green and black tourmaline, labradorite, magnetite, malachite, peridot, quartz, ruby, smoky quartz, annabergite, aragonite, galena
Associations	Law, administration
Metal	Lead, platinum
Colours	Very dark green, dark brown, grey, black, russet, indigo
Animals	Goats and all cloven-footed creatures, bears, bats
Foods	Onions, meat, salted nuts, potatoes, beets, barley, malt, starchy foods, quinces, spinach
Herbs	Comfrey, sarsaparilla, wintergreen, rue, slippery elm, thuja, shepherd's purse, fumitory, thyme, henbane
Trees	Pine, willow, elm, hemlock, poplar, camellia, japonica, yew, aspen, holly, white oak
Plants	Pansy, ivy, red and black poppy, hellebore, carnation, horsetail
Places	Afghanistan; Mexico; Macedonia; the Shetlands, especially Orkney; Greece; the former Yugoslavia; Belgium, especially Brussels; England, especially Oxford; mountains, hills, and high, barren and rocky places; low and dark places; quarries; storehouses; sheep and cow-pens; thresholds; tool sheds and old lumber piles; fallow fields and thorny places

AQUARIUS
The water bearer

Glyph	∿∿∿	The ripples of the Aquarius glyph symbolize the coming together of intuition and reason in humanitarianism.
Dates		21 January–18 February
Ruler		Saturn and Uranus
Natural house		Eleventh
Quality		Fixed
Element		Air
Polarity		Positive
Exaltation		None
Fall		Neptune
Detriment		Sun
Keywords		Humanity, detachment, dispassion, revolution, rebellion, reform, reason, eccentricity, idealism, brotherhood, objective, erratic, gregarious, scientific, progressive, eccentric

Appearance

Aquarius is a restless character with a wiry body and similarly wiry hair. Misshapen teeth are characteristic. The sartorial intent is to surprise, although not necessarily to shock. Outfits are often outrageous: high fashion or thrift-shop chic intermingle with army surplus.

Personality

This is a quirky persona that manifests itself differently depending on which of the rulers, Saturn or Uranus, is strongest. Unconventional and idealistic, cranky and perverse, unpredictable and chaotic, rebellious and stubborn, genius and misfit all at the same time, Aquarius can be lively, original and inventive.

The Aquarian model possesses a streak of perfectionism that craves order. Fanaticism and bigotry run deep below a sincere desire to help the world. Possessing a fervent desire for change and revolution as a youth, Aquarius may find a way of rebelling or follow a set of ideals, and then stick with that for the remainder of life. This is the 'old hippy' who cannot move on, or the anarchist

Science appeals to the rational and innovative Aquarian mind.

who didn't notice the end of the revolution. Then again, Aquarius can be one of the great movers and shakers of social change.

Mind

Intuition and intelligence blend in this sign. While the Aquarian mind follows logical thought processes, it is open to a bolt from the blue, a flash of insight that can take it far beyond established thought. The combination makes for a brilliant mind, bordering on genius. But as is often the way with genius, the far-sightedness and originality of the Aquarian mind is frequently misunderstood. All Aquarius is looking for is justice and equality. It just so happens that this involves widespread change, breaking free from convention and exploding the status quo.

Idealistic and perfectionist, Aquarians can be fixated on a particular ideal, and hold a definite mental picture of how things should be. It is as though Aquarius has framed that specific vision and the frame is placed around everything and everyone. If a person doesn't fit the picture, then it is the person who is scrapped not the idealized picture.

Emotions

Traditionally seen as a dispassionate, detached sign, in actuality Aquarius has chaotic emotions and conflicting

Meditation creates space for an unexpected flash of intuition to emerge and stills a busy mind.

emotional needs. Routine and stability are craved, and yet Aquarius can feel stifled in a committed relationship.

When the sign's perfectionist streak comes into play, it inevitably finds this mess of emotions wanting. Aquarius therefore has an enormous problem with intimacy, preferring to remain aloof.

Intuition-enhancing amethyst is one of Aquarius's birthstones.

Strengths

Strongly motivated by social conscience, Aquarius understands what the world will need in 20 years' time and begins to bring in change now. Without Aquarius there would be no evolution.

Weaknesses

Aquarius is prone to fad following, and can become stuck in a rut of eccentricity. At another extreme of the sign, the desire for change can rule to the detriment of everything else, so that the baby is thrown out with the bathwater.

Shadow

With two such powerful co-rulers, Aquarius can have one of two shadows. The Saturnine shadow is cold, rigid and disapproving, a perfectionist craving control, which it may achieve through anarchy. The second, dominated by Uranus, is unconventional and perverse with it, doing things simply for the sake of being different. Sometimes psychotic, this shadow figure aspires to anarchy and annihilation.

Far-flying birds symbolize the space that Aquarius craves.

Karma

Karma for Aquarius pertains to previous rebellion and conflicts with authority. The karmic challenge is to keep the best from the past, letting go of the rest and evolving flexibly.

Likes

Chaos, change, innovative technology, next year's fashions.

Dislikes

Dull conformity, rules and regulations, routine, last week's fashions.

Money

Aquarius is either tightfisted or an impulsive spender, depending on which planetary ruler is strongest. With Saturn strong, Aquarius never puts a bank statement away without checking it. This person knows to the penny how much he or she is worth. The Uranus-ruled personality presides over financial chaos, fueled by mounting debts and eccentric business schemes. A brilliant invention, borne out of a desire to help humankind, could well make Aquarius's fortune, in which case, profits would be shared with others. Any investments or get-rich-quick schemes would have to be strictly ethical.

As a parent

Aquarius is an unpredictable parent at best, and an unstable one at worst. This is the parent who tries out all the latest child rearing practices, and insists on a faddy nutritional programme that claims to promote genius. It's well intentioned, but the reasoning can be flawed. On the plus side, Aquarius always embraces the individuality and the shared humanity in his or her child.

As a child

Aquarius is born different. Any attempt to describe this emerging personality probably won't ring true. An Aquarian child often acts as a catalyst in his or her own surroundings, yet benefits from a stable routine. An unconventional educational setting is most appropriate, in which experimentation and invention are encouraged and science is god.

Career

The intention is to help humanity move forward so scientist, quantum physicist, systems analyst, technologist, electronic engineer, researcher, volcanologist, anthropologist, sociologist, social or charity worker, or astronomer suit well, as do ecological consultant,

The co-rulership of Saturn can occasionally lead Aquarius to explore the past.

radiographer, astronaut, inventor, cognitive therapist or reformer. As this sign exists in the future, a futures trader is appropriate and, with Saturn as co-ruler, so surprisingly is archaeologist.

Leisure activities

Aquarius likes racquet sports, running, skiing, dancing, socializing and, of course, protesting. Many Aquarians have unusual hobbies such as UFO-watching or astronomy, candlemaking, or restoring old cars. This sign also enjoys studying the mind-body-spirit link and complementary medicine. Most Aquarians have an affinity with computers. All find satisfaction in political or charitable work. Science fiction is the preferred genre when it comes to reading and comics are devoured.

Suitable gift ideas

Aquarius enjoys anything different. Clever gadgets of all kinds appeal, as would a subscription to a quirky Internet site. Happy with crystals or anything New Age, Aquarians also appreciate organic food, wine or health products.

Orchids are traditionally associated with Aquarius.

TRADITIONAL CORRESPONDENCES

Season	Winter
Day	Saturday
Number	4
Physiology	Shins and ankles, circulatory system, pineal gland
Birthstones	Aquamarine, amethyst
Crystals	Amber, angelite, blue celestite, blue obsidian, boji stone, chrysoprase, fluorite, labradorite, magnetite, moonstone, antacamite
Associations	Electricity, computers, chaos theory
Metal	Lead, uranium, aluminium, platinum
Colours	Sky blue, electric blue, turquoise
Animals	Peacocks and large, far-flying birds
Foods	Peppers, chillies, foods with sharp, distinctive flavours; health foods
Herbs	Snake root, southernwood, prickly ash, chamomile, catnip
Trees	Most fruit trees, elder, frankincense, myrrh, rowan, mountain ash
Plants	Orchids, golden-rain, mandrake, snowdrops, passion flower, skullcap, lady's slipper, valerian, hops
Places	Poland; Croatia; Scandinavia; Russia, especially Siberia; North America, especially Los Angeles; Ethiopia; the hippy trail; hilly and uneven places; places for machinery; quarries where minerals are extracted; vineyards; wells; recently cultivated ground; springs and conduits; surgeries and lecture rooms

PISCES
The fishes

Glyph	♓	Two fishes swim in opposite directions while tied together at the centre to represent the vacillating, fluid nature of Pisces.
Dates		19 February–19 March
Ruler		Jupiter and Neptune
Natural house		Twelfth
Quality		Mutable
Element		Water
Polarity		Negative
Exaltation		Venus
Fall		Mercury
Detriment		Mercury
Keywords		Compassionate, impressionable, receptive, vacillation, imagination, malleable, mysticism, transcendent union, dreamer, confusion, elusive, self-effacing

Appearance

Pisces is happiest living within reach of the ocean.

Pisceans are characterized by their beautiful eyes: hypnotic pools in which to drown. The gaze is often distracted, as though directed at other worlds. The typical complexion is pale; the face expressive and alluring. The body may be fleshy but exudes sexual attraction. The stance is languid and boneless, as though at any moment the body might drift away. Clothes are flowing and romantic.

Personality

The Pisces personality is typically vague and lacking in focus. Possessing permeable boundaries, Pisces is not sure where self ends and someone else begins. This personality acts like a psychic sponge, picking up feelings and impressions from all around.

Whilst gentle Pisces would not willingly hurt anyone, this unassertive personality finds it difficult to say no. Pisces often casts itself as victim, and excels at passive aggressive behaviour. Rather than displease someone overtly, this personality will take on tasks with no intention of fulfilling them, or make promises lightly only to break them almost immediately. Like the fishes of the glyph, Pisces gets pulled in two directions at once. One side of this personality is kindness personified, the other is passively manipulative. Wavering between the two, it is no wonder Pisces has difficulty dealing with everyday reality.

Mind

The Piscean mind is irrational and intuitive or illusory and deceptive. Allowed to flow where it will, it may enter the realms of the mystical and transcendent. Pisces seeks union with the divine and, plugged into universal energies, can access sources of information beyond the norm. Pisces can achieve a mind meld with another person that allows him or her to know exactly how it feels to stand in another's shoes.

Emotions

For Pisces, emotion underpins virtually everything in life. It is a fluid personality that reacts to any emotional stimulus without discrimination. Inner currents of feeling tug Pisces first this way, then that. Most Pisces have no idea what they actually feel because they so easily absorb other people's feelings and psychic impressions.

Pisces is a soft touch, easily pulled in by tales of another's misfortune. No other sign is as prone to guilt as this one. Exercising self-blame and flagellation, Pisces wallows in an anxiety created by the thought of all those who suffer and all those whom Pisces lets down.

Echinacea is traditionally associated with Pisces.

Romantic Pisces is a sucker for love – or a sob story.

Strengths

When Pisces is at his or her best, it is the most intuitive and empathetic sign of the zodiac, with vast imaginative and compassionate resource.

Weaknesses

Pisces finds handling the harsh realities of the world very difficult. When confusion sets in, this manipulative character finds it difficult to distinguish truth from reality and reneges on promises.

Shadow

The Piscean shadow is a martyr who feels put upon and used. This persona is created by an inability to discern when it is inappropriate to go on giving, and to stop doing everything for someone else. A major feature of the Pisces shadow is guilt and a consequent drive to atonement and self-immolation.

Karma

Karma in the Piscean sphere centres around the sign's tendency to play the saviour or victim, taking on atonement rather than at-onement. The karmic challenge is to learn to empathize without taking on someone else's pain.

Healing is often associated with Pisces.

Likes

Anything romantic, artistic and mystical; music, theatre and the arts; the sea.

Dislikes

Detail, time constraints, reality; telling the truth when it's going to hurt someone.

Money

The money flows in and then flows out. This impractical sign has no time for budgeting or making provision for the future. Details are overlooked, bank statements don't get checked and financial disaster looms around every corner. An extremely generous sign, Pisces always falls for a sob story and often gets tricked out of considerable amounts of money.

As a parent

The Piscean parent sees offspring as an extension of him or herself, without recognizing that a child's experience of life is different. This is a sensitive and caring parental model, which provides artistic stimulation and opportunities for play, but does not encourage individuality.

Discipline is difficult for Pisces and boundaries have a habit of shifting, making life challenging for any child who does not belong to an empathetic, water sign. Children may also feel overwhelmed by such an emotional style of parenting.

As a child

The Pisces child is a natural daydreamer. This active mind thrives in an artistic and imaginative educational environment, which disciplines gently. Since this is a soft-hearted child who cries easily and cannot bear pain, no matter whose it is, an inharmonious atmosphere can cause great upset.

Career

This sign is happy in an artistic role such as actor, dancer, artist, poet, fantasy writer, photographer or animator. A propensity to addictive behaviour can be worked out positively as a drug or alcohol counsellor, hypnotherapist or psychiatrist, nurse or doctor. Pisces enjoys the mystical side of life so priest, intuitive healer, tarot reader, astrologer or illusionist are all appropriate occupations.

Photography is an activity that can easily become a Pisces career.

The sign's connection to feet makes Pisces an excellent chiropodist or podiatrist; links to the sea suggest a cruise organizer, sailor, or fishmonger.

Leisure activities

Anything to do with water suits Pisces, so swimming, sailing, fishing or cruising are ideal. As an artistic character, Pisces also enjoys writing, poetry, ballet, acting, theatre, photography and watercolour painting. Other suitable activities include yoga, dance and solitary walking. This sign is often a film buff. Most Pisceans enjoy metaphysics, romantic dinners and magic of all kinds.

Suitable gift ideas

Pisces adores anything romantic: candles, crystals and perfumes are welcomed. A Piscean likes a touch of luxury, too, so champagne would be fitting. Handmade shoes are sure to please since this is a foot-orientated sign.

Fluid willow trees are traditionally associated with Pisces and with natural healing methods.

TRADITIONAL CORRESPONDENCES

Season	Early spring
Day	Thursday
Number	7
Physiology	Feet, lymphatic system, pituitary gland
Birthstones	Amethyst, moonstone
Crystals	Bloodstone, aquamarine, beryl, blue lace agate, calcite, chrysoprase, fluorite, labradorite, turquoise, smithsonite, sunstone
Associations	Drama, addiction
Metal	Tin
Colours	Soft sea green, pure white, mauve, purple, violet, silver
Animals	Fish, dolphins and all sea-mammals
Foods	Figs, fruit, vegetables with high water content
Herbs	Golden seal, myrrh, echinacea, eyebright, mugwort, kava kava, Irish moss (sea lettuce), angelica
Trees	Willow, fig, hazel, chaparral
Plants	Waterlily, seaweed, ferns, mosses, evening primrose, iris, orchid, violet
Places	Portugal, especially Lisbon; the Sahara; Scandinavia; France, especially Normandy; Spain, especially Seville; North America, especially Vermont and Hollywood; Alexandria; Warsaw; Jerusalem; watery places of all kinds, especially marshes, the sea or where springs flow, fishponds and places where waterfowl breed; watermills; houses near water; wells or pump houses; dams; moats; old hermitages

The elements

The energy of the planets is filtered by the four elements. Each element is related to a particular function of the self: earth to the body and matter, water to emotions, air to the mind and intellect, and fire to the spirit and intuition.

The balance of planets within the chart describes how much at ease within these specific realms of experience a person is. Some charts are balanced, with an equal number of planets in each element. Others have only one planet in an element or none at all, and a large number in another.

The elements represent different ways of perceiving life. In practical earth, the world is experienced via the physical senses; in water, it is experienced through sensing and emotion. Air arrives at understanding through thought and logical reason but fire is intuitive and knowing.

Signs that share the same element resonate with each other but independent fire signs find water too dependent and introspective, making relationships difficult; water feelings are expressed non-verbally, whereas the air signs communicate primarily with words. Earth signs are essentially practical and have little time for flights of fancy or emotional outbursts.

ELEMENTAL BALANCE

The number of planets placed in each element in an individual's chart shapes behaviour and indicates how that individual perceives reality. While a balanced number of planets in all four elements favours expression of the element in which the Sun is placed, a preponderance of elements that are not harmonious with the sun-sign can have a powerful effect on how the Sun is expressed, particularly if the Moon

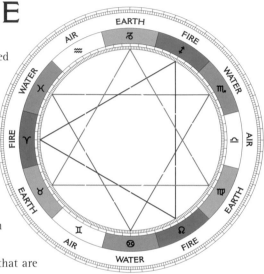

Three signs, equally spaced around the zodiac, each share the same element.

or Mars is placed in a dominant element. The Sun in Cancer – a water sign – and the Moon, Mars and Pluto in Virgo – an earth sign – suggests a practical, earthy person, who can keep control over the powerful emotional reactions characteristic of Cancer, for instance.

A strong emphasis on one or two elements in a chart can lead to a deficiency in others (see pages 368–81 for the effect on health), and specific combinations of elements give rise to a characteristic approach to the world.

ELEMENTAL COMBINATIONS

Fire–Earth   When working well, this combination suggests enormous staying power, as the fiery energy is harnessed and used for earthy, practical tasks. If the combination is not working well and earth restricts fire, there is risk of a sudden explosion.

Fire–Air   This is a volatile combination, characterized by explosive bursts of energy followed by burn out or mental exhaustion. It's a relationship that does well in the realm of ideas and imagination but less so in the everyday world.

Fire–Water   When fire and water are not working well together, the emotions tend to overheat, and the creative energy of fire can be quenched by excess emotion. When the combination works well it is intuitive and imaginative.

Earth–Air   Generally speaking, earth and air are not a good mix, as the slow and orderly processes of earth are anathema to air. However, on occasion this combination can lead to sustained and productive thought.

Air–Water   This combination points to personalities that live in their imagination. The ideas flow, but they are mostly impractical. It's a poetic combination that puts feelings into words.

Earth–Water   This combination may be dull and solid, or productive and hard-working. Earth tends to muddy water, restricting emotional expression and creating misunderstandings.

FIRE

Signs	Aries, Leo, Sagittarius
Planets	Sun, Mars, Jupiter, Chiron
Type	Intuitive
Polarity	Positive
Keywords	Energy, vision, creativity, intuition, conquest, enthusiasm, motivation, aspirations, burn-out, volatile, impatience
Physiology	Digestion, skin, body temperature, fever, inflammation, cuts, bruises, scars
Appearance	Medium stature, moles, freckles, pimples, tendency to redness
Disposition	Bold, hot-tempered, domineering and spontaneous
Associations	Creativity, life force, intuition, optimism, transmutation, insight, intelligence, heat, fruit and seeds

Living from the spirit

The fire signs – Aries, Leo and Sagittarius – are characterized by a great appetite for experience and a joyous approach to living. Fire is the element of creation, the life force made manifest. It is the most active and consuming energy of the zodiac. As the element of spirit, it roams far and wide in search of inspiration and meaning. Without its all-consuming vision, there would be no new horizons. This is the element of new possibilities and regeneration. Without fire there can be no transmutation.

People born under the element of fire have rapid thought processes and act on hunches. The fiery mind is intuitive, capable of plucking inspiration from the ether. Whether making great leaps of understanding or jumping to instant conclusions, fiery people have learned from birth to rely on their intuition.

Balanced fire

When the planets are placed on a chart in such a way that the effect of fire is balanced, the personality is optimistic, intuitive, spontaneous, affectionate and inspirational.

Imbalanced fire

Excess fire is angry, violent, overheated and accident-prone. Too much fire can lead to over-enthusiasm, a string of projects that are never completed, and burn-out.

Deficient fire results in low resistance to infection, poor digestion, coldness, lacklustre eyes and a lack of drive, courage or perseverance. Possessing neither energy nor creativity, it cannot regenerate itself.

THE FIRE SIGNS

Aries Ardent, passionate and ego-directed. This cardinal sign (see the Qualities, pages 140–41) is the most immediate expression of fire.

Leo With the heart at its centre, Leo expresses the warmth of fire. This fixed sign (see the Qualities, pages 142–3) may also display the despotic side of the element.

Sagittarius This is the most wide-ranging of the fire signs. For mutable Sagittarius (see the Qualities, pages 144–5), what matters most is the journey.

EARTH

Signs	Taurus, Virgo, Capricorn
Planets	Saturn
Type	Sensing
Polarity	Negative
Keywords	Form, productivity, practicality, fertility, sensuality, basic needs, security, the body, caution
Physiology	Anabolic processes, sense of smell, bones, teeth, nails, structure
Appearance	Firm, stocky body with well-developed physique
Disposition	Dignified and conservative with slow and deliberate speech
Associations	The physical body and the senses, fruitfulness, grittiness, permanence, practicality, plant roots

Living in matter

Earth is the security-conscious element and by far the most practical of the four. This element is concerned with bringing form out of chaos, moulding and shaping matter. Creations born of the earth are solid and enduring. As the fertile, tangible element, it is related to the physical body, to the physical senses and to sensuality.

Personalities with an emphasis on the earth element use the five physical senses to interact with and understand the world around them, focussing on practical, basic needs such as survival, security, food and warmth. This element can be relied upon to carry things through. While earth signs enjoy interaction with others, and recognize the value of physical contact, this is a self-sufficient element. Earthy personalities do not need other people in order to function.

Balanced earth

Balanced earth is tolerant, patient, steadfast and realistic, with a sound value system. With earth functioning at optimum levels, tasks are carried out efficiently and taken to their conclusion.

Imbalanced earth

Excess earth is inflexible and lethargic, slow to think and to understand. It indicates a tendency to oversleep and a strong resistance to change. The body and emotions become toxic, requiring regular cleansing.

Deficient earth results in toxicity on every level, especially in the body. This personality tends to be unstable, with scattered energy and an inability to show vision. Lack of earth promotes irrational behaviour, indicating someone who lives totally in his or her head, or who is immersed in emotion.

THE EARTH SIGNS

Taurus This is the most fixed and enduring of the earth signs, symbolizing immediate and tangible interaction with all that is physical.

Virgo Mutable Virgo organizes and refines, discerning the patterns behind matter. This is earth at its most adaptive.

Capricorn Takes matter out into the world. As a cardinal sign, it is driven to conquer and is involved with consolidating and shaping things.

AIR

Signs	Gemini, Libra, Aquarius
Planets	Mercury, Uranus
Type	Thinking
Polarity	Positive
Keywords	Intellect, communication, ideas, mental rapport, technology, concepts, insight, innovation, planning
Physiology	Nervous system, all ducts, canals and cavities; cognitive processes, respiration, coordination, movement, elimination
Appearance	Lean, slender, delicate, fine hair
Disposition	Lively and mercurial, with rapid speech
Associations	The mind, movement, communication, books, grace, fellowship, dislike of cold, computers, television, desert climate, flowers

Living in the mind

Air is the most intellectual and innovative of the elements. Unconcerned with the material side of life, it is a connective element that is driven by a desire to communicate and share thought. Air thrives on discussion, and places mental rapport above passion.

Individuals with innovative air strong in their chart are ideas-people. They see infinite new possibilities. Although not always the most practical of elements, usually relying on others to carry things through, air is the instigator. This is a rational but nevertheless intuitive sphere: air personality types typically gather in vast quantities of data, then process it to make huge leaps of understanding, without recognizing all the steps and connections involved.

Balanced air

Balanced air is graceful, objective, sociable and fair-minded. When air exerts the optimum influence, communication is open and, usually, honest. The mind is lively and intuitive, and yet functions rationally.

Imbalanced air

Excess air is restless, nervous, anxious, unstable and detached. Too much air results in a butterfly mind that flits between topics and is unable to concentrate. With this excess present, speech is rapid and not always lucid, and conditions such as stuttering or dyslexia are more likely.

Deficient air results in lassitude, introversion, stagnation and lack of perception. Without air, the mind may be irrational or slow to function. This condition is often associated with difficulties in making oneself understood.

THE AIR SIGNS

Gemini — Insists on communication and simply can't keep the words back. The mutable quality of this sign shows itself in an ability to adapt.

Libra — A sign that places emphasis on partnership, uses the mind to connect to other people. Intellectual compatibility is key for cardinal air.

Aquarius — Possesses prophetic insight, being concerned with what will be rather than what is. This mind can be surprisingly fixed and exceedingly difficult to change.

WATER

Signs	Cancer, Scorpio, Pisces
Planets	Moon, Neptune
Type	Feeling
Polarity	Negative
Keywords	Feelings, fluidity, cycles, passivity, sensitivity, empathy, reflection, compassion, imagination, intuition, illusion
Physiology	Lubrication and cooling systems: lymph, blood, plasma, secretions
Appearance	Plump, fleshy, with large, soft eyes and glossy complexion
Disposition	Tranquil, mild-tempered with monotone speech
Associations	Emotions, cleansing, empathy, smoothness, moisture, nurture, tree trunk or flower stem

Living in the emotions

Water is the most subtle and sensitive of the elements. The three introspective water signs flow with their own inner rhythm, heeding the call of powerful emotions. Water is concerned with feelings, cycles and fluctuations. Motivation is from within, often an unconscious reaction to an emotional stimulus. This is the least outwardly aware of the elements and the most irrational. These are the artists and poets of the zodiac. Water-sign people need to be needed, experiencing themselves most strongly through an exchange of emotions. Attuned to delicate nuances, they can be dependent and vulnerable, sometimes misreading the signals through the bias of their own emotion. When water intuition works well, it accesses an inner level of knowing that goes beyond the usual five senses. This is the element of 'gut instinct', of sensing and precognition.

Balanced water

Balanced water is calm, soft, gentle, sensitive and empathetic, with a steady disposition. Harmony in this element translates as someone who is emotional but not ruled by the emotions.

Imbalanced water

Excess water is excessively emotional, apprehensive, overly security-conscious, self-indulgent, waterlogged, dreamy, sensuous, and often overweight.

Deficient water leads to stiffness, an inability to empathize, lack of rhythm, and an absence of emotional connections. Without sufficient water, the emotions are detached, a condition that may be disguised as dispassionate objectivity.

THE WATER SIGNS

Cancer	Despite being an active, cardinal sign, Cancer is most protective of the water signs. Sensing emotional vulnerability, this caring sign is defensive and possessive.
Scorpio	Reflects the fixed and unfathomable depths of instinctual emotion, but reveals little, like a deep, still pool.
Pisces,	A mutable sign, finds free expression in the water realm, moving with the tides of emotion, but finding it difficult to establish boundaries.

The qualities

The qualities and polarities subtly regulate astrological energy. Cardinal signs are characterized by energy that flows in a straight line; fixed signs by box-like parameters, while mutable signs 'go with the flow'. The qualities influence how a person interacts with the environment, so signs that share the same quality tend to have the same approach to life.

The water and earth signs possess negative polarity, or *yin*, and fire and air signs possess positive or *yang* polarity.

and polarities

The polarity of a sign is mirrored in the sign that lies opposite to it in the zodiac.

In astrology, the concept of 'negative' is not a judgmental one. The negative signs are inward-looking and receptive. The positive signs are outgoing and self-expressive. These energies are complementary to each other. Neither is better nor worse than the other. Each is needed for a balanced flow of energy.

ENERGY FLOWS

The qualities and polarities are the shading within a chart, accounting for individual difference within an element. Each of the four elements encompasses one cardinal, one fixed and one mutable sign. There are two positive cardinal, fixed and mutable signs, and two negative of each type also. This arrangement gently directs how the elemental energy and that of any planets placed in a sign will flow, indicating whether it can move directly and spontaneously or will meet blockages,

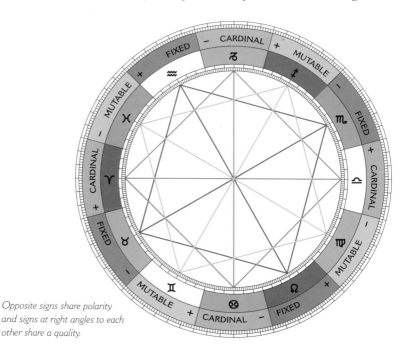

Opposite signs share polarity and signs at right angles to each other share a quality.

whether it adapts to change easily or resists. It also indicates whether the energy of a sign or planet is outwardly or inwardly directed.

Effect on the luminaries

Of the planets, the qualities and the polarities have greatest influence on the luminaries, the Sun and Moon. A cardinal and positive placement renders the Sun the most active of that element – making Aries the most spontaneous of the fire suns – whilst a cardinal negative Sun can help to overcome the timidity of the negative signs – so that the Cancer Sun is the most ambitious of the passive water Suns. A fixed Sun is the most rigid and a mutable Sun the most adaptable.

If the Moon is placed within a positive, cardinal sign, it can overcome a less assertive Sun, supporting any attempt to change. A fixed Moon leans towards the past and follows deeply entrenched emotional patterns, while a mutable Moon is changeable and adaptable.

Effect on the other planets

The qualities and polarities affect all the planets to some degree. Planets can show their nature more directly in cardinal and positive signs. In fixed signs the more intractable side of a planet shows itself. In adaptable, mutable signs, the planet finds its own natural mode of expression.

Several planets in one quality or polarity may well overrule the Sun in a different quality or polarity. Even if the Sun was passing through Aries at the time of your birth, making your sun-sign Aries, Venus, Mars and Jupiter placed in Pisces, a water sign, would suggest a much more emotionally sensitive character than the average Aries, because of the preponderance of water.

CARDINAL

Cardinal signs	Aries, Cancer, Libra, Capricorn
Cardinal houses	First, Fourth, Seventh, Tenth
Keywords	Action, enterprise, challenge, assertion, initiation, change, leadership, impetuosity

The cardinal personality

Concerned with initiating change and setting things in motion, cardinal signs are the most active and enterprising of the zodiac. Of the three signs within each element, the cardinal sign is the most vigorous and proactive of the three. Tough, assertive and sometimes aggressive, cardinal personalities lead others into action. As natural leaders, they do not take orders easily.

Preponderance of the cardinal quality

A chart showing four or more planets within cardinal signs indicates a strong will and a powerful desire to command. Such a preponderance of the cardinal quality can override the Sun's position in a more placid and receptive sun-sign and be the hidden motivation to succeed.

Effect on the planets

Placement in a cardinal sign energizes a planet and makes its expression more forceful. If the dynamic planets are placed in cardinal signs, then their effect is brought into relief. Mars, for instance, can be unstoppable in fiery, positive, cardinal Aries. The placid planets are also energized within cardinal signs but, rather than freely expressing their qualities, may become restless and irritated. Neutral planets tend to express themselves more forcefully when they take on the cardinal quality.

CARDINAL SIGNS

Aries	The most dynamic expression of fire. This sign embodies enormous personal drive. Enterprising Aries retains control by being one step ahead of everyone else.
Cancer	Cancer, which is dampened down by the water element, draws on cardinal energy in less obvious, but no less ambitious ways. This tenacious sign seeks emotional control, especially of home and family.
Libra	This seems the least pushy of the cardinal signs, lacking personal drive. However, Libra shows the cardinal quality in a desire to control relationships and the social environment.
Capricorn	Represents the cardinal element most markedly. The quality adds the personal drive that is normally lacking in the earth element, making this negative sign one of the most ambitious of the zodiac.

FIXED

Fixed signs	Taurus, Leo, Scorpio, Aquarius
Fixed houses	Second, Fifth, Eighth, Eleventh
Keywords	Consistency, intractable, rigid, resistant, stable, steadfast, loyal, entrenched, predictable, fixation

The fixed personality

Fixed signs are resistant to change, preferring a rigid routine and a stable lifestyle. These personalities want everything to stay the same – forever. They also draw on the strength and consistency of this most reliable of qualities. This is the loyal personality that carries things through, sometimes long after it would have been sensible to give up.

Preponderance of the fixed quality

Four or more planets in fixed signs make for an extremely stubborn person, who almost never changes his or her mind, and who hates change. Such a preponderance of fixed energy can overcome even the most fluid or flexible of sun-signs.

Effect on the planets

Planets are at their most intractable when placed in fixed signs, which
tends to bring out the worst in them. On occasion, however, such a
placement can add strength and stability to a dynamic planet and,
when it is used constructively, to the neutral one. Mercury, when
placed in fixed signs may spout dogma, but also suggests a capacity for
profound thought.

FIXED SIGNS

Taurus Perhaps the most entrenched of the fixed signs,
as the quality reinforces the earth element's desire
for stability at all costs. Although dependable,
this personality's cautious approach to life can be
life-negating.

Leo The least flexible of all the fire signs, Leo shows
little of the impetuosity of fire and finds it difficult
to adapt to change.

Scorpio This signs has an intensity that masks a deep
intractability. The fixed quality imparts
stubbornness to the usually acquiescent water
element, which can lead this sign into an
emotional rut.

Aquarius The fixed sign of air – an element noted for its
flexibility – can be extremely inflexible, as befits
its planetary co-ruler Saturn. Like Scorpio, this
sign can get stuck in fixed behavioural patterns,
so reflecting its other ruler Uranus.

MUTABLE

Mutable signs	Gemini, Virgo, Sagittarius, Pisces
Mutable houses	Third, Sixth, Ninth, Twelfth
Keywords	Flexible, adaptable, versatile, changeable, unpredictable, unstable, superficial

The mutable personality

Three of the mutable signs are dual signs. This means that they have two distinct sides to their nature, and slip seamlessly between the two or argue from two different perspectives. Virgo is the exception, preferring one viewpoint. This quality adapts and responds to the needs of the surrounding environment, creating versatile personalities that may be difficult to pin down. Mutable signs revel in exploration and change. These personalities find it difficult to stick to a routine because boredom soon sets in. They dislike following orders or protocols – especially if they see no sense in them. Mutable people make excellent team players as they work for the good of all.

Preponderance of the mutable quality

Four or more planets in mutable signs can indicate an unpredictable, unstable and unreliable personality – or, if the quality is properly channelled, exceptional skill at multi-tasking. A preponderance of the mutable quality can lead an otherwise stable and trustworthy sun-sign to be economical with the truth and less reliable than would otherwise be the case, depending on other planetary placements.

Effect on the planets

Mutability enables the planets to flow as they will, which is ideal for the dynamic planets that need no direction, but may be difficult for placid ones. An emphasis of planetary activity in mutable signs can lead the planetary energies to fire off in random bursts. The result may be internal conflict but, if harnessed to intuition, mutability can bring about unexpected solutions to seemingly intransigent problems.

MUTABLE SIGNS

Gemini	Enjoys mutability. The quicksilver nature of this sign means it easily adapts its ideas and responses.
Virgo	Mutability lightens the heaviness of earth in Virgo and adapts to the needs of the environment through service to others.
Sagittarius	This sign channels the mutable quality into an exploration of life's endless possibilities, so appeasing the sign's restless nature.
Pisces	Draws on mutability to adapt to changing emotions both in the inner and outer worlds. Pisces wears many disguises as it seeks to blend into the environment.

POSITIVE

Positive signs	Aries, Gemini, Leo, Libra, Sagittarius, Aquarius
Positive elements	Fire and Air
Keywords	Masculine, yang, active, extrovert, self-expressive, dominant

The positive personality

Positive signs are extrovert, having a forceful personality that expresses itself spontaneously and energetically. Orientated towards the external world, positive personalities initiate and change.

Emphasis on positive signs

If six or more planets are in positive signs, a person is more dominant and forceful in their self-expression regardless of sun-sign.

Effect on the planets

Dynamic planets, such as Mars and Uranus, find positive energy conducive to easy expression. Neutral planets become more active and communication more direct. Placid planets may be energized in a positive sign, depending on the nature of the sign.

A preponderance of dynamic positive planets may attract aggression or chaos or create a situation where someone feels invincible or becomes despotic.

NEGATIVE

Negative signs	Taurus, Cancer, Virgo, Scorpio, Capricorn, Pisces
Negative elements	Earth and Water
Keywords	Feminine, yin, receptive, reflective, repressed, submissive, introvert

The negative personality

Negative signs are essentially inward looking, compliant and acquiescent. Geared towards conservation, negative signs receive feelings or impetus from others and reflect these back.

Emphasis on negative signs

If six or more planets are in negative signs, a person is more introverted and repressed, making a positive Sun much more reflective and introspective than would otherwise be the case.

Effect on the planets

Negative signs slow the planets down. Dynamic planets find it harder to express themselves and may be experienced through projection on to others. When the Moon or Venus are in negative signs, the emphasis is on feelings and emotions. Used constructively, this can lead to greater self-understanding; experienced unconsciously, emotions are acted out without thought. A preponderance of negative planets can indicate a person who feels powerless.

The planets

The planets are the active ingredients of astrology: the factors that make a chart unique, because the planetary positions are different each day. These positions are plotted from the perspective of earth. Seven planets are visible to the naked eye: Mercury, Venus, Mars, Jupiter and Saturn, and the Sun and Moon. These 'personal' planets are closest to awareness, representing matters such as 'love' or 'will'. The invisible 'outer' or 'transpersonal' planets, Uranus, Neptune, Chiron and Pluto, indicate energies such as transformation, evolution and regeneration. Traditionally, planetary energies were seen as character attributes, or as forces that created events. In more recent times, the planets have been recognized as archetypes, or drives that underlie human behaviour, and the transiting planets – moving through space from day to day – as triggers. Whilst planets do not cause events, representing an inclination rather than a compulsion, nevertheless transiting Mars appears to push us into rash behaviour or conflict, and Neptune spreads a veil of illusion that can hide the true nature of things.

Planets have traditional associations with parts of the body, diseases, crystals and other matters.

PLANETARY MOVEMENT

The time it takes for a planet to travel once around, or orbit, the earth may be as brief as 28 days, in the case of the Moon, or as long as 248 years by Pluto. Not all the planets pass through the signs uniformly. Uranus, Pluto and Chiron have eccentric orbits that overlap and which move more slowly through some signs than others.

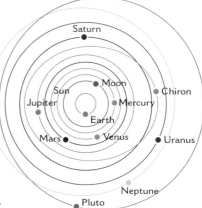

ORBITS

Sun	1 year	**Saturn**	29 years
Moon	28–30 days	**Chiron**	51 years
Mercury	1 year	**Uranus**	84 years
Venus	1 year	**Neptune**	164 years
Mars	2 years	**Pluto**	248 years
Jupiter	12 years	**The Nodes**	18 years

Retrograde movement

Viewed from earth, the planets (with the exception of the luminaries) sometimes appear to move backwards in the sky, as though reversing in orbit. This phenomenon is known as retrogradation. On an astrological chart, a retrograde planet is marked with an 'R'. Its effect is to turn the energies inward, making them less conscious or to reflect karmic stumbling blocks.

The effect of retrograde movement is most marked in transits. A retrograding planet may transit, or appear to pass over, a particular degree of the zodiac three times. Each time the retrograding planet does this, its influence becomes more marked, as though a lesson or opportunity were presenting itself ever more strongly until it is grasped. The energy of a retrograde planet can be most easily harnessed at the point when it 'turns direct', or begins to move forward.

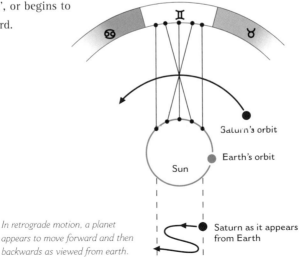

Saturn's orbit

Earth's orbit

Sun

Saturn as it appears from Earth

In retrograde motion, a planet appears to move forward and then backwards as viewed from earth.

PLANETARY RULERS

In traditional astrology, the seven planets visible to the naked eye were associated with particular signs. The Sun and the Moon each ruled one sign, whereas the others ruled two. As new planets were discovered, they were assigned as co-rulers to a sign with which their energy resonated. These new rulers often seem more appropriate than the old ones, but the underlying effect of the traditional ruler can still be felt. For instance, the tendency of Pisces to 'go over the top' around drink or drugs is related as much to Jupiter's influence as to Neptune's escapist tendencies.

THE RULING PLANETS

Sun rules **Leo**

Moon rules **Cancer**

Mercury rules **Gemini** and **Virgo**

Venus rules **Taurus** and **Libra**

Mars rules **Aries** and **Scorpio**

Jupiter rules **Sagittarius** and **Pisces**

Saturn rules **Capricorn** and **Aquarius**

Uranus rules **Aquarius**

Neptune rules **Pisces**

Pluto rules **Scorpio**

Fiery Mars was traditionally assigned to both Aries and Scorpio.

PLANETARY GLYPHS

The planetary glyphs represent abstract and metaphysical principles that underlie the universe. They are formulated from symbols that are combined to communicate deep occult truths.

The circle represents spirit. It is the totality of the energy in the cosmos and, as such, is eternal and infinite.

The semi-circle or crescent represents soul. It is the duality of existence and that which is created. It has the potential for growth and form.

The cross represents matter and the physical plane of existence.

A vertical straight line represents authority and the absolute.

A horizontal straight line links the life force between two points.

The dot is the divine that interpenetrates everything.

THE PLANETS

⊙ Sun

☽ Moon

☿ Mercury

♀ Venus

♂ Mars

♃ Jupiter

⚷ Chiron

♄ Saturn

♅ Uranus

♆ Neptune

♇ Pluto

☊ Node

SUN
The Self

Glyph	⊙	The eternal spirit encircles the divine spark that resides in everyone, giving life and symbolizing the self and ego.
Rules/Dignity		Leo
Detriment		Aquarius
Exaltation		Aries
Fall		Libra
Keywords		Life force, consciousness, power, creative principle, vitality, potential, individuality, self, identity, self-expression, self-integration, recognition, the father

The golden Sun represents the vital spark of creative soul energy.

The urge to express the Self

The Sun is the life force, vitality and the indestructible Self. It is the energy that holds together disparate parts of the personality until these can be integrated as an individual matures. The Sun represents the search for a unique identity, as expressed through the sign in which it is placed. Wherever the Sun sits in the chart, the urge for self-expression is channelled out to the world through the sign and house.

The quality, polarity and element in which the Sun is placed have a strong impact on how this self-expression will flow. In negative signs, self-expression may be reticent or inhibited, although not necessarily blocked. In positive signs, ebullient self-expression is natural. Watery Suns have difficulty in expressing aggression and in taking the lead, whereas this is an innate quality of fiery Suns. Earth Suns have little difficulty standing their ground, but are not innately aggressive, and airy Suns may be assertive but find difficulty in standing firm. A cardinal Sun is the most outgoing in any element group, although this has to be balanced against a negative sign's natural reticence.

Without the warmth of the Sun there would be no life on earth.

The creative principle

The Sun is the creative principle made manifest, as shaped by the element in which the Sun is placed. Earth Suns express the creative principle practically and productively, shaping matter.

In an Air sign, the creative principle is expressed intellectually and inspirationally, shaping thought and words. Water signs express the creative principle emotionally and sensitively, shaping feelings. Fire signs express this principle actively and spontaneously, shaping life.

Sunflowers are ruled by the Sun.

Vitality

The placement of the Sun in a chart shows the level of vitality that is available to the personality. In a receptive, negative sign, vitality flows gently and consistently but huge amounts of emotional energy are expended in water signs. In air, the energy is intellectual, in fire physical. In an active, positive sign, vitality flows strongly and abundantly, but reserves of energy become depleted and have to be renewed. The Sun also shows how the personality deals with disappointment. In fire and earth signs, resilience is strong. Ever optimistic, fire signs quickly bounce back; earth signs patiently endure. Water signs, however, can be wiped out, as their confidence is rarely strong enough to deal easily with disappointment. Air signs may need time to regroup until stimulated by something new.

The male principle

The Sun indicates how well the active, masculine part of the personality can flow. This energy is part of the psyche of both men and women, complementing feminine energy flow. When the Sun is placed in a positive sign, masculine energy impacts on the world; in negative signs it flows inwardly. So the Sun in positive signs is more able to assert itself. In passive signs a convenient surrogate in the outside world lives out the energy.

Gold is often used to symbolize kingship and authority.

The father

The Sun symbolizes the father, either as a parent or authority figure and significant male influences. An individual's expectation around fathering is described by the zodiac sign, coloured by the element. With the Sun in a fire sign, the expectation is of a warm, spontaneous father; in earth disciplined and dependable; in air authority figures are expected to be communicative and flexible; and in water sensitive and nurturing. Aspects to the Sun (see Aspects, pages 264–85) by the outer planets, indicate what kind of father or authority figure an individual expects. A difficult Saturn aspect, for example, points to a cold and controlling father, whereas Pluto suggests a father who is overpowering.

Disposition

Traditionally when the Sun is well placed, the disposition is noble, magnanimous, proud and humane. This is a faithful friend and a generous enemy. Adversely placed, the disposition is vain, boastful, arrogant, pompous and given to sycophantism.

SUN THROUGH THE SIGNS

Aries
Spontaneous self-expression. Self-orientated, selfish, energetic, brash and outgoing, the Sun in Aries indicates a personality that bounces back from setbacks, but abandons tasks.

Taurus
Practical self-expression. Pragmatic, conservative, reliable, persevering and stoical, the Sun in Taurus continues regardless of setbacks and never abandons tasks.

Gemini
Communicative self-expression. Restless, sociable, mind-orientated, versatile, highly-strung, the Sun in Gemini bounces back from setbacks, and multi-tasks.

Cancer
Cautious self-expression. Highly emotional, nurturing, possessive, introverted, the Sun in Cancer can withdraw after setbacks, but is generally tenacious over tasks.

Leo
Exuberant self-expression. Outgoing, enthusiastic, benevolent, playful, proud and autocratic, the Sun in Leo recovers quickly from setbacks and is a committed taskmaster.

Virgo
Competent self-expression. Practical, perfectionist, analytic, productive, functional and organized, the Sun in Virgo is committed and unperturbed by setbacks.

Libra
Affectionate self- expression. Sociable, dependent, artistic, pleasant and just, the Sun in Libra retreats from setbacks, dislikes criticism, but carries through tasks.

Scorpio
Secretive self-expression. Intense, perceptive, mysterious, passionate and powerful, the Sun in Scorpio continues regardless of setbacks and is focussed on tasks.

Sagittarius
Adventurous self-expression. Spontaneous, questing, questioning, philosophical and energetic, the Sun in Sagittarius bounces back after setbacks, but can burn out.

Capricorn
Controlled self-expression. Practical, authoritative, conservative, dogmatic, reliable and rule-abiding, the Sun in Capricorn is resilient in the face of setbacks and stalwart over tasks.

Aquarius
Unconventional self-expression. Innovative, progressive, inquisitive, radical, unpredictable and humanitarian, the Sun in Aquarius dislikes setbacks and is tenacious over tasks.

Pisces
Fluid self-expression. Impressionable, sensitive, vacillating, diffuse and deceptively passive, the Sun in Pisces withdraws after setbacks and vacillates over tasks.

TRADITIONAL CORRESPONDENCES

Day of the week	Sunday
Numbers	1, 8
Metals	Gold, brass
Mineral	Calcium
Vitamin	D
Musical note	C
Crystals	Diamonds, citrine, topaz, jasper, amber, rhodachrosite
Colour	Yellow
Physiology	Cardiovascular system including heart and pericardium, back, spine, thymus, life force, feverish complaints
Past life stumbling blocks	Misuse of personal power and authority
Associations	Head of state, the father, creativity, games, yellow apparel, articles of value, jewellery
Careers	Managing director, chief executive officer, ambassador, public relations, king, magistrate, jeweller, justice of the peace, superintendent, steward, goldsmith, brazier, coppersmith, minter of money, customs and excise officer
Trees	Mistletoe, almond
Plants	Succulents, stout stalks; reddish stems; deeply veined leaves; tap root; flowers that are yellow, orange or purple; aromatic plants with a pleasant taste; angelica, centaury, chamomile, eyebright, frankincense, helianthus, heliotrope, juniper, marigold, rosemary, rue, saffron
Foods	Rice, sunflowers, grapes, walnuts
Virtue	Hope
Vice	Indolence
Places	Palaces, magnificent buildings, dining rooms, towers, ostentatious apartments

MOON
The eternal feminine

Glyph	☽	The crescent of soul takes on form, linking spirit with matter and creating the womb, container of life.
Rules/Dignity		Cancer
Detriment		Capricorn
Exaltation		Taurus
Fall		Scorpio
Keywords		Emotional reactions, feeling, instincts, fluctuation, receptivity, reflection, habits, childhood, response, cycles, the mother, maternal instinct, the past, ancestral inheritance, the subconscious, moods

The Moon is traditionally associated with motherhood and pregnancy.

The urge to fulfil basic needs

The Moon is essentially a receptive and passive planet. Negative where the Sun is positive, it reflects life experience rather than initiating it. Fluctuating and cyclical, the Moon pertains to basic needs and survival instincts that arise out of the unconscious. It is the planet of ingrained habits and instinctual responses, of conditioning and patterns that we absorb without conscious thought. It is the planet of feelings and emotions.

The Moon exerts enormous influence over the tides of water and human experience.

As it is orientated towards survival, for many people the Moon's pull is stronger than that of the Sun. When the Moon is placed within a free-flowing sign, for example, it can overcome an inhibited, repressed sun-sign. In a controlling sign, expression of feelings can be blocked despite an outgoing sun-sign; and in a Moon-sensitive water sign, irrational feelings and unrecognized emotions can bring on an emotional outburst from even the coolest of sun-signs.

Lunar security

One of the strongest and most basic of human needs is for security. The position in which the Moon is placed in the chart indicates the area of life, the 'house', (see pages 228–63) in which the need for security is felt most strongly, and the element in which it is sought. In an earth sign, security is a physical matter, whereas in water signs it is an emotional one. For these signs, security lies in being needed, in the home or relationships, or in possessions or feelings. For fire and air signs, security is embedded in freedom from responsibility or duty and being oneself.

Lunar food

Food is another basic need. The Moon has great bearing on eating patterns and food habits. As well as the physical body, its placement describes what emotional, mental and spiritual 'food' a person needs to nourish the soul and shows ability, or lack of ability to self-nurture.

Conception and beyond

The highest tides are found at full Moon near the solstices.

The Moon represents habits and emotional inheritance, qualities and attitudes, strengths and weakness passes down through the family. Aspects (see pages 264–85) to the Moon from the outer planets show whether the *in utero* experience was positive or not. Pluto in aspect to the Moon suggests a hostile toxic uterus, whereas Neptune indicates a womb at its most nurturing.

Childhood has an enormous impact on future emotional maturity. The placement of the Moon and aspects to it, show whether childish emotional needs will be carried forward into adulthood to be replayed with a partner. For many people, adult relationships are driven by a lifelong quest to get those earlier, unfulfilled needs met or a fight to prevent being swamped by a partner or parent's needs.

The mother

The Moon represents the maternal instinct and the eternal feminine principle, indicating how strongly these manifest in an individual, man or woman. Its placement describes the type of mother that is expected and the qualities that are desired in a mother. No matter what sign she was born under, the mother is experienced in a style characteristic of her child's Moon sign. This experience may pertain to the positive qualities of the sign or the less constructive aspects.

Fire Moon people need a warm, outgoing mother who will help them explore the exterior world. Earth Moon people need a dependable mother who can provide a routine to make them feel secure. Air Moon people enjoy a mother who opens up the world through story and word play and who encourages free expression. Water Moon people need a mother who empathizes with their intense emotional experience and who is able to stimulate the imagination.

Disposition

Traditionally, when the Moon is well placed, the disposition is home-loving and well-mannered, but somewhat timid. When the Moon is poorly placed, disposition is idle, sluggish and discontented.

The Moon is concerned with genetic and psychic inheritance passing down the maternal line.

MOON THROUGH THE SIGNS

Aries   Emotionally headstrong and self-absorbed. Courageous, affectionate and sensitive, the Moon in Aries demands instant gratification, craves admiration and dislikes authority.

Taurus   Emotionally entrenched. Faithful, possessive and unimaginative, with ingrained habits and a powerful maternal instinct, the Moon in Taurus craves security and abhors change.

Gemini   Emotionally facile and fickle. Flexible, moody and intuitive, the Moon in Gemini rationalizes feelings, represses emotional needs and dislikes routine and does several things at once.

Cancer   Emotionally responsive. Empathetic, caring, moody, possessive, vulnerable, and strongly maternal or paternal, the Moon in Cancer has a deep need for security and refuses to let go.

Leo   Emotionally proud. Generous, confident, dominant, playful and self-indulgent, the Moon in Leo needs to feel special and dislikes being put down or ignored.

Virgo   Emotionally fastidious. Inhibited, self-critical, altruistic and lacking confidence, the Moon in Virgo analyzes feelings, has integrity and needs to be valued for services rendered.

Libra   Emotionally dependent. Peaceable, courteous, diplomatic, emotionally dishonest and critical, the Moon in Libra dislikes confrontation, is a people-pleaser and needs a partner.

Scorpio Emotionally intense. Perspicacious, compulsive, secretive, resentful and jealous, the Moon in Scorpio has the capacity for self-transformation but fears rejection or abandonment.

Sagittarius Emotionally restless. Independent, outspoken, uncommitted, warm-hearted, adventurous and impulsive, the Moon in Sagittarius needs freedom and dislikes emotional neediness.

Capricorn Emotionally controlled. Self-reliant, diligent, dependable, dutiful or authoritarian, and insecure, the Moon in Capricorn needs to control environment and family.

Aquarius Emotionally unpredictable. Independent, unconventional, isolated and uncommitted, the Moon in Aquarius prefers friendship to intimacy.

Pisces   Emotionally sensitive. Mendacious, compassionate, receptive, empathetic, imaginative, unreliable, gullible and self-indulgent, the Moon in Pisces has escapist tendencies.

TRADITIONAL CORRESPONDENCES

Day of the week	Monday
Number	2
Metals	Silver, aluminium
Mineral	None assigned
Vitamin	None assigned
Musical note	F
Crystals	Pearls, moonstone, opal, selenite
Colours	White, cream, silver
Physiology	Breasts, nipples, alimentary canal, digestive juices and lymphatic system; glands; nervous system; emotional disturbance
Past life stumbling blocks	Emotional excess and mothering issues
Associations	Mother, ancestors, emotion, rebirth, cycles, tides, baths, obstetrics
Careers	Sailor, navigator, traveller, fisherman, fishmonger, brewer, publican, milkman, miller, brewer, boatman, navy officer, midwife, nurse
Trees	Willow; trees rich in sap
Plants	Pale leaves; thick, firm, succulent and shallow roots; flowers that are bottle green, pale yellow or greenish white; plants with disagreeable odour or a sweetish or watery taste; chickweed, cleavers, white willow
Food	Cabbage, cress, cucumber, lettuce, melons, pumpkins, shellfish
Virtue	Chastity
Vice	Envy
Places	The oceans, lakes, fountains, seaports, rivers, fishponds, docks, springs, sewers, wharfs, dairies

MERCURY
The messenger

Glyph	The cross of matter sits below the circle of spirit and is surmounted by the crescent of soul. This is the triumph of mind over matter: active intelligence that can channel impulses from above and below.
Rules/Dignity	Gemini, Virgo
Detriment	Sagittarius
Exaltation	Virgo
Fall	Pisces
Keywords	Communication, travel, learning, knowledge, mind, thought, reason, logic, eloquence, perception, cunning, coordination, intellect, reason, writing, speech, gossip, wit, guile, trickster, adroit, expressive, memory

Fire Agate, a Mercury-ruled stone, encourages introspection.

The urge to communicate

Inquisitive Mercury is the planet of communication and the mind. It is concerned with intelligence in the sense of how quickly things are understood, although it also pertains to memory and reasoning. A well-placed Mercury takes in an enormous amount of information, synthesizes it and then, forming a net of connections, makes a great leap of intuition. This is the planet of writing, publishing, the media and

Mercurial people always have access to a means of communication.

telecommunications. As winged messenger of the gods, it also has association with roads, transport and commerce, the Internet and trips into the depths of one's psyche.

The dance of the Sun and Mercury

As Mercury is never far from the Sun, remaining within 28°, it acts as an interpreter in the process of self-expression. When Mercury falls in the same sign as the Sun, the effect of that sign is strengthened. If Mercury falls either side of the Sun sign, there is a clash of polarities: a negatively placed Sun is speeded up by a positive Mercury and a positively placed Sun is slowed down by a negative Mercury.

The elements also affect the Sun–Mercury dance. Mercury placed in a Water sign enhances emotional empathy and intuition, making a fiery Sun more aware of other people's feelings, whilst earth makes fiery self-expression more practical and restrains flights of fancy. Mercury in fire quickens the somewhat cautious self-expression of earth, making for a more spontaneous and outgoing personality; air urges cautious earth to faster speech and more communication. Earth deepens airy self-expression, so that it gives more thought to weighty issues; whilst water can drown an air Sun in an overly emotional reaction, but can also deepen intuition and encourage empathy. Air helps watery self-expression to become more rational and fire encourages a water Sun to be more self-expressive and self-assured.

Ways of thinking

Mercury's placement in the elements affects the way the mind works, indicating whether thinking is linear, following a well-defined pathway, or more intuitive and creative, exploring new pathways. In cerebral air or intuitive fire, Mercury is fast as lightning. This versatile placement suggests a person who can deal with many things at once but may overlook important details. In a watery sign, thought processes are irrational, and Mercury becomes the dreamer or the visionary. With Mercury in earth, mental processes tend to be more linear and slow to move beyond the boundaries of conventional thought.

Mercurial characteristics

Mercury-attuned people are characterized by their vivacity, youthfulness and boyish charm. Mercury has lightning reactions and a changeable nature. With this planet exerting influence, coordination between body and mind is good, and the hands are always talking. The mind is typically flighty and flexible.

Mercury is also the archetypal trickster. Things may not be what they seem when this untruthful character is at large. There is a need to perceive things from all angles, to keep an open mind and to be aware

Mercury is both winged messenger and patron of safe passage when travelling.

of the illogical, intuitive processes of the right brain as well as the logical, rational left brain. Difficult aspects (see pages 264–85) especially by Saturn and Uranus to Mercury usually lie at the root of impediments to speech or perception.

Adaptation to the environment

Mercury governs not only the autonomic processes of the body but also links the brain, central nervous system, the neural net and processes in the muscles and tissues so that instant adaptation to whatever is perceived by the brain is possible.

Disposition

Traditionally, when Mercury is well placed, the disposition is intelligent, subtle and logical, the personality witty and sharp. When poorly placed, the disposition is untrustworthy and unprincipled.

MERCURY THROUGH THE SIGNS

Aries   Personal communication. Outspoken, witty, impulsive, confident and argumentative, Mercury in Aries has a strong belief in its own ideas.

Taurus   Practical communication. With good concentration and a methodical, literal mind that is slow to form opinions or assimilate facts, Mercury in Taurus has a fixed outlook and refuses to change its mind.

Gemini   Quick-witted communication. Inquisitive, articulate, versatile, witty, intuitive and changeable, Mercury in Gemini simply has to communicate, at all times. Nervous tension is likely.

Cancer   Emotional communication. Intuitive, imaginative, thoughtful, subjective, with a highly retentive memory, Mercury in Cancer lives in a past coloured by emotional memories.

Leo   Creative communication. Confident, strong minded, boastful, prejudiced and conceited, Mercuy in Leo forms firm opinions quickly and holds on to them. This is a natural performer or show-off.

Virgo   Logical communication. Quick-witted and witty, analytical, perceptive, orderly, rational, discriminating and overly critical, Mercury in Virgo can get bogged down in the detail.

Libra   Shared communication. Fair-minded, logical, strategic, vacillating and judgmental, Mercury in Libra sees both sides of the argument and is dependent on the opinions of others.

Scorpio   Insightful communication. Strong-minded, perceptive, incisive, shrewd, manipulative and suspicious, Mercury in Scorpio is governed by instinctual beliefs and drawn to mysteries.

Sagittarius Philosophical communication. Broad-minded, tactless, with potential for bigotry or hypocrisy, Mercury in Sagittarius craves intellectual challenge and seeks the answers to life's big questions.

Capricorn   Conventional communication. Strong-minded, constructive, practical, controlled, calculating and sceptical, Mercury in Capricorn has a strong sense of how things ought to be.

Aquarius   Unconventional communication. Free-thinking, innovative, far-sighted, independent, original and erratic, Mercury in Aquarius separates feelings from thoughts.

Pisces   Intuitive communication. Imaginative, impressionable, gullible, deceptive and unfocussed, Mercury in Pisces has difficulty with boundaries, and confuses emotions with thoughts.

TRADITIONAL CORRESPONDENCES

Day of the week	Tuesday
Metal	Mercury
Mineral	Phosphorus
Vitamin	B complex
Musical scale	E
Crystals	Agate, tiger's eye
Colours	Light blue, azure, dove grey, violet
Physiology	Brain, nervous system, eyes, bronchial tubes, respiration, thyroid, thymus, organs of speech and hearing
Past life stumbling blocks	Slander, scandal, misunderstanding, lies, hearing or speech impediments
Associations	Intellect, vehicles, money, bills, paper, books, pictures, party wear, scientific instruments, penknives, inkstands, writing instruments, butterflies
Careers	Salesperson, broker, astrologer, writer, journalist, philosopher, mathematician, secretary, officer of state, poet, lawyer, printer, teacher, priest, orator, ambassador, artificer, scribe, public relations consultant, journalist, computer programmer, postal worker, driver, messenger
Trees	Filbert, hazel, mulberry, myrtle
Plants	Thin, feathery, ethereal and abundant flowers that are pleasing to the eye; deep, wide roots; plants with a subtle but penetrating odour; seeds in husks or pods, aniseed, dill, elecampane, fennel, horehound, lavender, liquorice, marjoram, parsley, southernwood, valerian
Foods	Hazelnuts, beans, mushrooms, fennel, pomegranate, carrots, celery
Virtue	Wisdom
Vice	Gluttony
Places	Schools, public assembly rooms, tennis courts, fairs, markets, bowling greens, studies, libraries, banks, legal offices

VENUS
Love

Glyph	♀	The circle of spirit surmounts the cross of matter, symbolizing union and love pouring into the world.
Rules/Dignity		Taurus, Libra
Detriment		Aries
Exaltation		Pisces
Fall		Virgo
Keywords		Relatedness, love, lust, sociability, desire, aesthetics, attraction, eroticism, female sexuality, harmony, charm, vanity, intimacy, rivalry, beauty, covetousness, gratification, lasciviousness, voluptuous

Venus always appears low down in the evening sky, as if waiting for the night, or low down in the dawn sky greeting the day.

VENUS

The urge for relationship

The brightest object in the sky after the Sun, Venus stays close to its solar companion, never straying more than 48°. Approaching closer to earth than any other planet (with the exception of the Moon), Venus represents one of the most obvious drives behind human behaviour: the need for relationship. The position of Venus in a chart indicates capacity for closeness and intimacy with others, and for relationship with oneself. The potential for self-esteem, this planet is a reminder that someone who cannot love and value his or her own self is unable to give and receive love or share affection or enter into intimacy.

Venus is a sociable planet, symbolizing the need to meet oneself through external relationship. With Venus in a compatible sign, especially with easy aspects (see pages 264–85), relationships flow freely and easily. Venus in an incompatible sign can point to a surface coolness or to transient relationships that mask a deep fear of intimacy.

Desire

Venus personifies desire – for emotional satisfaction, for all that is beautiful, aesthetic and valuable, for money in the bank. Venus serves as a reminder that what is valued externally is a reflection of what is most loved within oneself and what is attracted may be what is most feared.

Venus is erotic desire and comfortable relationships.

In art, Venus is often accompanied by her son Cupid, who fires love's darts.

Venus' position in the chart indicates what someone values and whether they believe they are worth loving and whether they deserve happiness. This planet also reveals the type of person with whom there is natural attraction and harmony. This may be lover or a friend, but most Venus-attuned friendships have something sexual and erotic at their heart, even if it is not acted upon.

Male and female Venus

In a man's chart, the position of Venus indicates what he is attracted to in a partner, the qualities he seeks, what turns him on and what he desires. Venus is his anima and his ideal woman – an idealized picture of the feminine which may turn sour.

Closely bound up with her sense of self and her own femininity in a woman's chart, sensuous Venus indicates how a woman presents herself to the world, the body language she uses to express her femininity, what she values in herself and how comfortable she feels with herself as a female. It is the need to look good.

In both men and women, Venus is sensuality, the capacity to enjoy gratification of the senses and to indulge the body. It is the urge to be glamorous, voluptuous, hedonistic, erotic, cosy, comforting, lustful or frigid, according to its sign.

Venus characteristics

A Venus-attuned person has a pleasing appearance and charming manner. Overtly or covertly, seductive Venus imparts a magnetic sexuality that is hard to resist. On the surface, this pleasure-attuned planet puts out the message 'come and get me'. Whether that message is blatant or subtle depends on the sign in which Venus is placed.

Beneath that superficial attractiveness, Venus is dark and erotic, possessing a compulsive drive that can manipulate mercilessly or even kill to obtain what it desires. The side of Venus that emerges is in part governed by outer planet aspects, but it is possible for the planet's duel nature to emerge at any time.

Disposition

Traditionally, when Venus is well placed, the disposition is charming, equable, quiet and placid, but easily aroused to jealousy. When Venus is poorly placed, the disposition is shameless, lascivious and profligate.

Venus represents the urge to look and feel good.

VENUS THROUGH THE SIGNS

Aries
Desires attention and flattery. Passionate, erotic, idealistic, hedonistic, impulsive and demanding, Venus in Aries falls in love quickly and is attracted to dominant partners.

Taurus
Desires sensual satisfaction. Affectionate, passive, faithful, possessive and jealous, finding deep satisfaction in marriage, Venus in Taurus falls quickly in lust, cautiously in love and is attracted to voluptuous partners.

Gemini
Desires mental stimulation. Charming, flirtatious, fickle and emotionally detached, inconstant Venus in Gemini falls in and out of love fast and is attracted to lively, intellectual partners.

Cancer
Desires emotional satisfaction and constancy. Sensuous, clinging, moody and emotionally possessive, Venus in Cancer falls cautiously in love and is attracted to maternal types with money in the bank.

Leo
Desires adoration. Erotic, dramatic, amorous, warm-hearted, demanding, generous and vain, Venus in Leo falls instantly in lust, slowly in love and is attracted to strong personalities.

Virgo
Desires perfection. Reserved, sensuous, controlled and critical of his or her partner, Venus in Virgo over-analyzes feelings, falls cautiously in love and is attracted to the 'perfect' partner.

Libra
Desires a 'significant other'. Charming, accommodating, romantic, unrealistic and self-indulgent, Venus in Libra falls easily in love and is attracted to a charmer.

Scorpio
Desires intensity and drama. Passionate, rapacious, jealous, erotic, manipulative and faithful, Venus is Scorpio falls permanently in lust or love and is attracted to temptresses or darkly handsome types.

Sagittarius
Desires companionship. Sociable, flirtatious, lusty, generous, independent and promiscuous, Venus in Sagittarius falls rapidly in and out of love and seeks a 'courtesan', an entertaining companion.

Capricorn
Desires respectability. Undemonstrative, cool until sexually aroused, and faithful, Venus in Capricorn falls cautiously in love, rapidly in lust and is looking for a status symbol.

Aquarius
Desires emotional freedom. Companionable, dispassionate and magnetic, Venus in Aquarius falls reluctantly in love and is attracted to unconventional, intellectual types.

Pisces
Desires emotional melding. Romantic, accommodating, seductive and elusive, Venus in Pisces confuses lust with love, falls quickly into both and is attracted to a fantasy.

TRADITIONAL CORRESPONDENCES

Day of the week	Wednesday
Number	3
Metals	Copper, bronze
Minerals	Iodine, sodium
Vitamin	Bioflavonoids
Musical note	A
Crystals	Malachite, tourmaline, emerald, green aventurine, rose quartz, kunzite, sapphire
Colours	Blue, pink, white, purple, green, turquoise, pastel hues
Physiology	Throat, kidneys, lumber region, parathyroids, venereal disorders, glandular swellings of the neck
Past-life stumbling blocks	Misuse of sexual attraction, failure to love
Associations	Arts, music, colour, love, social life, women's clothing, jewellery, bed linen, white wine, adultery
Careers	Musician, artist, model, sex-therapist, lap-dancer, courtesan, haberdasher, draper, painter, jeweller, embroiderer, chorister, escort, interior designer
Trees	Alder, fruit trees, ash, birch, pomegranate
Flowers	Large leaves; rich green plants; early flowering, roseate, abundant and beautiful plants with a pleasing odour and sweet taste; archangel, burdock, coltsfoot, daisy, lady's mantle, marshmallow, meadowsweet, mint, mugwort, pennyroyal, plantain, tansy, rose, thyme, vervain, yarrow
Foods	Potatoes, strawberries, wheat, sugar, nectarines
Virtue	Love
Vice	Lust
Places	Bedchambers, ballrooms, dining-rooms, gardens, fountains, wardrobes, banqueting houses, theatres

MARS
Will

Glyph	♂	In the ancient symbol, the cross of matter sat above the circle of spirit, symbolizing the creative force imposing its will. In the modern symbol, the cross is replaced by the arrow of desire.
Rules/Dignity		Aries, Scorpio
Detriment		Libra
Exaltation		Capricorn
Fall		Cancer
Keywords		Will, action, assertion, aggression, virility, self-preservation, lust, passion, male sexuality, energy, heat, anger, angst, rage, machismo, vigorous, impatience, burning

Mars is known as 'the red planet' – easily visible from earth.

The urge to act

Symbolizing a primitive, initiatory force, the position of the planet Mars on a chart reveals how assertive an individual is. This dynamic planet personifies the lust for conquest and the survival instinct. It is concerned with virility, passion, masculinity and potency.

Wilful Mars is so wrapped up in its own personal needs that it can appear anti-social. The urge to go out and make things happen or to defend and preserve what has already been gained, can manifest as assertion or aggression depending on how Mars is placed. Its force can be felt as an energizing, cleansing flame of anger or as a festering sore of rage and resentment. When Mars is placed in a sign that is already strongly self-defensive, its effect is to exacerbate this characteristic.

Faces of Mars

When Mars is well-placed, it cuts through to the core and gets things done. This Mars stands firm in the face of obstacles. With challenging aspects, however, Mars can display cruelty and uncontrolled aggression. People with strong Mars or a Mars in a fire sign are typically quick to lose control. Tempered by earth, the

Mars symbolizes lustful conquest and desire.

179

anger burns more slowly but it is spectacular when control is lost. In fixed signs, Martian anger becomes long-held rage and resentment. An irritable planet, especially in an air sign, a damped down Mars is expressed in whingeing or misdirected bursts of anger.

A blocked Mars feels helpless, powerless and impotent and is frustrated or apathetic. In fire signs, assertion quickly ignites into aggression. Fire signs do not get drawn into conflict against their will, but fight to the death to defend what they think is right. In water signs, the will may appear fluid – although, paradoxically, both Scorpio and Cancer have a strong will. In air signs, the will may be unfocussed, so that time is spent in planning and not in activity. Notwithstanding this Mars can assert itself through clear communication and is open to reason no matter how heated matters become. For air signs, self-preservation comes through as guile and cunning. With Mars in strong-willed earth signs, inertia may be a problem. However, earth is geared to self-preservation and will stand up to challenges if necessary.

Female and male Mars

Mars describes the type of man a woman attracts and is attracted towards. It indicates the strength of her libido, how directly this is expressed, and how comfortable she is with the masculine side of her nature. In a man's chart, Mars indicates how comfortable he is with his masculinity and what he projects out to the women in his life. (See also Relationship Astrology, pages 346–7.)

Mars can be a flaming sword, cutting rhough all the opposition.

Mars underlies the urge to go to war and fight for what one wants.

Passion

The passion of Mars is about embracing life in its fullness. In dynamic fire signs, Mars is volcanic: passion bursts out spontaneously and there is little build-up. In romantic water signs, whilst the passion may be as strong, it will not be as apparent. Water signs like to lead up to things gradually, savouring the passion of each moment. In pragmatic and sensual earth, Mars is more straightforward, indicating a personality with few hang-ups when it comes to expressing lust. Mars-in-air people tend towards mental rather than physical passion.

Martian characteristics

A strongly placed Mars indicates a competitive nature that boldly asserts itself. But Mars is thoughtless as well as honest. Impatient, insensitive and crude, Mars-attuned people may tread on toes in the process of getting things done. An aggressive urge towards self-preservation is mediated through the sign in which Mars is placed and may operate clandestinely or blatantly.

Disposition

Traditionally, when Mars is well placed, the disposition is courageous and fearless but irascible. This is a natural fighter. Poorly placed, the disposition is violent, quarrelsome and treacherous.

MARS THROUGH THE SIGNS

Aries
Brash assertion. Bold, competitive, aggressive, virile, impatient and reckless, Mars in Aries goes all out for what it desires and is attracted to macho men or dominant women.

Taurus
Tenaciously assertive. Determined, immovable, obstinate with an indolent streak, Mars in Taurus is slow to anger but has a ferocious temper, and is attracted to earthy types.

Gemini
Verbally assertive. Changeable, highly-strung, passionate about words, restless and impatient, Mars in Gemini skirts issues, wastes energy and is attracted to smooth talkers.

Cancer
Cautious. Emotionally demanding. Circuitous, diffident, fiercely protective and crabby, Mars in Cancer disguises strong will, never approaches directly and is attracted to protective partners.

Leo
Dramatically assertive. Self-confident, creative, lusty, proud, quick-tempered and arrogant, Mars in Leo wants to be top of heap and is attracted to power.

Virgo
Quietly assertive. Restrained, cautious, lacking vitality, hard-working and practical, Mars in Virgo pays attention to the smallest detail and is attracted to practical partners.

Libra
Rarely assertive. Adaptable and persuasive, laid-back, and peace seeking, Mars in Libra goes all out to please and is attracted to charmers.

Scorpio
Powerfully assertive. Attractive, sexy, unstoppable, jealous, energetic and with a strong libido, Mars in Scorpio steamrollers the opposition and is attracted to enigmatic partners.

Sagittarius
Boisterously assertive. Enthusiastic, energetic, bold and tactless with a tendency to exaggerate, Mars in Sagittarius is an inveterate traveller, attracted to free spirits.

Capricorn
Ambitiously assertive. Determined, practical and relentless, with a powerful sex drive, Mars in Capricorn cannot tolerate incompetence and is attracted to success.

Aquarius
Erratically assertive. Strong-willed, idealistic, radical and unpredictable with a scientific bent, Mars in Aquarius channels passion into ideals and is attracted to mavericks.

Pisces
Fluidly assertive. Impractical, self-sacrificing, imaginative and easily sidetracked, Mars in Pisces embraces martyrdom and has a strong sex drive, and is most attracted to fantasy lovers.

TRADITIONAL CORRESPONDENCES

Day of the week	Thursday
Number	5
Metals	Iron, brass
Mineral	Iron
Vitamin	E
Musical note	G
Crystals	Bloodstone, carnelian, cinnabar, pyrite, magnetite, ruby, garnet, hematite
Colour	Scarlet
Physiology	Muscular and urogenital systems, ovaries and testes, adrenals and suprarenals, red blood corpuscles, kidneys; resistance to disease; elimination of toxins
Past-life stumbling blocks	Overly aggressive, misuse of will, failure to overcome anger
Associations	Heat, action, arms, pepper, anything red, sharp instruments, cutlery, marauders, scissors, weapons, male sexuality, insect bites and stings, scalds, accidents
Careers	General, officer, soldier, physician, pharmacist, surgeon, gunner, butcher, bailiff, smith, baker, watchmaker, barber, cook, carpenter
Trees	Box, hawthorn, pine
Plants	Hard and long leaves (often spiked; serrated, pointed or pendulous leaves) and thorns; abundant red or yellow flowers and fruit; plants with an acrid or pungent odour and burning taste; agnus castus, aloes, anemone, arnica, belladonna, broom, bryony, capsicum, garlic, ginger, hops, mustard seed, nettles, pepper, wormwood
Foods	Chives, onions, leeks, peppers, radishes, rhubarb, tobacco
Virtue	Courage
Vice	Wrath
Places	Anywhere connected with fire, war or blood, laboratories, furnaces, distilleries, bakehouses, ovens, smiths, butchers' shops

JUPITER
The Mage

Glyph	♃	The crescent of soul rises above the cross of matter, symbolizing the soul triumphing over earthly experiences and consciousness freed from illusion.
Rules/Dignity		Sagittarius, Pisces
Detriment		Gemini
Exaltation		Cancer
Fall		Capricorn
Keywords		Expansion, optimism, good fortune, faith, philosophy, ritual, hope, knowledge, excess, abundance, luck, travel, inflation, creative visualization, largesse, generosity, wastage, cornucopia, opulence, generosity, conscience

Jupiter is one of the largest planets as befits this expansive energy.

The urge to expand

Jupiter is the drive towards expansion and success in the outer world. If this planet's power is used wisely, it is an opportunity to prosper. Used unwisely, Jupiter leads to over-extension and excess. As one of the planets of travel, Jupiter is also associated with the mental opening up that new horizons can bring. The mage is the eternal seeker after truth, and the urge towards new opportunities. The position this planet occupies in the chart highlights a need to grow in that area of life.

Jupiter is the traditional ruler of organized religions and religious sites.

Jupiter is linked to religion and belief systems, in the sense that they encourage a broader perspective. It is the planet of morality and law, faith and optimism as well as philosophical impulses. Everyone needs something to believe in and Jupiter indicates how and where this is sought, whether in the forces of materialism and consumerism or in something greater. With flowing aspects (see pages 264–85), Jupiter's call to expansion is effortless but if the aspects are challenging, knowledge can be hard won.

Jupiter and diet

The physical body also responds to Jupiter's call to expand. If self-indulgent Jupiter is placed in a needy sign, it can engender a lifelong habit of comfort eating. Food cravings or addictions are in part

Jupiter's domain, as the planet points to an out-of-control place that runs with an unconscious desire for more. Weight fluctuates according to Jupiter's transit cycle around the chart. There are parts of the cycle when it is easy to be disciplined and diet-conscious, and others, such as its transit over the Ascendant (see Transits, pages 300–309), when it becomes much more difficult.

Abundance

Ever the optimist, for Jupiter the glass is always half full rather than half empty. One of this planet's symbols is the cornucopia, the horn of plenty. It symbolizes the fertility and abundance that this planet can bring, sometimes as though from thin air. Trust is a Jupiter quality and this planet helps to make the most of a 'bad' situation.

Jupiter is never afraid to take a chance, which is why it is the planet of gambling. However, Jupitarian luck is capricious: it may appear like a bolt out of the blue and run out as suddenly as it arrived.

Creative visualization

Jupiter symbolizes the power of creation and manifestation. With Jupiter's assistance, something seen in the mind's eye can be brought into being. What Jupiter manifests is to some extent predetermined by the aspects (see pages 264–85): difficult aspects indicate an expectation of negative events, which naturally causes them to happen; easy aspects suggest a positive outlook. If necessary, the tendency can be turned around with Jupiter's assistance. This is what lies at the heart of making one's own luck. If you visualize something with passionate intensity, you can seize the opportunity when it arises and make it happen (see the Jupiter cycle, Transits, page 308).

In myth, Jupiter was an attractive, amoral seducer of innocent young women.

Jupiter characteristics

Jupiter strongly placed within a chart indicates a personality that is jovial, cheerful, optimistic and expansive – if the aspects are favourable. This is someone who always wants to go further, who pushes for more, who risks everything on the throw of the dice and who may well go over the top.

Jupiter with difficult aspects, on the other hand, suggests a tendency to exaggerate and procrastinate, and is associated with extravagance, conceit and the possibility of fraud and lawlessness. This Jupiter may be the gambler or the extremist.

Disposition

Traditionally, when Jupiter is well placed, the disposition is wise, magnanimous, liberal and prudent. When Jupiter is poorly placed, the disposition can be bigoted and hypocritically religious.

JUPITER THROUGH THE SIGNS

Aries
Expansion through challenge. Headstrong, willful and often over-the-top, Jupiter in Aries views life as an endless opportunity to grow.

Taurus
Expansion through possessions and good living. Ambitious, acquisitive, hedonistic and ostentatious, Jupiter in Taurus has a tendency to put on weight.

Gemini
Expansion through new concepts. Exceedingly talkative, Jupiter in Gemini tells tall tales, exaggerates abilities and distributes fresh beliefs.

Cancer
Expansion through nurturing. Sympathetic, protective and dedicated to caring for others, Jupiter in Cancer uses food as emotional sustenance.

Leo
Expansion through holding court. Dramatic, flamboyant and self-confident, with enormous pride and personal dignity, Jupiter in Leo makes a big impression.

Virgo
Expansion through mental productivity. Gentle, unassuming and idealistic, Jupiter in Virgo is quietly ambitious.

Libra
Expansion through pleasure. Seeking pleasure and companionship, sociable Jupiter in Libra has a hedonistic streak and wants to be popular.

Scorpio
Expansion through hidden knowledge. Placing strong emphasis on sexual activity, Jupiter in Scorpio nevertheless pushes back the boundaries of esoteric knowledge.

Sagittarius
Expansion through knowledge. Optimistic, lucky and prone to wild exaggeration, Jupiter in Sagittarius is happy to take a gamble, enjoys life to the full.

Capricorn
Expansion through breaching boundaries. Ambitious and success-orientated, Jupiter in Capricorn may be far-sighted and wise, or feel hemmed in by rigid rules.

Aquarius
Expansion through helping humanity. Tolerant and far-sighted but prone to eccentricity, Jupiter in Aquarius is attracted to causes.

Pisces
Expansion through imagination. Artistic, lacking discipline and direction, and religiously inclined, Pisces in Jupiter may escape into wild fantasies.

TRADITONAL CORRESPONDENCES

Day of the week	Friday
Number	6
Metal	Tin
Minerals	Silica, chromium
Vitamin	None assigned
Musical note	B
Crystals	Turquoise, chrysocola, topaz, citrine, jasper
Colours	Purple, red with green, green, yellow, turquoise
Physiology	Liver, pancreas, pituitary gland, sciatic nerve, tumours, disposition of fats, obesity and excess
Past-life stumbling blocks	Failure to respect religious teachings or to live up to the demands of the spiritual path, over-indulgence and excess
Associations	Abundance, prophecy, religion, philosophy, knowledge, expansion, universities, foreign travel, books, honey, oil, silk, fruit, men's clothing, merchandise, horses, domestic fowl, gambling, excess and over-indulgence
Careers	Judge, senator, professor, counsellor, lawyer, preacher, investment banker, professional gambler, doctor, bishop, minister, chancellor, woollen draper, entertainer, mentor, diet counsellor
Tree	Oak
Plants	Smooth leaves with veins not deeply marked; greyish-blue-green leaves; flowers that are ruddy, blue, purple or yellow; small roots; plants with a subtle odour; agrimony, borage, dandelion, sage
Foods	Chervil, endive, asparagus, figs
Virtue	Faith
Vice	Pride
Places	Churches, oratories, palaces, altars, courts of justice, wardrobes, magnificent abodes, woods and orchards

SATURN
The way-shower

Glyph	♄	Authority and the cross of matter is imposed on the soul, symbolizing the responsibilities and challenges that mortality imposes.
Rules/Dignity		Capricorn, Aquarius
Detriment		Cancer
Exaltation		Libra
Fall		Aries
Keywords		Limitation, control, consolidation, structure, boundaries, thrift, conservation, strength, discipline, direction, wisdom, resilience, karma, the shadow, self-condemnation, time, fear, denial, hardship, responsibility, mentor

Saturn is bounded by its rings.

Saturn symbolizes limits and boundaries of all kinds.

The urge for conservation

Cold, hard and stern, Saturn points the way along the path of duty and destiny. A hard taskmaster, in medieval astrology it was the edge of the known, and Saturn still stands for boundaries and limitations. Its placement in the chart shows where resources have to be hoarded to conserve energy, what traditions have to be adhered to, where the status quo should be upheld and what responsibilities need to be taken seriously. Used positively, this somewhat cold and hard planet gives structure and form to everyday existence.

Saturn also represents the point at which limitations become unacceptable and restrictions need to be breached. It is where responsibility has to be taken for oneself, where karma has to be transcended, where inner discipline is formed and the soul can grow. If this resilience is not developed, then something 'out there' is likely to impose discipline and restriction. Authority figures of all kinds pertain to Saturn. When Saturn is worked with constructively, strength and discipline develop, and the soul is tempered so that it can bend instead of breaking. As the way-shower, Saturn points to where the soul must live in accord with its inner purpose and its destiny.

Saturn represents law and order at many levels: personal, societal, collective, karmic and cosmic. It is concerned with convention and conservation of the old order, bureaucracy and government. In this role, it gives Uranus (see page 202–207) something to rebel against.

The Lord of Karma

Saturn is the law of cause and effect in action. Life is not a random process, but is based on the result of previous actions: the credits and deficits of the soul's journey. As such, Saturn embodies a balancing and shaping drive, concerned with reparation and reward, recompense and fairness. Karmic justice says that if the soul is able to take responsibility for itself, it creates a positive future. If it cannot, it appears that punishment is inflicted by a vengeful god.

The Keeper of Time

Saturn watches over the allotted span on earth and calls the soul home when it is ended. In this role, Saturn is controller and conserver, balancing the expansion of Jupiter. Without Saturn, things would get out of hand, but a fearful Saturn resorts to over-tight control.

Saturn is Old Father Time, the Lord of Death.

This is also the planet of old age. Saturn is happiest in maturity, when burdens and responsibilities weigh least. Age confers wisdom, the sagacity that develops through experience.

The shadow

Saturn also represents the unacceptable, shadow side of personality. It is all that is repressed and disowned, pushed down into the unconscious mind. Saturn stands at the boundary of the known and the unknown and offers insight that has to be hard won from the depths. By accepting the despised qualities of the shadow, the soul becomes whole, freed from fear and self-condemnation.

Saturnine characteristics

People with Saturn strong in their natal chart are seldom young, even as babies. They bear the mantle of Saturn: responsibility and seriousness. This is someone with a highly developed sense of duty. In extreme cases, the Saturn-dominated child learns through deprivation and poverty, developing an inner strength that manifests later in life.

Stern and disciplined, Saturnine personalities have little time for play, but they are always just. Saturn is not swayed by spurious debate. Used positively, this planet imparts great strength of character and resilience. Used negatively, Saturn creates fears and a deep reluctance to try anything new or challenging.

Disposition

Traditonally, when Saturn is well placed, the disposition is reserved, dignified and solicitous. When poorly placed, the disposition is grim, covetous, mistrustful and pedagogic.

SATURN THROUGH THE SIGNS

Aries
This placement holds natural impulsiveness in check, frequently resulting in frustration, but also providing the discipline to move forward once motivated.

Taurus
This placement provides dogged determination and enormous tenacity. Feelings are tightly controlled and progress is made cautiously.

Gemini
This placement can result in unusually slow but deeply serious thought-processes and restricted speech patterns. Communication may be inhibited or disabled.

Cancer
This security-conscious placement clings firmly to the past, creating rigid boundaries to protect loved ones. Depression and moodiness are possible.

Leo
This placement may limit or delay creative expression or channel it into a rigid outlet. Life may be difficult because the pleasure principle is effectively blocked.

Virgo
This placement is extremely methodical, highly conscientious and hard-working. It is pedantic and critical and failure is its biggest fear.

Libra
This placement may have difficulty in relating to others. Coolly objective, with infinite patience, it holds back from intimacy and is lonely as a consequence.

Scorpio
This placement has strongly controlled or repressed emotions. Highly secretive and reserved, it is resentful and extremely slow to forgive.

Sagittarius
This placement often undertakes long periods of disciplined study, but may be mentally restricted by a rigid belief system. Lack of education can hamper self-belief.

Capricorn
This placement is extremely cautious and careful, possessing the ability to plan and stick to long-term strategies for success. Rigid, traditional views hold sway.

Aquarius
This placement follows a solitary path, often as a lone idealist with rigid although unconventional views or may fit awkwardly into society.

Pisces
As planet and sign are diametrically opposed in this placement, restrictions cause much frustration. Isolation is feared as is fluidity.

TRADITIONAL CORRESPONDENCES

Day of the week	Saturday
Number	4
Metals	Lead, iron, steel
Minerals	Calcium, phosphorus, sulphur, asbestos
Vitamin	None assigned
Musical note	D
Crystals	Diamond, onyx, green calcite
Colours	Black, green, grey, orange
Physiology	Skeleton, gall-bladder, spleen, skin, teeth, nails, vagus nerve, joints, bile secretion
Past-life stumbling blocks	Failure to carry out duties, fulfil expectations or accord respect to authority; refusing to take a risk and grow
Associations	Structure, crystallization, old age, blockages, anything dark, wool, heavy materials, agricultural implements, wheelbarrows, spades, farm houses and buildings, cold
Careers	Law-maker, barrister, judge, banker, business person, comedian, scriptwriter, clown, bricklayer, miner, potter, plumber, brewer, sexton, gardener, farmer, shoemaker, dyer, excavator, archaeologist, tanner
Trees	Aspen, blackthorn, buckthorn, cypress, elm
Plants	Hardy, dry, hairy or prickly leaves; flowers with a black tinge; spreading roots; plants with a fetid odour, especially ones that are toxic or poisonous;; comfrey, fumitory, shepherd's purse, hemlock, henbane, aconite, belladonna, hellebore
Food	Barley, beetroot, safflower, parsnips, spinach
Virtue	Prudence
Vice	Covetousness
Places	Deserts, woods, valleys, caves, sepulchres, church yards, ruins, coalpits, sinks, wells, muddy or dirty places, institutions

CHIRON
The wounded healer

Glyph	The most commonly accepted glyph for Chiron – a K over the circle of spirit – illustrates how this planet acts as a channel for spiritual authority to manifest on Earth, healing the duality of existence.
Rules/Dignity	Rulership not yet assigned, possibly Virgo
Detriment	Not yet assigned
Exaltation	Not yet assigned
Fall	Not yet assigned
Keywords	Woundedness, suffering, fragmentation, healing, paradox, dilemmas, renunciation, initiation, fusion, the shaman, the key, the maverick, integration

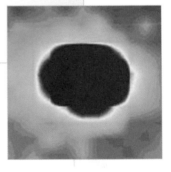

An astronomical puzzle, it has been suggested that Chiron may be a comet, a 'planetoid' or even a very large meteorite.

The urge for integration and healing

The most recently accepted of the astrological planets, Chiron is a paradox. The mythological Chiron was both healer and warrior. He was immortal and yet was mortally wounded, so endured constant pain. In the end, he renounced his immortality, took on someone else's pain, and was elevated to a place in the heavens.

With the head of a man and the torso of a horse, the centaur represents a fusion between the instinctual self and self-consciousness. This planet is the urge to resolve the dilemmas and paradoxes of the disparate parts of the self. In uniting opposites and embracing extremes, Chiron offers the gift of healing. Its placement in the chart indicates what must be integrated into and eliminated from life in order for an individual to achieve wholeness. With his sword held ready to cut away all that is diseased and outworn, Chiron can cut through the patterns of the past to offer creative solutions to seemingly insoluble problems. This is the planet that accompanies transitions and inner healings, and that aids rebirth into the Aquarian age of equality.

The cosmic messenger

From an astronomical point of view, Chiron is not a planet at all. This maverick visitor to the zodiac moves in an erratic, elliptical orbit that passes between Saturn and Uranus, and then between Saturn and Jupiter, bringing impersonal energies from beyond consciousness into awareness. When placed between Saturn and Uranus, Chiron raises the vibrations in the physical body and stimulates the chakras, the body's energy centres. When it moves into orbit between Saturn and Jupiter, it seeds potential from the outer planets, and can act as the conduit by which their energies pour down to Earth. In the role of cosmic messenger, Chiron acts as a bridge between the worlds and urges integration of the known with the unknown.

The lost comet

Chiron is believed to be a comet that became trapped within the solar system. In esoteric literature, comets came into the solar system and swept up the collective psychic debris that had been generated across aeons of time. This debris was incinerated and transmuted in the comet's tail. Chiron's

Chiron taught the arts of healing and warfare. Many of his pupils became great heroes.

entrapment suggests that humanity can no longer rely on this cosmic clearing process. It is necessary for each individual to take responsibility and recognize that suffering is largely created out of ignorance and greed. Much of our plight is caused by a refusal to be part of the greater whole, or of the whole Self, resulting in fragmentation. Chiron urges the giving up of this separation and the fusing of the instinctual nature with the spiritual self.

The soul's wound

Chiron's placement in the chart symbolizes the soul's wound. In past-life astrology, Chiron represents the pain that is carried forward from life to life. It shows where healing is needed and where suffering must be set aside. This healing is not merely a question of 'making it better'. True healing goes to the core and may entail a descent into darkness and acceptance of a part of the self that will always be wounded – and yet in embracing that pain rather than rejecting it, healing is found.

Chiron characteristics

Someone with Chiron strong in their chart meets suffering early in life. But whether the wound is physical or mental, the potential is there to reach beyond it. Chiron is strong in the charts of healers and shamans. Shamans link the unseen forces, the spiritual realm, with the physical world and act as a go-between. Having passed through many levels of initiation and died to the old self, the power of the spirit is activated. (See also the Chiron transit cycle, pages 308–309.)

Disposition

When well placed, the disposition is kindly and caring, often leading to a role as teacher or mentor. When poorly placed, the disposition is pained and wounded, an alienated outsider or scapegoat.

Chiron has strong links with healing of all kinds, but especially with complementary medicine.

CHIRON THROUGH THE SIGNS

Aries
Wound is in the ego or the Self. It may be necessary to renounce the ego. Healing comes through being centred in one's Self.

Taurus
Wound is in the body or in loss of a sense of security or self-worth. Body and soul have to be integrated. Healing comes through finding inner security.

Gemini
Wound is in making oneself heard and may affect breathing. Healing comes through speaking one's truth and avoiding wounding words.

Cancer
Wound is emotional and may manifest as psychosomatic illness. Healing comes through emotional detachment and nurturing one's Self.

Leo
Wound is in the heart or in self-expression. Healing comes through being empowered and in resolving the head–heart paradox.

Virgo
Wound may manifest at a mental or nervous level with perfectionism and self-criticism as likely causes. Healing comes through service to others.

Libra
Wound is in relationship with others or with one's Self. Healing comes through reconciling the needs of the self with the needs of another.

Scorpio
Wound may lie in unhealed, past-life experiences around death and other death-related trauma. Healing comes through recognizing and integrating the dark parts of the soul.

Sagittarius
Wound may have been caused by a previous adherence to a particular belief system or may lie in present-life attitudes, such as closed mindedness. Healing comes in mental reprogramming.

Capricorn
Wound may be carried in the skeletal system or relate to past-life authoritarianism. People with this placement may achieve a great deal at a young age, but remain closed to the suffering of other people until brought graphically to their attention. Healing comes in finding inner authority rather than accepting the authoritarianism of society.

Aquarius
Wound is in not being accepted in society. This placement suggests the alienated outsider or scapegoat for the troubles of the world. Healing comes in reconciling the needs of the individual with those of society.

Pisces
Wound is loss of union with the divine. Healing comes through recognizing one's Self as divine and integrating this into everyday life.

TRADITIONAL CORRESPONDENCES

Day of the week	None assigned
Metal	None assigned
Musical note	None assigned
Crystal	Charoite
Colour	None assigned
Physiology	Immune system, thighs, genitals
Past-life stumbling blocks	Unhealed wounds and fears, personality splits, role as victim or scapegoat
Associations	Holistic health, chiropody, chiropractic, herbs, healing tools, shamans, renunciation, keys, horses, spiritual warrior, war
Careers	Doctor, nurse, counsellor, warrior, paramedic, holistic healer, therapist, chiropractor
Trees; Plants; Food; Virtue; Vice	None assigned
Places	Greece, hospitals, schools, war zones

URANUS
The awakener

Glyph	♅	The dual soul of humanity is separated by the cross of matter, linking the human to the divine, supported and energized by the circle of spirit.
Rules/Dignity		Aquarius
Detriment		Leo
Exaltation		Scorpio
Fall		Taurus
Keywords		Chaos, change, vibration, originality, unpredictability, non-conformity, deviance, revolution, rebellion, higher mind, intuition, change and transformation, liberation, research, breakdown, genius, invention, technology

This maverick planet has a highly eccentric orbit and axis spin.

The urge for transformation

The great mover and shaker, symbolizing change or chaos, Uranus seeks to transcend limits, to move beyond the boundaries of established thought and to crack resistance, opening the way. It is the rebellious energy that throws off the past to make room for the new. As such, the position of Uranus in a birthchart reveals where the soul needs to break free from restriction. But when Uranian energy flows out of control, revolution runs wild. The greatest challenge for Uranus is to preside over orderly evolution that takes the best of the past into the new and makes crisis into opportunity.

Uranian thought processes

As the higher vibration of Mercury – the universal not personal mind – Uranus shares some of that planet's qualities. Whereas Mercury follows rational, logical thought processes, Uranus is intuitive and illogical, arriving at unexpected solutions. Uranus symbolizes independent,

Uranus is the urge towards revolution and overwhelming change.

creative thought that makes itself known through dreams and during inattentive moments. This planet strikes out of the blue as a flash of inspiration. Although this energy cannot be restrained, it can be channelled constructively.

The outsider

This wayward planet is different from any other. It has a rapidly oscillating magnetic field and its orbit is highly eccentric. It revolves on its axis at a right angle to the other planets, so that its poles seem to lie

Uranian science is not always beneficial for humanity.

where other planets have their equators. As such, this planet represents the part of the psyche that is the outsider, the misfit and the genius. Despite its inner patterns of constant, harmonic vibration, Uranus brings the unexpected and cannot be pinned down.

Vibration and innovation

In the ancient creation myths, earth was formed out of the void and continually threatened to return to chaos. It is Uranus that holds the balance. Uranus is the planet of vibration and magnetism, attraction and repulsion. It is a dynamic unifying force that holds the universe in motion. If vibration is out of sync or in disequilibrium, Uranus brings it back into rhythm. If it is too rigid, Uranus shakes it loose. Drawing on its links with vibration, and also inventiveness, Uranus is the planet of technology. It symbolizes all that is new and challenging, and all that threatens to tear apart the fabric of society or the planet.

Uranian characteristics

Uranian people can seem wired, as though crackling with static. This is an innovator, a rebel, a non-conformist – anyone who challenges accepted norms and conventions. Detached and perhaps aloof, someone with Uranus strong in his or her birthchart feels no need to be socially accepted. This personality nevertheless has a deep sense of social awareness. This is someone who lives a step ahead of the rest of humanity and, as such, is frequently misunderstood. While a passive sun-sign might tone down a strong Uranus, a Uranius-attuned person always finds a way to challenge injustice, to fight for the underdog and to pursue causes that will change the world.

Associated with eccentricity, Uranus also symbolizes all that is freakish and bizarre. Strong or difficult aspects to Uranus are translated in a need to be different, perverse and unorthodox. When Uranian power goes awry in this way, it indicates someone who is antisocial and anarchic.

Disposition

Traditionally, whether well or poorly placed, the disposition tends towards chaotic and eccentric. Well-placed Uranus is inventive and revolutionary, whilst a poorly placed Uranus is rebellious and unstable.

Uranian creativity is next season's trend.

URANUS THROUGH THE SIGNS

Aries
This placement is a loose cannon. Original, unpredictable, disruptive and independent, it indicates great personal ingenuity and a tendency to seek change regardless of cost.

Taurus
In this placement, irresistible force meets an immovable object that creates enormous tension; something has to blow. It is inventive in a practical way.

Gemini
This placement is highly intuitive, verbally unpredictable and inventive, with original but logical thought-processes. It sees new possibilities but does not always act on them.

Cancer
This placement seeks emotional independence from family and needs to break free from caring for others. It may be emotionally unstable or erratic.

Leo
This placement may display charismatic leadership or supreme arrogance. It indicates creative and original ideas.

Virgo
This placement promotes an interest in unconventional healing and health fads. It seeks to modernize outdated and inefficient practices and can revolutionize creativity.

Libra
This placement urges expression of individuality in relationships, which may be explosive or highly unconventional. Social values may be revolutionized.

Scorpio
This placement seeks a new understanding of life and death, with leanings towards metaphysics. It can be cruel and emotionally unpredictable.

Sagittarius
Unconventional beliefs direct life for this freedom-loving placement, associated with revolutionary ideals and an urge to expose hypocrisy and humbug.

Capricorn
This highly-strung placement seeks to transform society and government. It can indicate brilliant business and political strategies, or eccentric ideas.

Aquarius
This placement wants to revolutionize humanity, securing equal rights for all. Thought processes are ingenious and could resort to terrorism.

Pisces
This placement indicates powerful intuition at the mercy of strong emotions, resulting in confusion and misdirection. Visionary insights into the nature of consciousness overturn established knowledge in favour of a new perception into the nature of reality.

TRADITIONAL CORRESPONDENCES

Day of the week	None assigned
Number	22
Metal	Uranium
Minerals	Magnesium, manganese
Vitamin	None assigned
Musical note	None assigned
Crystals	Lapis lazuli, sapphire, aquamarine, azurite, chalcedony
Colours	Electric blue, plaids, checks, mingled tones
Physiology	Nervous and circulatory systems, electricity in the nerve cells, gonads, pineal gland, acute psychiatric problems
Past-life stumbling blocks	Failure to initiate reforms or rebellion, misuse of science, misuse of magical powers
Associations	Electricity, science and technology, chaos and violent upheaval, astrology, steam engines, coal, machinery, coins, baths, fishponds, anything dangerous, computers, magnets, inventions, perversions, cramp
Careers	Quantum physicist, researcher, welfare worker, antiquarian, astrologer, teacher, scientist, chemist, lecturer, sculptor, metaphysician, hypnotherapist, computer programmer
Trees; Plants; Food; Virtue; Vice	None assigned
Places	Railways, banks, gas vessels, psychiatric hospitals, hospitals, offices, dispensaries, fortified places

NEPTUNE
The visionary

Glyph		The semi-circle of the soul is pierced by the cross of matter, representing the interface between the spirit and the material world. The three prongs symbolize facets of consciousness: the unconscious mind, everyday awareness and cosmic consciousness.
Rules/Dignity	Pisces	
Detriment	Virgo	
Exaltation	Leo	
Fall	Aquarius	
Keywords	Unboundedness, dissolution, inspiration, illusion, ecstasy, romantic love, escapism, enlightenment, addiction, nebulousness, glamour, deception, mysticism, disintegration, impressionability, confusion, guilt, intangible, sacrifice, glamour	

Neptune's surface is diffuse and deceptive, it wears a veil of illusion that is impossible to penetrate.

The urge to transcend

Neptune embodies the urge to transcend the boundaries that keep the soul separate from the whole. This planet moves between the greatest extremes: from the highest spiritual awareness through imagination, fantasy and illusion, to the depths of deception and disillusionment. The planet of mysticism, glamour and enchantment, Neptune exerts a hypnotic fascination. It is the urge to transcend the everyday world, to

Watery Neptune was ruler of the oceans.

move into higher states of consciousness and to merge with the divine or to escape reality. When Neptune operates positively, it endows an individual with the ability to reach out and bring inspiration down into form, creating the poet and the visionary. But although the planet aspires to enlightenment, it may lead to ecstasy or madness. People with a strong Neptune seek dissolution of the ego, the small self, but all too often the intention dissolves into not knowing who or what the self really is. Many such personalities end up in institutions of one kind or another, living under the illusion that they have found divine inspiration.

Unconditional love

As the higher vibration of Venus, Neptune shares some of that planet's qualities. It is the archetypal romantic, someone who seeks an ideal and idealized love. Although this trait can lead to co-dependency, Neptune carries with it the potential for truly unconditional love that accepts the other person as they are.

Victim-martyr-saviour

One of the most powerful drives that underlies Neptune is that of the victim-martyr-saviour. Neptune wants to save the world or one person. There is nothing Neptune likes more than self-sacrifice. But all too often and too easily Neptune slips into victim or martyr role. This impractical planet is easily taken advantage of, especially when it comes to doing things in the name of love.

Neptune has to do with mysticism and the search for enlightenment.

Addiction

Neptune's diffuseness makes it difficult to grasp. It is as though the planet wears a veil of illusion. Its energy is unfathomable, slipping away into uncharted depths. Neptune remembers that the soul was once part of infinite oneness and urges reunion. This is why Neptune is so often linked to escapism of all kinds. It is the planet of addiction and disintegration, as well as imagination, seeking spirit in a bottle.

Neptune characteristics

Neptune-attuned people possess glamour in the old sense of the word: the ability to bewitch. They are also impossible to categorize or pin down, demonstrating the planet's elusive quality. Lacking strong boundaries, Neptune-attuned people are susceptible to outside influences. They may feel alienated or isolated in an uncaring world, or may be saints or gurus, or ordinary people with an artistic or musical vision. Neptune is highly compassionate, ruling psychics and dreamers as well as psychotics. But it is also the planet of illusion, so confidence tricksters are included under its mantle.

Disposition

Traditionally, when well placed, the disposition is gentle and visionary, given to the arts and music. When poorly placed, the disposition is addictive, escapist and prone to delusion.

Music and artistic pursuits are under the influence of Neptune.

ZODIAC POSITIONS

Approximate sign positions of Neptune

1916–1928	Leo
1928–1943	Virgo
1943–1956	Libra
1956–1970	Scorpio
1970–1984	Sagittarius
1984–1998	Capricorn
1998–2011	Aquarius
2011–2025	Pisces

NEPTUNE THROUGH THE SIGNS

Note: Due to its long orbit, which means that Neptune won't reach these signs until far in the future, Neptune in Aries, Taurus, Gemini or Cancer are not included.

Leo
This placement aspires to grandiose creativity, but ideas may be nebulous or impractical. Dramatic self-expression is common but the image of self may be an illusion.

Virgo
This placement aspires to service and sacrifice for the good of the whole. Neptune may distort perception but Virgo can be a constructive channel for inspiration.

Libra
This placement aspires to romantic love but falls prey to delusions and deception. Relationships are idealized, in the mistaken belief that charm is all it takes. This combination used positively, however, can lead to a new level of interdependent relationship.

Scorpio
This placement carries the urge to sublimate personal power into religious or spiritual experiences but is subject to delusion. Escapist tendencies are heightened and hidden secrets revealed. Extreme cruelty is possible.

Sagittarius
This placement urges the expansion of consciousness and supports spiritual rather than religious practices. The illusion lies in false gurus and inappropriate gods, but the potential exists for spiritual vision.

Capricorn
This placement wants to shape inspiration. The delusion lies in worshipping the false gods of materialism and a culture that seeks success at all costs and where the end justifies the means.

Aquarius
This placement aspires to humanitarianism and has a vision for a better world. The danger lies in confusing ideologies with rational thought.

Pisces
This placement aspires to total merging, a return to the source. The danger lies in being unable to distinguish between escapism and true spiritual inspiration.

TRADITIONAL CORRESPONDENCES

Day of the week	None assigned
Number	7, 11
Metal	Neptunian
Minerals	Zinc, potassium
Vitamins	C and A
Musical note	None assigned
Crystals	Amethyst, fluorite, jade, sugilite, coral, aquamarine
Colours	Sea-green, indigo, violet
Physiology	Cerebrospinal fluid, pineal gland, lymphatic and nervous systems, thalamus, spinal canal, mental processes, addictions, schizophrenia, psychoses, infectious diseases
Past-life stumbling blocks	Failure to develop spiritually, displaying weakness or practising deception, retreat into fantasy, misuse of psychic gifts
Associations	Photography, music, drink and drugs, gas, religion, poetry, mimicry, addictions, cameras, anaesthetic, telepathy, dancing
Careers	Musician, actor, designer, artist, painter, jeweller, vintner, brewer, chorister, pop singer, photographer, engraver, psychic, metaphysican, psychic counsellor, poet, hypnotherapist, confidence trickster
Trees; Plants; Food; Virtue; Vice	None assigned
Places	Anywhere near or beneath water

PLUTO
The renewer

Glyph		The crescent of soul hovers above the cross of matter, surmounted by the spirit, symbolizing the descent of spirit through the soul into matter, and the unconscious mind experiencing the fire of transformation.
Rules/Dignity	Scorpio	
Detriment	Taurus	
Exaltation	Not yet ascertained	
Fall	Not yet ascertained	
Keywords	Power, abuse, birth-death-rebirth, regeneration, elimination, taboo, pollution, transmutation, subversion, obsession, compulsion, the unconscious mind, decay, dictator, orgasm, religious conversation, psychoanalysis	

Although small and far away, Pluto nevertheless exerts a powerful influence.

The urge to regenerate

Pluto embodies the drive to confront all that is deepest and darkest in the psyche. The planet of pollution, inner and outer, it is the toxicity of emotional and psychic abuse, and the repository of all things that are deemed unacceptable and 'evil' in oneself and in the world. Pluto is all that must be eliminated, including the festering resentment, envy and jealousy

Pluto is the seed that germinates in darkness and then bursts through into new life.

that lurks in the depths of the psyche. The planet forces such things out into the open so that the psychological processes that lie at the root of the behaviour can be understood – and transformed. It tempers the gold within the soul. This planet has much to offer those who are prepared to explore the places where others fear to tread. Used wisely, Pluto can transmute the blackest of experiences to release a potent creative force. All that has decayed becomes fertile compost for new growth. Seeds are sown and germinate in darkness. Pluto brings new life forcefully if necessary. Used unwisely, Plutonian darkness festers, leading to an orgy of destruction. When unresolved, explosive Plutonian rage leads to war.

The cycle of life

Pluto has powerful links with the conception-birth-death-rebirth cycle in which energy is constantly reborn, dies and is renewed. The planet is connected with death of all kinds, especially endings and beginnings. Pluto is also intimately associated with the kind of sexual act in which the ego dies in an intense, orgasmic experience that goes way beyond mere physical gratification.

Pluto rules volcanoes and all that explodes from the depths.

Explosive influence

Pluto is the higher vibration of the warrior Mars, signifying universal aggression rather than its expression on a personal level. Although its devious aspect is often hidden, Pluto has the same dynamic charge as Mars and occasionally brings things bursting volcanically to the surface. Pluto can have this effect both on the generation who are born with the planet in their sign, and on everyone who lives through a Plutonian period.

Power

Plutonian power is more refined and purposeful than raw Martian energy. It's unstoppable, but subtle. Pluto concerns itself with the use, abuse and misuse of power. Wherever one person has power over another, Pluto is at work. Whenever someone is empowered, Pluto is operating positively. When Pluto is expressed negatively in a chart, it indicates abuse or ignorance. Intolerance, coercion, manipulation and fanaticism all arise out of an unconscious use of Plutonian power.

ZODIAC POSITIONS

Approximate sign positions of Pluto

1914–1939	Cancer
1939–1957	Leo
1957–1972	Virgo
1972–1984	Leo
1984–1995	Scorpio
1995–2008	Sagittarius
2008–2022	Capricorn

The rape of Persephone

One of the mythological Pluto's most oft-cited acts was the abduction of the young innocent Persephone. Persephone represents naïvety and undifferentiated consciousness. In his function as separator, Pluto brings her into consciousness of self. Impregnating her with the creative force, he triggers her own power. Emerging from the depths, Persephone is initiated into higher consciousness and becomes Queen of the Underworld. This is Pluto's greatest gift. He reveals the treasure at the heart of personal darkness.

Plutonian characteristics

Pluto is intense, obsessive and compulsive. The planet also imparts a certain fearlessness, granting Plutonian people the courage to confront and accept their own depths and to face their mortality. Life, for Pluto-attuned people, is not to be taken lightly.

Disposition

Traditionally, when well placed, the disposition is charismatic, intense and perceptive. When poorly placed, the disposition is malicious, suspicious and power-hungry.

Pluto abducted the innocent Persephone, but she became the Queen of the Underworld.

PLUTO THROUGH THE SIGNS

Due to its long orbit, making these placements irrelevant, Pluto in Aries, Taurus, Gemini, Aquarius and Pisces is not included.

Cancer	Pluto passing through Cancer was a period of emotional transformation, sandwiched between two World Wars that took millions of lives. It signalled the demise of the extended family, forcing a reluctant Cancer to let go emotionally.
Leo	With Pluto in Leo, the 'Me Generation' was born. The desire of the individual to be a self-directed, unique part of society separate from the collective was paramount. The nuclear family fragmented.
Virgo	This period encompassed the battle of 'free love' with conventional attitudes to marriage. Many children were adopted until developments in birth control brought control over fertility and changed attitudes drastically. Life and health issues came to the fore, the pollution of planet earth was recognized as a major issue and modern medicine was born.
Libra	Pluto in Libra challenged the basis on which social structure and relationships were built. Ideas around global responsibility took root, as did fundamentalism. The challenge was to transform relationships throughout humanity.
Scorpio	In this period, old taboos came forward to be confronted and social change was accelerated. AIDs showed itself as the modern plague. Psychotherapy took its subscribers on trips into the Plutonian depths to shine the light of consciousness within.
Sagittarius	With Pluto in Sagittarius, humanity's idealism is intensifying. However, unworkable ideologies and old ways of being need to be confronted and transformed.
Capricorn	The opportunity to transform society opens up, highlighting the conflict between conservatism and new political and economic policies that could bring the developing world into the modern world as equals.

TRADITIONAL CORRESPONDENCES

Day of the week	None assigned
Metal	Plutonium
Mineral	Selenium
Vitamin	E
Musical note	None assigned
Crystals	Smoky quartz, black obsidian, jet, pearl
Colours	Deep red, magenta, violet
Physiology	Reproductive and excretory organs, destructive processes, the unconscious
Past-life stumbling blocks	Misuse and abuse of power, lack of courage of in one's convictions, misuse of occult power/black magic, sacrifice of others for personal ends
Careers	Doctor, surgeon, detective, undertaker, midwife, nuclear physicist, metaphysician, psychologist, psychiatrist, management consultant
Associations	Transformation, death, birth and rebirth; underworld, riches, earthquakes, big business, kidnapping, murder, detection, invisibility, eruptions, volcanoes, enforced change
Trees; Plants; Food; Virtue; Vice	None assigned
Places	Anywhere dark, hidden and underground; drains, cesspits, sewers, anywhere radioactive or near a nuclear establishment

THE MOON'S NODES

The twin Nodes of the Moon are not tangible bodies, but are opposite points in space, marking a complex astronomical interaction between the earth, Sun and Moon. They move slowly backwards through the zodiac, as the Moon makes its monthly journey around the earth, crossing the annual path of the Sun (the ecliptic). The intersection points are the Nodes. The Nodes complete an entire retrograde cycle every 18 to 19 years. In astrological terms, they embody the drive for evolution. To reach the deepest possible understanding, both sign and house placement must be considered.

The Moon dragon

In Chinese astrology, the Nodes are referred to as the Dragon's Head and the Dragon's Tail. The Dragon's Head (the North Node) is where nourishment is taken in and the Dragon's Tail (the South Node) where waste is excreted. Whenever the Sun or Moon move close to the Nodes, the powerful Dragon swallows up the luminary, creating an eclipse.

The Nodes do not exist as tangible bodies, they are points in space where the Moon's path crosses the ecliptic.

Karmic astrology

The Nodes are particularly important in karmic or past-life astrology. The South Node represents a deeply ingrained way of being that has arisen from the past (in the present life or a previous one). Its house (see pages 224–7) and sign placement illustrates where the soul is comfortable; everything here is familiar. The North Node represents potential and the path of evolution the soul has chosen for the present life. The karmic challenge is to take all that has been learned in the South Node, the past, and combine it in the North Node, otherwise the soul will be torn apart by the polarities involved.

When the move into the North Node is made, a profound shift in orientation takes place. The South Node then performs its function of eliminating all that the soul has outgrown, and the North Node receives the nourishment of moving in harmony with the soul's purpose. Equilibrium is restored and a new point of balance reached.

Nodal connections with the luminaries

If the North Node is placed in the same sign as the Sun, the positive qualities of that sign are emphasized. The soul's evolution is urgent; the purpose strong. When the North Node is in the same sign as the Moon, on the other hand, or the South Node in the same sign as the Sun, the positive qualities of the sign have to be capitalized upon for the soul's evolution. The soul knows how to do this but the less constructive energies may hold it back. If the South Node is placed in the same sign as the Moon, it indicates difficulty in breaking out of a past pattern. Extra effort is needed.

NORTH NODE
The life path

Glyph	☊	The glyph represents the Dragon's head.
Keywords		Life purpose, destiny, striving, evolution, latent potential, choices, growth

The path of evolution

The North Node is what must be done to fulfil the soul's purpose. It is the life path, destiny or dharma. Since it represents what the soul must become, it is unknown territory and not always a particularly comfortable place. The path is untravelled and at the beginning of the journey the soul almost inevitably falls back into the South Node. At such times, the soul must pick up the innate talents it has developed in the past, lodged in the South Node, and bring them into the service of the North.

NORTH NODE THROUGH THE SIGNS

Aries The path of self-development. The soul is learning to be a separate, self-sufficient individual, centred around the Self, with the courage to initiate change and to evolve independently.

Taurus The path of inner security. The soul is learning the strength that comes from awareness of Self as an immortal soul on a human journey. This is the only security that can be taken out of life at death.

Gemini The path of effective communication. The soul is learning to express itself without ambiguity or ambivalence. This is a path of truth.

Cancer The path of nurture. The soul is learning to nurture and care about itself and those around it.

Leo The path of the heart. The soul is learning to keep an open heart, to be heart-centred in all that it does, and to be empowered from the heart.

Virgo The path of service. The soul is learning to be of service to others without thought of reward, recognition or validation.

Libra The path of relationship. The soul is learning how to be an equal partner in relationship, so that the needs of each party are taken care of in a balanced interweaving of souls.

Scorpio The path of mastering power. The soul is learning how to use its considerable power for the good of all. This is also the path of self-mastery and the application of power.

Sagittarius The path of the seeker. The soul is on a quest for knowledge of the true meaning behind the universe and physical incarnation.

Capricorn The path of self-discipline. The soul is learning how to control the world by being in control of itself. The soul must learn to listen to its own authority rather than the authority figures it has formerly relied upon.

Aquarius The path of evolution. The soul is assisting the evolution of humanity to a new vibration that brings equality for each and every soul.

Pisces The path of enlightenment. The soul is seeking at-oneness and must learn the difference between this and atonement. This is the path that leads back to the divine.

SOUTH NODE
Gateway to the past

Glyph	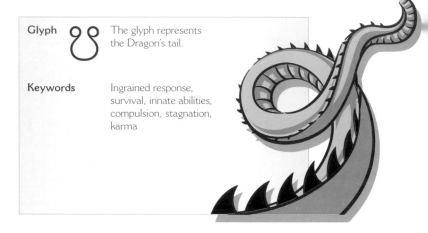	The glyph represents the Dragon's tail.
Keywords		Ingrained response, survival, innate abilities, compulsion, stagnation, karma

The path to the past

The South Node symbolizes all that has gone before. Like the Moon, it represents entrenched, instinctual behaviour that arises from innate reaction. As such, it is an ancient part of the psyche. This is a place of unfinished business; where survival strategies have been formulated, emotional stimuli and automatic reactions lie and unconscious compulsions and rigid behaviour patterns arise. The abilities with which the soul is most familiar lie in the South Node. It is also the point where the soul stagnates, where in response to the challenge to evolve, it says: 'Yes, but...', and turns back to the past. The challenge is to take what is good from the South and leave behind all that is negative.

SOUTH NODE THROUGH THE SIGNS

Aries
The soul has learned courage and become a separate Self, but must leave behind self-centredness, self-absorption and selfishness.

Taurus
The soul has learned inner security but must leave behind possessiveness and attachment to material goods.

Gemini
The soul has learned how to communicate and to question. Now it must find a way to live by its beliefs with integrity.

Cancer
The soul has learned to nurture and care for others but must now leave possessiveness and attachment in the past.

Leo
The soul has learned about personal power and how to keep an open heart. It must now leave emotional games and pride behind.

Virgo
The soul has learned how to serve others and must take forward its ability to discriminate, leaving behind criticalness and the futile search for perfection.

Libra
The soul has learned how to relate but must leave behind the tendency to lose sight of itself in relationships, taking forward the ability to make a creative compromise.

Scorpio
The soul has been through traumas and dramas. The emotional pain must be left behind, while the ability to survive can be carried forward.

Sagittarius
The soul has explored many philosophies and lived by many different beliefs. Now it must learn to simply be.

Capricorn
The soul has gained authority but must leave behind authoritarianism and the tendency to exercise tight control over everything.

Aquarius
The soul has worked for the evolution of humanity but must leave behind the tendency to rebel or to be different simply for the sake of being different.

Pisces
The soul has merged itself in at-oneness or dissolution. It must leave behind the pattern of victim-martyr-saviour and learn to discriminate, taking forward the knowledge that it is part of the divine.

THE NODES THROUGH THE HOUSES

North Node in first house This placement indicates a need to express individuality, becoming centred around the self. It has learnt harmony through relationships.

South Node in first house The challenge is to let go the ego and move to a self-orientated approach that encompasses the needs of others.

North Node in second house The task is to develop inner security, drawing on karmic resources and values, on an eternal, rather than a material level.

South Node in second house The challenge is to detach from things that have given security in the past, drawing on positive resources and an instinct for survival.

North Node in third house All that has been learned must now shine through. Karmic debts, lessons and promises are confronted with, or through, a sibling.

South Node in third house Reliance has been placed primarily on the intellect or guile, but communication skills have been developed nonetheless.

North Node in fourth house The task is parenting beyond the immediate family, to nurture in the widest possible way. Karma is met through family, or previous interaction with family can be harnessed towards soul's growth.

South Node in fourth house Shedding a past tendency to live life through children or family, now the soul has to live for itself.

North Node in fifth house The soul needs to learn to use power creatively, becoming empowered from the heart.

South Node in fifth house The challenge is to shift from creating at a biological level to spiritual and mental creativity. There may be karma from past love affairs.

North Node in sixth house The task is to give altruistic service to humanity, by whatever means. This Node may be learning through a health condition or a vocation.

South Node in sixth house The task is to leave behind a role of servitude or servility, which may have been mistaken for true service.

North Node in seventh house The task is to relate to others without repressing the soul's needs. Relationship and partners of all kinds bring to light karmic issues.

South Node in seventh house The soul has lost sight of its right to develop as appropriate for its own needs. It has learned to harmonize with others, so making relationships easier.

North Node in eighth house Karmic evolution demands that the soul explores sex, birth, death and rebirth, sharing resources with others.

South Node in eighth house The soul has an unshakeable certainty that it will survive no matter what. Evolution for the soul in the future needs to be a steady process, and not be borne of trauma, as in the past.

North Node in ninth house The soul is on an eternal quest for meaning and must align with divine purpose.

South Node in ninth house The soul has been on a life-long quest to find out who and what it is. The challenge is to stop and hear the voice that says 'simply be'.

North Node in tenth house The soul's task is to develop inner and outer authority and to find success through a career.

South Node in tenth house The soul may carry authoritarian parenting patterns that need release. Karma can be met through parenting or the family of origin.

North Node in eleventh house The urge is to change things, to make a fairer and equal community, and to work through interaction with others.

South Node in eleventh house The soul has tried to change things for many lifetimes and may have suffered as it misunderstood what was on offer.

North Node in twelfth house The urge to get off the karmic round, to reach a state of grace. The soul may deal with considerable karma – collective or personal.

South Node in twelfth house The soul has been seeking at-oneness but confused this with atonement, and can now move beyond karma.

The houses

The birthchart is divided into 12 houses, which are the *where* of astrology. Each house acts as a focus finder, indicating the area of life in which planetary energies operate. The angles function as orientation points along the way. The Ascendant marks the eastern horizon at the moment of birth, while the Descendant marks the western. The Midheaven, or MC, marks the highest point the Sun traverses on its path around the chart, and the Imum Coeli, or IC, its opposite point. The division between houses is

and angles

known as the cusp. The journey around the houses begins on the Ascendant, the cusp of the first house, going counter-clockwise through each house in turn. On the Ascendant, the soul is at the point of incarnation and expressing identity; as it moves through the houses it undergoes a symbolic progression from an initial sense of self as a separate entity, through childhood, work and play, to contact with others, then moving into community and then back into wholeness.

SPHERES OF LIFE

The houses represent spheres of life. Each provides an arena in which planetary energies are experienced. Houses are coloured by the sign on the cusp and the planets placed within them. Planets act dominantly in the first house, concretely in the second, communicatively in the third, protectively in the fourth, creatively in the fifth, altruistically in the sixth, in partnership in the seventh, intensely in the eighth, philosophically in the ninth, with significant impact in the tenth, socially in the eleventh and deviously in the twelfth.

Calculating houses

Astrologers use several methods to calculate houses. In the Equal House system, each house takes up a 30° segment of the chart. The MC may fall in the ninth, tenth or eleventh house, according to the latitude at which

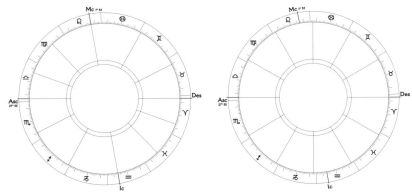

An example of Placidus house division, a quadrant system.

An example of Equal house division, with the MC in the tenth house.

SIGNS OF LONG AND SHORT ASCENSION

Some signs rise over the horizon in less than an hour (short ascension), while others take about three hours (long ascension).

Long ascension in northern hemisphere   Cancer, Leo, Virgo, Libra, Scorpio, Sagittarius

Long ascension in southern hemisphere   Capricorn, Aquarius, Pisces, Aries, Taurus, Gemini

Short ascension in northern hemisphere   Cancer, Leo, Virgo, Libra, Scorpio, Sagittarius

Short ascension in southern hemisphere   Capricorn, Leo, Virgo, Libra, Scorpio, Sagittarius

an individual was born and the time of year. In Quadrant Systems, which include Placidus (the system followed in this book), the MC always forms the cusp of the tenth house. The house divisions are unequal, and can include up to three signs. The sign on the cusp is the most significant, but all the signs manifest in the sphere of life to which the house relates. The size of a house indicates the importance of that sphere of life.

The rising sign

The Ascendant marks the eastern horizon at birth. The Sun falls on the Ascendant if birth is at dawn; if birth is between sunset and sunrise, the Sun is in the bottom half of the chart; between sunrise and sunset, the Sun is in the top half of the chart.

House rulers and elements

Houses have planetary rulers and elements. The first house, ruled by Mars, is a fire house, the second, ruled by Venus, an earth house and so on.

ASCENDANT
ASC

Keywords	Self-awareness, individuality, appearance, adaptation, reaction, embodiment, boundaries, meeting, the environment

The mask

The Ascendant, or rising sign, is the sign that was rising over the horizon at the moment of birth. This is the face that a person presents to the world as a shield to protect his or her inner sun-sign self. As the first thing others notice, an Ascendant can effectively mask true personality.

The Ascendant also affects how much of the innerself is revealed to the world. With an extrovert Ascendant, someone may *appear* to share their life story within the first five minutes of meeting. However, if the sun-sign is essentially introspective, this impression of openness will be a false one – what is 'revealed' will be a façade.

The Ascendant indicates how easily adaptation to the external environment takes place. Earth Ascendants appear to be practical, well-organized and efficient; fire Ascendants seem confident, ebullient and outgoing; water ascendants seems more reserved and sensitive; air Ascendants are lively, curious and talkative.

Appearance

The Ascendant reveals how adjustment is made to incarnation in a physical body. A Sagittarian Ascendant, for example, can be clumsy, whereas Taurus is well-coordinated. The Ascendant also has a bearing on physical appearance. A Gemini Ascendant has a twinkle in the eye, Scorpio a penetrating gaze and Pisces a dreamy look. Libra is beautifully dressed, whilst Aquarius aims to shock.

Boundaries

The Ascendant describes how well personal boundaries function. Aries knows: 'this is me', Libra says 'this is me, this is you' and asks 'how can we combine?', whilst Pisces is unsure: 'where do I end and you begin?' The negative signs tend to have weaker boundaries than the positive signs, although some negative signs, such as Cancer, are aware of this and take appropriate steps for self-protection.

THROUGH THE SIGNS

Aries Wants to make an impact and conquer the world.

Taurus Experiences the world, steadily, through the senses.

Gemini Wants to communicate with the world.

Cancer Circuitously protects and nurtures the world.

Leo Perceives loyal subjects waiting to applaud.

Virgo Sees the world as a place in which to serve and organize.

Libra Wants to relate to the whole world, but can be indecisive.

Scorpio Is inscrutable, but wants to master the environment.

Sagittarius Sees the world as an exciting place to explore.

Capricorn Wants to control the environment.

Aquarius Sees a different world

Pisces Flows to and fro in response to the environment.

DESCENDANT
DES

Keywords	Interaction, awareness of others, the partner, contact, projection, urge for relationship, intimacy, commitment, cooperation

Relationship to others

The Descendant marks the place of relationship in the widest sense of the word: interaction and cooperation with another. This is the point where an individual reaches out to make contact, and the sign on the Descendant reveals how easily someone else is related to and how successfully another's viewpoint can be seen.

The Descendant also indicates capacity for commitment and intimacy. In a self-protective or repressive sign, relationship is more of a challenge than if the Descendant is self-expressive and outgoing. A sign that naturally reaches out will find it easier to adapt to being in a partnership than a sign that is self-orientated. So the Descendant is the need to come to terms with being part of a couple and to reconcile the needs of 'you' with 'me'.

Living through others

The Descendant also indicates what attributes are projected on to others: the facets of the personality that are lived out through a partner, friend or colleague rather than owned in oneself. By recognizing the unacceptable qualities that the personality would prefer to disown, or which were rejected by parents, the task of integration and acceptance is begun.

The way in which an individual interacts with others is strongly coloured by the planets placed near to the Descendant in his or her chart, especially if these are outer planets. Neptune near the Descendant, for example, suggests idealization, illusions, delusions and deceptions, while the intensity of Pluto can indicate manipulation and domination, and Uranus a lack of intimacy and sudden endings.

THROUGH THE SIGNS

Aries Finds it difficult to be in a close one-to-one relationship.

Taurus Sees partnership as a symbol of status and security.

Gemini May have more than one partner at the same time.

Cancer Holds on to a relationship at all cost.

Leo Wants to be looked up to in unequal partnership.

Virgo Is dedicated in a relationship but can be hypercritical, as any partner is bound to be less than perfect

Libra Wants the perfect partnership and is willing to sacrifice everything to gain this.

Scorpio Is loyal but reveals little in a relationship.

Sagittarius Suspects the grass is greener someplace else.

Capricorn Takes the responsibility of partnership seriously.

Aquarius Finds commitment and intimacy extremely difficult.

Pisces Idealizes and romanticizes, wanting to merge with another and become one.

MIDHEAVEN
MC

Keywords	What is visible, outer self, career, ambition, recognition, separation, extroversion, striving

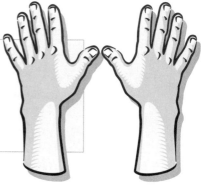

Making an impact

The Midheaven, or MC, symbolizes what is striven for, the drive to 'go for it' and how self-absorbed the personality is in pursuit of success. In Equal House systems, the house in which the MC falls indicates the sphere of life in which the mark has to be made. The element of the MC indicates whether the effort is sustainable. Fire and air MCs are great ideas people, but they tend to lack the stamina to carry the ideas through. Earth signs may have difficulty getting started, but once they do, they are most likely to stay the course. The water signs are the most likely to be swayed by emotions – although the highly sensitive Cancer MC is also one of the most ambitious.

MC and career choice

Since the MC describes the way in which someone pursues recognition, it is frequently linked to career choice. A Scorpio MC is linked to detection and medicine, a Capricorn MC has links with government and law and order, whilst a Libra MC is often found in positions that require diplomacy, or else design. An Aquarius MC seeks a better world for all, and may develop intuitive qualities in order to find new solutions to world problems or, in pursuit of the strange, may become an outcast from society.

The visible self

The MC marks the point where someone is packaged for consumption by the outside world, depending on the introverted or extroverted energy of the sign. As such, it indicates whether or not someone is motivated by what others think, and whether there is a 'team' or 'I' orientation. Individualistic signs thrust forward and make a stand, whilst more compliant signs try to melt into the background. The MC indicates qualities that are valued and which will be pursued and developed on the journey of life.

THROUGH THE SIGNS

Aries MC Is assertive and outgoing, wants to make an impact, but lacks stamina.

Taurus MC Gets there by stubborn determination.

Gemini MC Talks its way to the top.

Cancer MC Approaches goals obliquely.

Leo MC Courts success.

Virgo MC Gets there by hard graft but may remain subservient.

Libra MC Is laid back but gets there.

Scorpio MC Manipulates its way to controlling the world.

Sagittarius MC Fires off arrows but rarely targets them specifically. This is the perpetual student who never stops learning.

Capricorn MC Seeks authority and stability and resolutely pursues success.

Aquarius MC Has its eyes fixed on a better world for everyone.

Pisces MC May well float off on another tack when success is in sight.

IMUM COELI
IC

Keywords	What is hidden, inner Self, roots, introspection, home, introversion, security, origins

The abode of the Self

The imum coeli, or IC, is the root of the innermost Self. It symbolizes base security, what a person needs to feel safe. It also describes a person's home, family of origin and how easily a person fits into the family. What feels 'safe' for one person may not be safe as others would understand it. Someone with a Scorpio IC, for example, will have grown up surrounded by trauma and drama, and so finds security in that; and Aquarius expects upheavals. Because these experiences occur early in life, they are familiar – and are unconsciously recreated later. The IC is where self-destructive patterns originate and, as such, explains why violence or trauma may have such seductive appeal.

The inner Self

The inner Self is found deep within the solitude of the IC. It is what must be sought to know one's Self fully. The inner landscape may be safe or threatening, dull or exciting, imaginative or pragmatic, orderly or elastic according to the sign and the IC shows how introspective someone is and how easily the inner depths are explored.

THROUGH THE SIGNS

Aries IC Wants to be valued as an individual and is often the loner within the family.

Taurus IC Needs an unchanging routine to feel safe. Rock-solid Taurus is the pivot around which the family revolves.

Gemini IC Likes having someone there to listen. Gemini communicates the family's concerns.

Cancer IC Needs time to withdraw back to the womb and reflect. This clingy IC is family-orientated and has difficulty in cutting ties.

Leo IC Finds security in being thought special and in taking centre stage. Leos are expected to shine and seldom disappoint their family.

Virgo IC Finds security in orderly routine and tidy surroundings. This person may have been over-protected as a child, or be part of a family with impossibly high standards.

Libra IC Finds security in being part of a harmonious family, but is expected to be a people-pleaser who does not express individuality.

Scorpio IC Is self-contained and something of a mystery to the rest of the family.

Sagittarius IC Finds security in freedom, hating to be tied down.

Capricorn IC Needs a secure environment and to be in control on the inner levels. A great deal is expected from dutiful Capricorn.

Aquarius IC Needs space and a secure base to return to. Aquarius IC may be the family outcast or valued as an independent individual.

Pisces IC Has great difficulty in distinguishing between self and the rest of the family.

FIRST HOUSE

Sphere	Individuality
Polarity	Masculine
Element	Fire
Quality	Cardinal
Position	Angular
Physiology	Head, face
Places	Place of birth, immediate environment
Colour	White
Keywords	The Self, incarnation, self-image, separateness, individuality, physical characteristics and personal appearance, expectations, environment

Expressing individuality

The first house is where identity is formed. It also describes the circumstances surrounding birth, and the reception the child's arrival engendered. A planet in the first house has a profound impact on an individual's early life and the developing personality. With Pluto in the first, for example, the process of birth may have been life-threatening; Uranus or Mars indicates a sudden appearance; whereas Saturn can point to a long, slow or difficult birth, or a cold reception or the family may be materially or emotionally impoverished.

How directly individuality is expressed is coloured both by the sign of the first house and the planets within it. But people are not always what you would expect, given the nature of the planets. Pushy Mars may give the appearance of dynamism but, if it is masking a placid sun-sign, not much is actually going to get done. Venus in the first house may cloak a ruthless nature, and placed in pleasant Libra masks the deviousness of a power-hungry Scorpio Sun. When two signs fall in the first house, a planet such as Mars in the second sign may reveal an unexpectedly aggressive nature behind an apparently subservient façade.

The first house is the mirror that reflects the personality out to the world.

Expectations

Planets and signs in the first house pervade the whole of life, describing particular expectations and the way in which interaction with the world takes place. Capricorn and Saturn expect early life to be onerous, whilst Leo and the Sun anticipate a much happier time. Mars is pushy and impatient, Saturn slow and cautious, making someone with both these planets in their first house at times over-hasty and at others over-cautious. Chaotic Uranus expects sudden upheavals and upsets, Jupiter looks forward to fun, whilst Neptune inhabits a dreamy, or deceptive, environment. Pluto in the first house suggests that a great deal goes on beneath the surface and that life will be intense.

SECOND HOUSE

Sphere	Personal resources and possessions
Polarity	Feminine
Element	Earth
Quality	Fixed
Position	Succedent
Physiology	Neck, throat
Places	Banks
Colour	Green
Keywords	The material world, wealth, worldly goods, personal resources, possessions, security, values, self-worth, material values, spending

Values and resources

The second house is where the sense of individuality is reinforced through personal possessions and bolstered by a solid sense of worth. Describing what is valued and obtained in everyday life, it is where identity is extended through material accumulation and a psychological sense of worth. The sign on the cusp of this house describes a person's attitude to money and things that are owned. It indicates whether money comes easily or has to be worked for, and reveals how much someone values who they are.

This house also shows what resources a person has to draw on to achieve success – potential to be developed. Planets in the second house feel comfortable, and describe things that come naturally. Jupiter placed in the second house, symbolizing abundance, suggests a 'lucky' person on whom blessings shower and whose gambles always pay off. Mars in the second house has courage and knows how to get what it wants, while Saturn has reserves of strength and wisdom. Venus or Libra in the second house point to artistic abilities or a pleasing personal appearance, which may well constitute a tangible asset.

Security

The second house is concerned with security. For some people, this security comes from external possessions that give a sense of personal substance, most usually a house or a car. For others, security is an inner quality, so that they can live anywhere, with very little, and yet feel safe and secure. The sign and element on the cusp indicate whether an individual seeks security in the tangible or intangible. On the whole, earth and water signs value material possessions, and air and fire signs value knowledge, ideas and inner qualities.

The second house has to do with attitudes to money and what is valued.

THIRD HOUSE

Sphere	Communication
Polarity	Masculine
Element	Air
Quality	Mutable
Position	Cadent
Physiology	Hands, arms, shoulders
Places	Schools
Colour	Yellow
Keywords	Communication, siblings, short journeys, learning, immediate environment, neighbours, manner of speech

Self-expression

The third house embodies the beginning of self-expression. The sign and planets placed here either facilitate or restrict the flow, whereas the sign on the cusp indicates whether clear communication or confusion can be anticipated and how easy it will be to learn. Linked to the rational, left brain (the ninth house being abstract thought), the third house also describes the concrete function of a person's intellectual processes. If there is a strong emphasis on this house in the chart, acquiring new skills will be a motivating factor throughout life.

Mercury in the third house of a person's chart suggests a natural communicator. But if Saturn is in the third house, learning or communication may be difficult, particularly in early years. Chiron in the third house may well indicate someone who is deeply wounded by what people say or who is, for one reason or another, prevented from speaking a unique, personal truth.

Siblings

The third house is also the house of siblings. If the Sun is in the third house, the sibling in question may be the child who shines in the family, whereas the Moon suggests sibling empathy or siblings who act as surrogate parents. Saturn also points to a sibling who acts as a substitute parent, keeping discipline in the family, or a sibling who is carrying, or who becomes, a burden. Chiron is the wounded sibling, often the carrier of the family's pain. Mercury usually indicates a talkative, companionable sibling but Neptune is more elusive. Mars can signal sibling rivalry and Venus suggests a deep love between siblings. Pluto may indicate a sibling who holds power and Uranus usually refers to the family rebel.

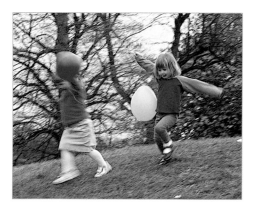

The third house covers siblings, communication and short journeys.

FOURTH HOUSE

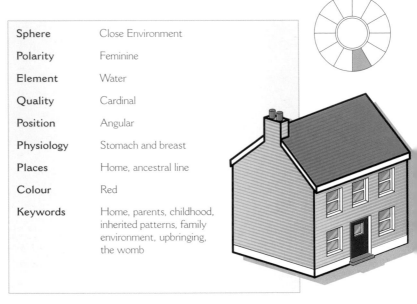

Sphere	Close Environment
Polarity	Feminine
Element	Water
Quality	Cardinal
Position	Angular
Physiology	Stomach and breast
Places	Home, ancestral line
Colour	Red
Keywords	Home, parents, childhood, inherited patterns, family environment, upbringing, the womb

Home base

The fourth house is home, the base from which to venture out into the world. If it coincides with a water sign, the likelihood is that home is charged with emotion and the act of leaving a fearful one. Fire signs are the most confident in this realm, whereas air homes have their basis in mental rapport and earth homes are places of comfort and support.

The home is where we feel most secure. Like the IC, that doesn't necessarily mean the fourth house is a gentle, easy environment. Some

The fourth house often represents the mother or care-giver.

people are 'at home' on a battlefield. The internalized sense of home and security will depend on initial childhood experience, as described by the planets, sign(s) and house ruler. Scorpio in this house indicates that disturbing but unvoiced undercurrents permeated the home, whilst Cancer points to a nurturing home, but one that may well have included a possessive mother. This early experience of home is sought out and replicated in adult life.

The archetypal parents

The fourth house indicates which parent will provide primary nurturing care. Planets in the fourth house represent archetypal parents, sowing their particular energy into a person's psyche, which resonates when that energy is met. The child recognizes what he or she is programmed to expect, so whenever an actual parent behaves in that way, the archetype is reinforced. This is especially so with outer planet placements. Pluto is powerful, dominating and manipulative; Uranus unstable, disruptive and unpredictable; Neptune an elusive vision of perfection who cannot be relied upon; the Moon indicates a nurturing parent who understands a child's feelings; Chiron a parent who is wounded in a way that colours the home environment.

FIFTH HOUSE

Sphere	Creation
Polarity	Masculine
Element	Fire
Quality	Fixed
Position	Succedent
Physiology	Heart and back
Places	Theatres, nightclubs, leisure and sports centres, hotel rooms
Colour	Anything dark
Keywords	Self-expression, recreation, creativity, offspring, pleasure, love affairs, children, speculation

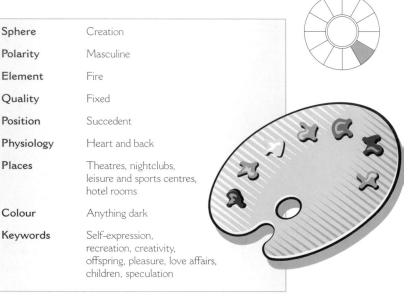

Creation and recreation

A self-expressive house, the fifth house encompasses everything that is creative, including ideas, dreams, music and art. This is where the soul goes forth into the world, where the inner landscape is made visible. The sign on the cusp describes how easily creative energies flow, as do the planets in this house. Saturn often indicates difficulty in getting projects underway.

Saturn may also indicate difficulty in conceiving a physical child, as children are an important part of the fifth house. The sign and planets placed here describe interaction with children, and how easy an individual finds it to enter into a child's world. The fire signs are perpetual children at heart, while earth signs may not have had the opportunity to express their own child-nature fully. An air sign values the individual creativity of a child, seeing children as friends of equal standing, whereas water signs find it virtually impossible to recognize a child as separate, seeing instead an extension of themselves.

Love affairs

The fifth house represents more than biological reproduction or the sexual urge. Love affairs also come under this house, because they make a person feel special. With links to Leo, this house is where someone plays and discovers the inner child, and develops a sense of wonder.

Recreation

The sign on the cusp of the fifth house and the planets within it point to the kind of recreation and leisure activities that are enjoyable and life-enhancing. With an active, outgoing sign or planet, or a strong earth or fire element, sport or dance are likely to be important, whilst an indolent sign points to someone who prefers inactivity. Air enjoys mind-based, empathetic activities, and water signs anything that brings them into emotional communication with others or water itself.

For some people strenuous activity is life-enhancing, for others it is not.

249

SIXTH HOUSE

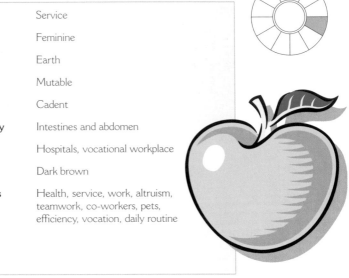

Sphere	Service
Polarity	Feminine
Element	Earth
Quality	Mutable
Position	Cadent
Physiology	Intestines and abdomen
Places	Hospitals, vocational workplace
Colour	Dark brown
Keywords	Health, service, work, altruism, teamwork, co-workers, pets, efficiency, vocation, daily routine

Work and service

The sixth house is where we become aware of others. Linked to Virgo, this is where innate talents and abilities are used in a productive way and vocations arise. The signs and planets placed in this part of the chart describe how unselfishly or not someone can act. The Sun placed in the sixth, for example, indicates dedication to a life of service, but the sign determines whether that takes place in a hospital, a shop, a government department or for a charity.

The service carried out in the sixth house comes from the heart, without thought of reward or recognition. This is what must be done because it must be done. However, if personal identity and self-worth have not been developed sufficiently, the sixth house may still seek recognition for its good works, to be told how worthy it is being.

Teamwork

This house also pertains to co-workers and describes how harmoniously someone is able to blend into a team and how work will be organized and approached. Without a strong sense of self, boundaries become elastic and there is no separation between 'you' and 'me' in the workplace. If personal boundaries are too strong, cooperation is impossible and isolation is inevitable.

The sixth house often points to an enjoyable vocation.

Health

The sixth house is linked to health, which in turn is dependent on how much at home someone is with their body, mind and emotions, and how much of the Self can be expressed. This is a truly holistic house: a state of health reflects an inner harmony while dis-ease indicates inner disharmony. (See also Planets, Health and the Sixth House, pages 380–81.)

SEVENTH HOUSE

Sphere	Interaction
Polarity	Masculine
Element	Air
Quality	Cardinal
Position	Angular
Physiology	Loins
Places	Marital home
Colour	Blue-brown
Keywords	Relationships, matrimony and partnerships, unity, other people, projection, public enemies, lawsuits

Self meets other

In this sphere, the soul reaches out to another in a mutually beneficial relationship. How easily someone reaches out and how well they balance their needs with that of another person is described by the sign(s) and the planets. Uranus or Aquarius suggests problems with commitment, whilst Saturn craves certainty.

The seventh house also describes the qualities someone seeks in a partner and the kind of person to whom someone is attracted. Mars placed in this house suggests that the chart's owner seeks an assertive partner, but an aggressive one may be attracted, depending on the sign on the cusp. The Sun or Moon in the seventh house may indicate an unconscious search for a father or mother substitute.

Questions of relationship

The seventh house raises and answers some important questions. 'Will relationships be easy, supportive and life-sustaining, or difficult and life-negating?' 'How much can I adapt and will we become united?' The planets and sign indicate how much you struggle to maintain personal boundaries within a relationship, and how able you are to share your humanity with another. (See also The Seventh House and Relationships, pages 346–7.)

Marriage is a function of the seventh house.

Projection

The seventh house is where we seek feedback to reinforce the sense of Self, as reflected back through the eyes of another. This is why it is the house of open enemies as well as partnerships. We may project our expectations or fears on to another, seeing qualities in them that they *may not necessarily have*. It may be that what we seek in a partner is what we need to feel complete and, as such, is an indication of what still has to be owned in ourselves.

EIGHTH HOUSE

Sphere	Transmutation
Polarity	Feminine
Element	Water
Quality	Fixed
Position	Succedent
Physiology	Reproductive organs
Places	Funeral parlours, cemeteries, labour wards, ancestral property
Colour	Black
Keywords	Interaction, shared resources, birth-death-rebirth, regeneration, sexual union, integration, self-sacrifice, expanded awareness, inheritance, other people's money, metaphysics

Mortality and metaphysics

In the complex eighth house, the secrets of the universe are revealed. This is the point at which we move beyond self-awareness to universal awareness. In its Plutonian reaches, death is met – the one great certainty of life and the most feared – and expanded states of consciousness are encountered.

At the mundane level, the eighth is the house of shared resources and monetary gain and of things inherited. The sign on the cusp describes how easily resources are shared and how altruistic someone can be.

Inheritances may be on the physical or psychic plane, including ancestral patterns and potential. An elusive Pisces or Neptune in the eighth house may indicate an inheritance that slips through one's fingers, or continuation of a family pattern of addiction; Capricorn or Saturn could suffer loss, inherit a substantial legacy or a flair for business.

Giving of one's Self

Intimately connected with sexual union, one of the most fundamental processes of the eighth house, this is a place of openness to giving and receiving. It is where the individual loses the sense of separate identity and learns to merge with another person. For some people this is a transcendental experience, for others, painful.

The eighth house also describes sexuality and choice of sexual expression, the sign pointing to how intimacy is experienced, and to expectations around sexuality. Uranus in this position, for example, indicates deep ambivalence and ambiguity around gender and sexual preferences.

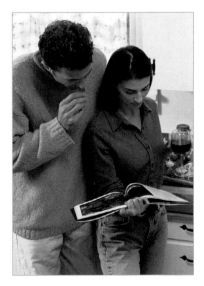

The eighth house indicates how resources are shared with others.

NINTH HOUSE

Sphere	Philosophy
Polarity	Masculine
Element	Fire
Quality	Mutable
Position	Cadent
Physiology	Hips, thighs
Places	Universities, publishing houses, newspaper offices, foreign shores
Colours	Green, white
Keywords	Higher learning, philosophy, distant horizons, ethics, vision, beliefs, religion, long journeys, in-laws, foreign affairs

Seeking meaning

In the philosophical ninth house, the search for meaning begins. This is where we reach out to something greater, and where universal truth is pursued. This is the house of higher education, philosophical debate and great questions of life, such as 'What am I doing here?' and 'What does it all mean?' Journeys are made to distant horizons – physical or of the mind.

Once an individual becomes conscious of being part of something larger, the next step is to try to order the world for the good of that whole, hence this house's connection to morality and law. This is where the mores of society are encountered, and where rebellion takes place against collective beliefs. Signs and planets placed here indicate conformity or conflicts with established belief systems – and show how forcefully someone is prepared to impress personal views on others. This is also the house of publishing and dissemination of information.

Religion or spirituality

In this house there is an opening up to something *other* – if the planets are propitious. If not, the vision cannot be shared nor the process of life fully engaged in. The ninth house is the sphere of organized religion, dogma, doctrine or spirituality. Planets placed here illustrate the response to the call of the spirit. If Neptune is in residence, the call is towards ritual and mysticism – or the illusions that pass for it; Saturn, on the other hand, favours religious certainty and dogma. Pluto's predilection for fanaticism and fervour finds a natural home in the ninth, whilst Uranus brings a new belief system – or none at all.

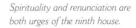

Spirituality and renunciation are both urges of the ninth house.

TENTH HOUSE

Sphere	Outer environment
Polarity	Feminine
Element	Earth
Quality	Cardinal
Position	Angular
Physiology	Knees, bones
Places	Workplace, home, government buildings, law courts
Colours	Red, white
Keywords	Outer environment, public life, social status, ambition, parents, career, trade or profession, recognition, authority figures

What is striven for

The tenth house is the point at which we try to make a mark on the world. It describes what we desire to achieve, not only in the material world but also in intangible spheres. The planets in this house and the sign on the cusp indicate motivation, or a lack of it, to strive for success. With Saturn in this position, progress may be slow but persistent, whilst Mars aims straight to the top, and the Sun simply has to shine. In tenth-house terms, career is about making an impact. This house may indicate the profession followed, although it is normally

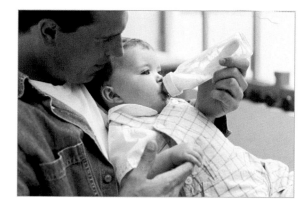

The tenth house often represents the father or male care-giver.

supported by other factors in the chart. Mars and Aries are traditionally associated with aggressive professions, and Mercury and Gemini with careers that involve writing. Saturn and Capricorn can indicate a teacher or upholder of the law, and Jupiter, Sagittarius or Pisces a travel agent or actor.

Parents

The tenth house is one of the parental houses (the other being the fourth) In the past, it was associated with the father as he interacted with the world. Now, however, the role of the mother in socially conditioning a child is recognized, so the tenth house is also assigned to the mother. It signifies which of the parents has most influence on career choice and who propels the drive to the top. Career choice may be a question of seeking approval and acceptance from a parent and, if this is so, the sign and planets in the tenth house will point this out. The house also describes experience with authority figures in general, and the expectations built up around them.

ELEVENTH HOUSE

Sphere	Community
Polarity	Masculine
Element	Air
Quality	Fixed
Position	Succedent
Physiology	Legs, ankles
Places	Social and tribal gatherings, the workplace
Colour	Deep yellow
Keywords	Group activities, society, friends, hopes, wishes, aspirations, social consciousness

Social awareness

The eleventh house is where a personal sense of identity is extended into the greater group: the extended family, a professional class, a tribe or a race. This is the house of group interaction and organized society, where a social conscience is developed, the rules governing human conduct are examined and, if necessary, change is affected. As such, the planets in the eleventh house describe how well or otherwise a person fits into society. Isolated, introspective signs and planets find it difficult to move beyond the confines of their own Self in order to mix in the wider group, whilst outgoing signs and planets quickly embrace this extension of Self.

Traditionally, the eleventh house is also the domain of hopes and wishes. It is what is envisioned and aspired to for the good of society. For those with social awareness, the dream is for the good of the community, but for those who have not yet developed a sense of social integration, all dreams centre around the Self.

Fitting into the bigger picture

The eleventh house is where someone sees themselves reflected in the eyes of the group and recognize their place in the bigger picture. Groups can be a source of conflict or offer an opportunity to find resolution. Pluto in the eleventh house suggests that power struggles may be faced within the group – or dominance attained over it. But this can also be a place of friendship and acceptance. The eleventh house can facilitate cooperation leading toward the achievement of a group objective, and can be a place where the group pushes beyond accepted convention to reach greater awareness.

The eleventh house is the most sociable of the houses.

TWELFTH HOUSE

Sphere	Reintegration
Polarity	Feminine
Element	Water
Quality	Mutable
Position	Cadent
Physiology	Feet, toes
Places	Prisons, institutions
Colour	Green
Keywords	Return, karma, family secrets, hidden enemies, reconnection, confinement, reparation, sacrifice, surrender, institutions, the collective unconscious

Return to the whole

The twelfth house is the house of secrets. It offers an opportunity for the soul to reconnect to the whole, and to bring into the light of consciousness all that was previously obscured. It is where the task of reintegration is completed, the boundary of individuality is relinquished and the Self surrendered back into the collective whole. Surrender back into the whole may be voluntary or involuntary. This is also the house of institutions, madness and disintegration, of deception and illusion, of family secrets. The way may be lost, a blurring occurs and the psyche does not know who or where it is. If the soul has not yet established a strong sense of self-identity, there is nothing to surrender, except delusions, and these may take over. If a powerful sense of individuality has been constructed, then merging back will be a painful process. This is a place of reparation for past wrongs. Much depends on the sign and planets in the twelfth house as to whether that surrender is constructive or destructive.

The twelfth house is one of mystery and secrets.

Karma

The twelfth house is the house of karma and past lives, where the results of past actions, personal and collective are met. Planets lurking in this house indicate the type of karma involved, where the karma is met, the issues that the soul is dealing with, and the drives and unconscious reactions that have to be controlled.

The Sun indicates karma pertaining to the father. The Moon points to the mother, Mercury the mind, Venus love, Mars aggression, Chiron wounding, Uranus revolution and upheaval, Neptune illusions and deceptions, and Pluto translates as power. Saturn indicates a heavy karmic load whilst Jupiter is the old priest or priestess or excess.

The aspects

The geometric relationships between planets, measured around the wheel of the zodiac, are known as aspects. An aspect is the angular distance between the degree of one planet and that of another, indicated by the lines across the birthchart. Aspects create a web that draws the different planetary drives together, linking two different 'substances' to form a chain reaction that subtly – or strikingly – alters the way the planetary energies function.

A psychological process in motion, aspects describe how planetary drives are enhanced or frustrated. This is particularly noticeable when the aspect is between an inner and outer planet. The planetary energies involved may combine into one driving urge or conflict may occur between two opposing needs. As a general rule, 'easy' aspects allow the planetary energies to flow more easily, whilst 'hard' aspects draw the planetary drives into conflict. Even if the aspect is a negative one, the potential for constructive expression of that particular combination of energies is always there.

FINDING ASPECTS

Measuring aspects

Each of the 12 signs of the astrological zodiac is allotted 30°. A planet that is placed at 0° Sagittarius, to use this sign as an example, therefore falls at the very beginning, the cusp, of Sagittarius, whereas a planet that is placed at 29° 59 minutes Sagittarius falls at the very end of this sign (the divisions that make up a degree are known as minutes).

To discover whether two planets are 'in aspect' – they may not be – first ascertain the position of each in degrees. If they are found to form an aspect – that is, if the angle, or number of degrees between the planets on the zodiac wheel is significant – an aspect line connects the planets on the chart. Some aspects have much more influence than others (see 'Minor and Major Aspects' overleaf).

If planets are situated within the same element, the aspect between them is either a conjunction or a trine. If placed in the same quality, the aspect is a square or conjunction. Opposition aspects draw together planetary energies on opposing sides of the zodiac.

Aspects sometimes occur 'out of sign', meaning that the planets activate different elements or qualities, causing a clash. These aspects are more of a challenge to integrate.

Orbs

An aspect is called 'exact' when both planets are placed at the same degree – a planet at 15° Taurus would, therefore, form an exact square with a planet at 15° Leo. However, astrologers allow some leeway when measuring aspects, so an aspect does not have to be exact to exist. The usual allowance for an orb (the overlap in planetary positions) is 8° for a conjunction, square, trine and opposition, meaning that a planet placed at 15° would make one of these aspects to any planet placed between 7° and 23° of a sign, except those immediately adjacent on both sides. The orb for sextiles is 6°, and 2° for all minor aspects. A quincunx in traditional astrology is given an orb of 2°, but in past-life astrology, the orb is 8°, since this is a major karmic aspect.

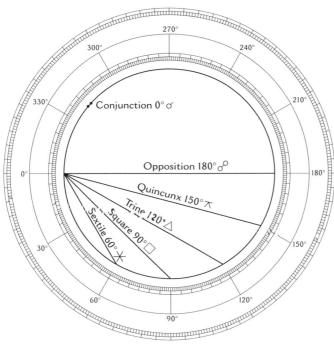

The aspects are measured around the outside of the zodiac circle, but the lines are drawn across the centre.

MINOR AND MAJOR ASPECTS

Aspects are classed as either major or minor. The relationships described by the major aspects have the strongest effect on how planetary energies flow.

MINOR ASPECTS

Semi-sextile, 30°

This somewhat stressful aspect unites two signs with no natural relationship. The resulting energy is often experienced through the behaviour of others rather than the self.

Semi-square 45°

A tension aspect similar to the square but weaker in its effect.

Quintile 72°

A one-pointed aspect of potential, sometimes indicating rare genius, especially pertaining to the mind.

Sesquiquadrate 135°

Another tension aspect with the nature of a square, but with a weaker effect.

Biquintile 144°

A harmonious but weak aspect of promise and potential.

MAJOR ASPECTS

Conjunction 0°

This relationship brings together planetary energies in a very immediate way, which will work well if the planets are harmonious. If the planets represent incompatible drives, the conjunction creates stress. If the orb is close, the energy of one planet may be overwhelmed by the other.

Sextile 60°

Traditionally an aspect of ease and harmony, considered less powerful than the other major aspects, the combination of energies in the sextile is comfortable, creating little obvious stress. The relationship may be so comfortable, however, that it ceases to be productive, and can actually be a source of conflict or tension.

Square 90°

An aspect of obvious tension, in which the planets are placed at odds with each other. This aspect may force an issue or pose a challenge. It can have an energizing effect or create a block, depending on the planets concerne.

Trine 120°

As a flowing aspect that usually links the same element, trines are able to harmonize the energies. Although they embody potential, they tend to be laid back, needing a transit (passing planet) to kick-start them. They offer a challenge as to how potential can best be expressed.

Quincunx 150°

A point of major tension and learning in the chart, the quincunx pulls together discordant energies that must be integrated and balanced.

Opposition 180°

This aspect sparks off dynamic tension as the energies of the planet meet head-on. When the aspect brings conflicting energies together, the resulting tension forces a resolution. When it draws together compatible energies, the interaction is invigorated and strengthened.

ASPECT PATTERNS

Repeating aspects, or a combination of different aspects, come together
to create easily recognizable patterns in a chart. These patterns have a
noticeable effect, depending on the planets concerned, and usually offer
a challenge to integrate the planetary energies and use them wisely.

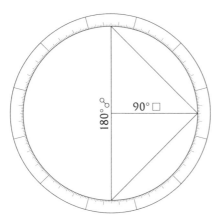

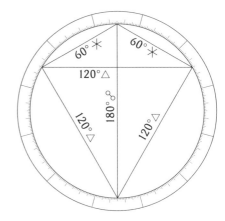

T-square *An opposition with a planet
in square to it: a pattern of tension that
puts stress on the 'missing leg'.*

Kite *The addition of an opposition
to the grand trine formation adds
tension and the possibility of a
constructive outlet for the energies
involved.*

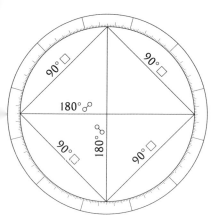

Grand cross *Two oppositions linked by four squares: a tense pattern indicating what must be faced in life, but holding the potential for great success.*

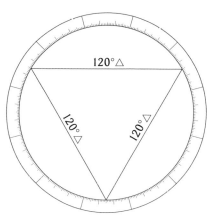

Grand trine *Three linked trines: a flowing pattern of enormous potential, although energy may flow round and round, finding no outlet.*

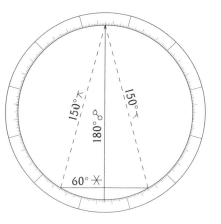

Finger of fate *Two quincunxes linked by a sextile: a tense pattern requiring integration. If a planet falls in opposition to the 'tip', release is facilitated.*

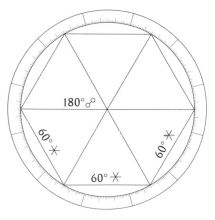

Grand sextile *A flowing aspect of great potential, which can nevertheless cause considerable tension if the energy is not released.*

PLANETS IN ASPECT

The nature of the aspect – flowing or difficult – affects how the planetary energies can be expressed.

☉ ASPECTS TO THE SUN

Sun to Moon The unconscious drive to behave according to old patterns and instincts meets the conscious urge to grow and express the self. This aspect also describes how parents are experienced.
Positively expressed: a settled nature and harmony at home.
Negatively expressed: inner conflict pertaining to deeply ingrained habits, turbulent emotions and difficult parental relationships.

Sun to Mercury The drive to communicate and express oneself.
Positively expressed: a creative and strongly self-expressive personality.
Negatively expressed: mental arrogance, feeling overwhelmed or exhausted.

Sun to Venus The drive for love.
Positively expressed: a charming, affectionate and artistic person, who thrives on affection and intimacy in a partnership and actively seeks relationships.
Negatively expressed: self-centred vanity.

Sun to Mars The drive to assert oneself.
Positively expressed: a self-assertive, courageous, energetic and bold individual with an excellent constitution and strong libido.
Negatively expressed: impatience, excessive recklessness, pugnacious with an egotistical tendency to overwork and extreme sex drive.

Sun to Jupiter The drive to expand oneself.
Positively expressed: an inspired, good-humoured, generous, optimistic and 'lucky' personality.
Negatively expressed: imprudence, exaggeration, misjudgement, conceit and extravagance.

Sun to Saturn The drive to control oneself.
Positively expressed: a self-disciplined, conscientious, resourceful, persistent and self-controlled personality.

Negatively expressed: depresssion, inhibition, low sense of self worth; poor relationship with father; physical or emotional separation; a child who is loved only for what is achieved. Difficult life circumstances to overcome.

Sun to Chiron The drive to heal one's self image.
Positively expressed: potential for a healing vocation; relationship with father is healing.
Negatively expressed: wounds in early life lead to a poor sense of self; may refer to a wounded father.

Sun to Uranus The drive for freedom and independence.
Positively expressed: unconventional, original, 'genius': independent, idealistic and intuitive individual with a flair for science and understanding of subtle vibrations.
Negatively expressed: disruption; deviant, chaotic and willful personality; eccentric loner or misdirected genius.

Sun to Neptune The drive to transcend.
Positively expressed: an imaginative, sensitive, artistic and intuitive person attracted to spiritual side of life.
Negatively expressed: vague and muddled, impressionable, self-deception, escapism, addiction or unproductive self-sacrifice.

Sun to Pluto The drive to transform oneself.
Positively expressed: a dynamic personality, dedicated to transformation of all that is outgrown. The challenge to claim one's own power.
Negatively expressed: obstinacy, paranoia or someone dedicated to ruthless advancement and elimination.

Sun to North Node The drive to evolve.
Positively expressed: the impetus to develop the positive qualities of the sun-sign and to follow the soul's purpose.
Negatively expressed: emphasis placed on the less constructive, egotistical side of sun-sign.

☽ ASPECTS TO THE MOON

Moon to Mercury The drive to communicate feelings.
Positively expressed: someone who expresses feelings eloquently, can perceive other people's feelings accurately and has an excellent memory.
Negatively expressed: a mind that dwells on the past and makes assumptions based on outdated emotions; poor memory; ingrained mental habits.

Moon to Venus The drive to nest.
Positively expressed: a sociable, pleasing person who is affectionate and orientated towards home, family and the arts.
Negatively expressed: indecision, attachment to the past, confusion about emotional needs.

Moon to Mars The drive to act on feelings.
Positively expressed: an emotionally courageous, passionate and robust personality.
Negatively expressed: moodiness, intolerance, a quarrelsome nature prone to emotional battles; parents may be in conflict.

Moon to Jupiter The drive for 'more'.
Positively expressed: a generous, optimistic nature that attracts good fortune.
Negatively expressed: extravagance, a constant need for more results in compulsions and obsessions (including eating disorders).

Moon to Saturn The drive for emotional control.
Positively expressed: a faithful and reliable person, who willingly takes on responsibilities and carries them out conscientiously.
Negatively expressed: lack of self worth, difficulty in emotional expression, sense of being weighed down by responsibilities; may be physical or emotional separation from mother; men attracted to older women; needs a stable home; difficult relationships with women; controlling mother archetype.

Moon to Chiron The drive to heal wounded emotions. Denotes a healing mother or a need to transform matriarchal patterns.
Positively expressed: the potential for emotional healing and integration; a channel for collective nurturing. An alchemical Moon that incorporates feelings into the spiritual dimension.
Negatively expressed: emotional insecurity; emotional wounding, especially by mother or women; extreme sensitivity and openness to outside influences or interference.

Moon to Uranus The drive for individual expression of emotional needs.
Positively expressed: an intuitive, emotionally independent personality, who needs personal freedom and experiences many emotional upheavals in life.
Negatively expressed: emotional terrorism, chaos, cold and distant, unreliability, possible explosive psychiatric disturbances and frequent, often unproductive breaks with the past; mother is unpredictable or emotionally detached.

Moon to Neptune The drive for empathy; the search for the perfect mother.
Positively expressed: highly imaginative artistic individual, who may be a visionary or mystic; compassion and a tendency towards self-sacrifice; a desire for something 'greater'; wants to refine feelings.

Negatively expressed: extreme emotional sensitivity, unrealistic fantasies or escapism; unavailable, idealized mother-figure.

Moon to Pluto The drive for emotional transformation.
Positively expressed: psychic and healing abilities, great emotional intensity under surface; an individual who needs strong emotional commitment from family and a supportive environment in which to flourish; emotional energy can be used constructively or destructively to achieve total transformation.
Negatively expressed: trauma and emotional drama, abandonment and rejection; 'devouring mother' archetype.

Moon to North Node The drive to rework the past.
Positively expressed: the positive qualities of the sign are reinforced and harnessed to soul growth.
Negatively expressed: the past prevents growth and soul evolution.

☿ ASPECTS TO MERCURY

Mercury to Venus The drive to express affection.
Positively expressed: an affectionate, charming, fair-minded person who expresses feelings with eloquence.
Negatively expressed: excess rationalization leading to separation from feelings.

Mercury to Mars The drive for mental assertion; the need to know.
Positively expressed: a strong-minded, forceful and incisive personality, with a flair for research.
Negatively expressed: sarcasm, irritability, overwork and mental burn-out.

Mercury to Jupiter The drive to expand the mind.
Positively expressed: a philosophical, optimistic personality, who has a thirst for knowledge and is open to new ideas.
Negatively expressed: extreme, over-the-top views; sweeping generalizations, exaggeration, poor judgment; potential difficulties with the law.

Mercury to Saturn The drive to conform mentally.
Positively expressed: a serious-minded, conservative personality with excellent concentration and logical reasoning skills, liking surety and routine.
Negatively expressed: rigid thought patterns, blockages to communication, inhibited self-expression, lack of confidence in one's own ideas.

Mercury to Chiron The drive to heal the mind.
Positively expressed: an original mind, intuitively logical, with a deep understanding of the causes of dis-ease; potential for teaching; someone who makes things happen as though by magic.
Negatively expressed: difficulty in communicating, psychosomatic dis-ease, deeply entrenched attitudes and beliefs; potential to be ridiculed.

Mercury to Uranus The drive for mental enlightenment.
Positively expressed: free, unfettered and intuitive mind, with strong powers of invention, attuned to technological solutions and innovations.
Negatively expressed: inability to concentrate, impractical ideas, eccentricity, severe nervous tension.

Mercury to Neptune The drive for spiritual enlightenment.
Positively expressed: imaginative, artistic, idealistic visionary.
Negatively expressed: 'head in clouds' mentality, gullibility, confusion, deception and escapism.

Mercury to Pluto The drive for mental mastery.
Positively expressed: a powerful, penetrating and perceptive mind, prone to black humour.
Negatively expressed: dark moods, fanaticism, obstinacy, manipulation, coercion and enforced conversion; possibility of deep-seated neurosis.

Mercury to North Node The drive for mental evolution.
Positively expressed: the mind is harnessed to spiritual purpose and growth; an openness to new ideas.
Negatively expressed: the mind expresses the negative qualities of the sign and evolution is slowed.

♀ ASPECTS TO VENUS

Venus to Mars The drive to unite male and female.
Positively expressed: sensuality and passionate feelings, romantic idealism; someone who demonstrates affection easily.
Negatively expressed: difficulty in relationship, excessive eroticism, desire for self-gratification; parents may be in conflict.

Venus to Jupiter The drive to grow through love.
Positively expressed: ardent, charming, sociable, hospitable and generous person.
Negatively expressed: selfishness, excessive emotional demands, vulgarity, exaggeration.

Venus to Saturn The drive toward emotional control.
Positively expressed: a coolly affectionate, faithful and socially responsible personality.
Negatively expressed: mean spiritedness, coldness, loneliness; disappointment in love; someone who does not believe themselves worthy of love.

Venus to Chiron The drive to find healing relationships.
Positively expressed: relationships that heal emotional pain.
Negatively expressed: abuse and wounding of or by partners, especially emotional abuse.

Venus to Uranus The drive for emotional independence.
Positively expressed: magnetic charm; constructive emotional independence; an excellent friend and companion.
Negatively expressed: commitment phobia, emotional isolation, sexual ambiguity and ambivalence; tendency to unconventional friendships and values, involving sexual ambivalence or ambiguity.

Venus to Neptune The drive for unconditional love.
Positively expressed: artistic, romantic, intuitive and idealistic personality; the soul practises unconditional love.
Negatively expressed: idealization and idolization, deception and co-dependence; an individual who seeks perfect love but finds illusions.

Venus to Pluto The drive for emotional power.
Positively expressed: deep, intense feelings; a charismatic and magnetic personality who seeks constructive emotional power.
Negatively expressed: obsessions and neuroses; manipulation, secrecy; someone who seeks destructive emotional power and is excessively needy.

Venus to North Node The drive to evolve through relationships.
Positively expressed: relationships are a rich source of evolution and growth.
Negatively expressed: old relationship patterns or outworn values hold back growth.

♂ ASPECTS TO MARS

Mars to Jupiter The drive to manifest.
Positively expressed: an expansive and enthusiastic person who attracts abundance and has an ability to manifest what is needed.
Negatively expressed: greed, superiority complex, rash speculation, negative expectations; potential gambler.

Mars to Saturn The drive for controlled self-assertion.
Positively expressed: self-assertive, hard-working, concentrated will.
Negatively expressed: feelings of powerlessness and helplessness; inconsistency; blockages and delays.

Mars to Chiron The drive to heal the will.
Positively expressed: dynamic with potential to energize others.
Negatively expressed: compulsive disorders, wounded will, disorder.

Mars to Uranus The drive toward self-will.
Positively expressed: individualistic, enterprising and energetic personality, possibly with fanatical courage.
Negatively expressed: extreme willfulness; rebellion; an unpredictable, irritable and accident-prone person; possibility of sexual difference.

Mars to Neptune The drive to spiritualize the will.
Positively expressed: a highly imaginative, artistic or musical individual.
Negatively expressed: impractical, irrational fears; probability of addiction.

Mars to Pluto The drive for power.
Positively expressed: dynamic, persistent, highly sexed personality, with a powerful survival instinct; attachment to a cause.
Negatively expressed: abuses and misuses of power; explosive temper, buried rage; possibility of fanatical dedication to a cause.

Mars to North Node The drive toward evolved will.
Positively expressed: will and assertion constructively expressed through the energy of sign and house.
Negatively expressed: will and assertion negatively expressed through the sign and house.

♃ ASPECTS TO JUPITER

Jupiter to Saturn Expansion-contraction dilemma.
Positively expressed: innate wisdom, expanding boundaries, growth through practical spirituality.
Negatively expressed: an inability to accept personal limitations resulting in compulsive eating or spending, gambling or depression; someone who swings between miser and spendthrift.

Jupiter to Chiron Growth through pain.
Positively expressed: an ability to overcome and grow through past pain and a capacity to inspire others.

Negatively expressed: pain caused by fragile belief system; someone prone to painful excesses.

Jupiter to Uranus The drive to explore new horizons.
Positively expressed: disciplined expansion; optimism; adventurous, original ideas and an independent mind.
Negatively expressed: anti-social tendencies; constant need for variety.

Jupiter to Neptune Unbounded imagination.
Positively expressed: a creative, intuitive, philosophical and compassionate individual, possibly with religious vision.
Negatively expressed: escapist fantasy, sensation seeker, tendency to sacrifice oneself for great causes, scatter-brained.

Jupiter to Pluto Growth through self-transformation.
Positively expressed: the ability to regenerate oneself, especially through dramatic transformation.
Negatively expressed: an overwhelming desire for personal power as compensation for personal inadequacy.

Jupiter to North Node The drive toward personal and spiritual expansion.
Positively expressed: growth is effortless.
Negatively expressed: the desire for growth leads to behaviour that is out of control.

♄ ASPECTS TO SATURN

Saturn to Chiron The drive to break bonds.
Positively expressed: potential for healing karma: channelling healing energy to earth and resolving negative ancestral patterns.
Negatively expressed: a sense of fear and isolation with no way out.

Saturn to Uranus Change-maintenance dilemma. immovable object meets irresistible force.
Positively expressed: an innovative, original, ambitious and determined personality who challenges the status quo constructively.
Negatively expressed: swings between order and chaos; authoritarianism or anarchy; extreme ideologies or cruelty; bi-polar disorder.

Saturn to Neptune Mystic-pragmatist dilemma.
Positively expressed: transcendence of the known; disciplined imagination and practical mysticism.

Negatively expressed: impractical, swings between pragmatic and heightened awareness or escapism, leading to emotional frustration and neurosis.

Saturn to Pluto The drive to transcend limitations.
Positively expressed: a deep desire for self-improvement and overcoming of strong emotion; constructively self-controlled and powerful.
Negatively expressed: obsession, compulsion, violence, fear of annihilation, destructive self-control; a totalitarian state.

Saturn to North Node The urge toward disciplined evolution.
Positively expressed: sincere and dedicated pathway of personal evolution.
Negatively expressed: false boundaries and beliefs that constrict evolution.

⚷ ASPECTS TO CHIRON

Chiron to Uranus The drive to heal chaos.
Positively expressed: a unique sense of individuality and inevitable transformation; channels energy from another dimension.
Negatively expressed: eccentricity and chaos.

Chiron to Neptune The drive to heal illusions.
Positively expressed: someone who surrenders illusions, is compassionate, self-sacrificing and prophetic; can indicate redemptive karma and the possibility of collective healing karma or burning of old self; channels energy from spiritual dimension.
Negatively expressed: self-immolation, scapegoating, over-sensitivity, emotional crucifixion.

Chiron to Pluto The drive to find the deepest meaning and healing.
Positively expressed: the potential to heal issues pertaining to power and environmental degradation; resolution of ancestral patterns; can channel or transform energy from collective level.
Negatively expressed: environmental abuse, abuse of power; growth may be blocked until autocratic parent dies.

Chiron to North Node The drive to heal the karmic wound.
Positively expressed: a pathway dedicated to healing and integrating karmic patterns; a vocation for healing.
Negatively expressed: wounds from the past prevent personal growth.

♅ ASPECTS TO URANUS

Uranus to Neptune The drive toward visionary transcendence.
Positively expressed: dynamic creativity and inspiration; a highly intuitive, imaginative, inventive and spiritually inspired personality, open to new technologies; a desire to usher in change.
Negatively expressed: self-deception, neurosis, chaos.

Uranus to Pluto The drive for dynamic change.
Positively expressed: the potential for enormous creative change.
Negatively expressed: the potential for violent destruction on a huge scale.

♆ ASPECTS TO NEPTUNE

Neptune to Pluto The drive for evolutionary growth.
Positively expressed: the potential for visionary transformation, bringing about a shift in collective spiritual awareness or personal revolution; emotionally intense.
Negatively expressed: religious or ideological breakdown, upheavals, chaos, confusion; disintegration as though caused by external forces.

Neptune to North Node The drive to spiritualize the path of personal growth.
Positively expressed: a spiritual pathway assists the soul to grow.
Negatively expressed: the soul encounters illusions and deceptions that masquerade as a path to evolution; may be totally ungrounded.

♇ ASPECTS TO PLUTO

Pluto to North Node The drive for evolutionary transformation.
Positively expressed: total dedication to the pathway of transformation and growth through empowerment.
Negatively expressed: dedication to obtaining power and mastery over others.

CONJUNCTIONS TO THE ANGLES

Sun on Ascendant a powerful personality that accentuates the Ascendant qualities but which may be self-centred.

Sun on Descendant self is expressed through relationship.

Sun on MC a strong need to make one's mark on world; may indicate egocentricity.

Sun on IC a home-orientated person who needs roots.

Moon on Ascendant reflective and responsive or reactionary personality.

Moon on Descendant someone whose emotions and past colour relationships.

Moon on MC a desire to nurture the world through the qualities of the sign.

Moon on the IC someone who is deeply attached to home and family.

Mercury on Ascendant a cerebral, self-expressive personality who may be restless and excitable.

Mercury on Descendant communication and companionship are more important to this personality than love.

Mercury on MC the ego has to express itself out to the world through words.

Mercury on IC the child who expresses the family's feelings.

Venus on Ascendant charming, affectionate, easy-going persona that blends with the environment.

Venus on Descendant relationships are extremely important and must be harmonious.

Venus on MC someone who has an artistic or pleasurable impact on the world.

Venus on IC the child who needs a harmonious, loving family.

Mars on Ascendant a forceful personality who can be selfish and quick-tempered.

Mars on Descendant the possibility of conflict with partners or dynamic partnership.

Mars on MC someone who makes a dynamic impact on the world.

Mars on IC the child who may experience conflict within family.

Jupiter on Ascendant or MC a desire to grow and expand, which is usually achieved, but may be hedonistic.

Jupiter on Descendant growth through partnership.

Jupiter on IC the family assists growth.

Saturn on Ascendant or MC someone with a controlled or controlling impact on the world.

Saturn on Descendant a controlling or older partner. The partnership is karmic.

Saturn on IC a controlling parent or restrictive home.

Chiron on Ascendant or MC a healing vocation or wounded personality.

Chiron on Descendant a need to heal relationship wounds.

Chiron on IC a painful home environment or a child who is not comfortable at home.

Uranus on Ascendant or MC the charismatic bringer of chaos or revolution.

Uranus on Descendant commitment issues; the potential for several partners.

Uranus on IC an unpredictable, changeable home.

Neptune on Ascendant or MC difficult to see, as though observed through a fog; extreme sensitivity and openness to environment.

Neptune on Descendant partners are idealized and may not be what they seem.

Neptune on IC parents are idealized and may be something other than perceived; family secrets.

Pluto on the Ascendant or MC an intense, somewhat obsessive persona that is power-orientated.

Pluto on Descendant power struggles in relationships.

Pluto on IC a powerful, controlling parent.

PLANETS THAT STAND ALONE

A planet that is not paired in an aspectual relationship with another planet stands alone in the chart and is known as a singleton or unaspected planet. and may not appear on the surface façade of the personality. It is not that the planetary energy is absent, more that it lacks connectiveness to the whole and is therefore unable to manifest. An unaspected planet bides its time and then emerges, often explosively and seemingly out of character. These potent loners are a hidden influence within the chart. Dynamic solo planets such as the Sun, Mars, Uranus or Pluto represent powerful unconscious drives at work within the personality. Placid and receptive solo planets such as the Moon, Venus or Neptune readily absorb outside influences, but find difficulty in releasing them.

Unaspected planetary energies are frequently projected on to other people, as though reclaiming the 'missing' energy through a relationship. Or an unaspected planet may represent a past-life persona that could one day break through with great force.

UNASPECTED PLANETS

Unaspected Sun A poor sense of self-identity and lack of self-confidence may be masked by apparent egotism and bravado. An unaspected Sun in a chart indicates a personality with little sense of self; it is as though two people seem to inhabit the same skin.

Unaspected Moon Deep emotions remain buried, but will one day be triggered explosively. Powerful unconscious forces conflict with the surface personality. This person may well be detached from home, family and feelings.

Unaspected Mercury Mental processes may be potent, according to the sign, but expression of those thoughts is difficult, blocked or inappropriate.

Unaspected Venus Social and romantic relationships are difficult when Venus is unaspected, although if Venus is placed in a sensual or sociable sign, excessive promiscuity or sociability may be used to mask a feeling of disconnection.

Unaspected Mars Motivation is difficult and outbursts of excessive anger or aggression can be a problem if Mars is isolated in Aries, Taurus, Leo, Scorpio or Capricorn.

Unaspected Jupiter An inability to connect with the abundance of life manifests when Jupiter is isolated; or the over-the-top side of this planet may be played out uncontrollably.

Unaspected Saturn Boundaries and limitations are a challenge when Saturn stands alone, although this person may exhibit a determined will or strong self-discipline.

Unaspected Chiron A powerful past-life wound can create considerable problems until the source is recognized and a means of healing and integration found.

Unaspected Uranus The chaotic and unstable side of Uranus frequently manifests when this planet is unaspected, and although genius and intellectual brilliance may be factors, it may be difficult to find a creative outlet for these.

Unaspected Neptune When Neptune cannot find outlet for its mystical energies, the planet encourages escapism, out-of-control psychism and self-destruction. These urges can be channelled constructively, giving rise to a dedicated artist or mystic.

Unaspected Pluto Strong compulsions and obsessions are likely when Pluto is unaspected. An outlet must be found for the intense, emotional urges of this planet or implosion could result.

CHART SHAPES

The distribution of planets within a chart may show itself as a random
spread, but very often the planets fall in a discernable pattern. The
shape they create illustrates the way in which the planetary energies
are experienced (see example charts below).

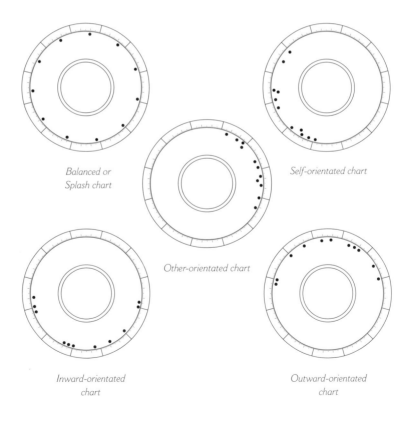

Balanced or
Splash chart

Self-orientated chart

Other-orientated chart

Inward-orientated
chart

Outward-orientated
chart

Balanced or Splash: even distribution of planets. Planetary energy flows throughout all areas of life. This distribution holds enormous potential, but the energies may be stretched too thinly as many goals are pursued at once.

Self-orientated: planets in the vertical half towards the Ascendant. A birthchart with this shape points to a self-directed personality for whom individuality is important, particularly when out in the world (the upper quadrant of the chart).

Other-orientated: planets in the half towards the Descendant. The emphasis here is on relationships, with the suggestion that others are more important than self.

Inward-orientated: all the planets in the bottom half. Planetary energy flow is introverted and focussed inwardly.

Outward-orientated: planets in top half. Planetary energy is flowing out to the world, but looks into an empty centre and wonders what is there.

Bowl: occupies one half of the chart. A bowl shape may indicate a receptive personality, depending on the angle. An upside-down bowl suggests someone who looks inward, seeking spiritual sustenance. A bowl on a slight angle, allowing constant replenishment, is ideal.

Bucket: a bowl with a planet that acts as a 'handle', a conduit between the self and the world. If receptive, it can channel inspiration and spiritual sustenance into the bowl.

Bundle: all the planets lying within four signs or 120°. A bundle indicates a specialist, who focuses on the areas of life in which the planets fall. It can also imply one-sidedness and unfulfilled potential.

See-saw: two groups of planets opposing each other. The planetary energies in this shape are pulling in two different directions, indicating a need for balance in conflicting areas of life.

Locomotive: spread evenly over eight signs or 240°. This shape leaves one sector empty and unexpressed. The leading planet tends to be most active, pulling the others behind it.

Splay: tight bunches of planets in several signs. A splay focuses attention in several areas of life, presenting a choice as to which will be fully expressed.

Angel's wings: two triangles spreading out from a shared base planet In this presentation, the incarnating soul wishes to rise above the mundane level of the chart to higher awareness (see chart on page 291).

Split: planets positioned in two unconnected areas. This distribution implies that energy is split and a personality that swings between the two.

Piecing it all

The different facets of an astrological chart resemble pieces of a jigsaw. Only when all the pieces have been weighed up and fitted together does the whole picture emerge. This skilful act of interpretation and integration is the art of astrology: recognizing what is dominant and what lies under the surface. Generally speaking, the strongest energies in a chart or horoscope are the Sun, the fire element, positive signs, and cardinal or fixed qualities. The Ascendant and the planets in the first house tend to be

together

dominant – at first glance. On an unconscious level, the Moon, the IC, or a preponderance of an element, polarity or quality, can also exert a powerful influence on behaviour. Much depends on which signs and elements are emphasized in a chart, and which of the planets is making itself felt. A fire Ascendant overrules a watery or airy Sun and an earth Ascendant gives a practical face to an otherwise impractical watery or fiery Sun. Aspects indicate whether the full force of a planet is felt, or whether their power is restrained.

HOW TO INTERPRET A CHART

Most astrologers follow a standard pattern when examining a chart for the first time. By breaking interpretation down into easy steps, it is possible to recognize what is dominant and what is passive, and to pick up on conflicts and contradictions. The main themes in the chart are then gathered together and laid out for synthesis. Interpretation is a combination of analysis and integration – with a measure of intuition to leaven the brew. With practise, weighing up a chart becomes an automatic process, but it is helpful to make notes initially.

The following steps show you how to interpret a chart. Each step is accompanied by an example that refers to the chart on page 291.

1 General shape Take in the overall shape of the chart (see pages 286) to ascertain approach to life and areas of life that are activated. *Example chart:* Balance of planets slanted towards the Ascendant but the chart falls into two distinct halves. 'Angel wings' formation.

2 Elemental balance The balance or imbalance of the elements may indicate a predilection for one way of perceiving the world over another (see pages 124–35). Note that Chiron and the Nodes are discounted in the balance of elements, polarities and qualities. *Example chart:* Emphasis on Earth (4) supports the Sun and Moon signs indicating a predilection for practical, body-based, sensory perception.

EXAMPLE CHART
08:23, 21 SEPTEMBER 1958, LONDON

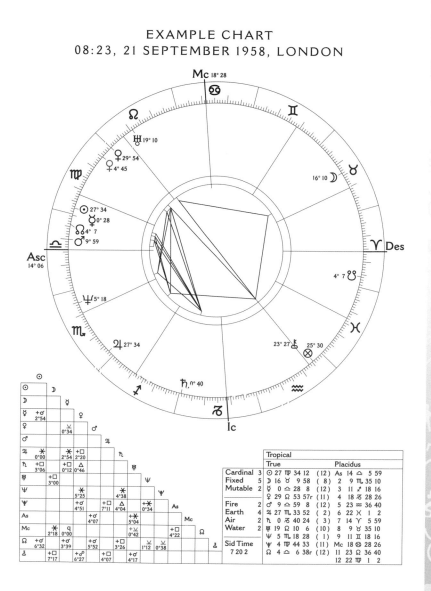

	Tropical		
	True		Placidus
Cardinal 3	☉ 27 ♍ 34 12	(12)	As 14 ♎ 5 59
Fixed 5	☽ 16 ♉ 9 58	(8)	2 9 ♏ 35 10
Mutable 2	☿ 0 ♎ 28 8	(12)	3 11 ♐ 18 16
	♀ 29 ♌ 53 57r	(11)	4 18 ♑ 28 26
Fire 2	♂ 9 ♎ 59 8	(12)	5 23 ♒ 36 40
Earth 4	♃ 27 ♏ 33 52	(2)	6 22 ♓ 1 2
Air 2	♄ 0 ♑ 40 24	(3)	7 14 ♈ 5 59
Water 2	♅ 19 ♌ 10 6	(10)	8 9 ♉ 35 10
	♆ 5 ♏ 18 28	(1)	9 11 ♊ 18 16
Sid Time	♇ 4 ♍ 44 33	(11)	Mc 18 ♋ 28 26
7 20 2	☊ 4 ♎ 6 38r	(12)	11 23 ♌ 36 40
			12 22 ♍ 1 2

3 Polarities A chart that has planets placed in mainly negative planets suggests an inward focussed and introverted personality, while a chart that has mainly positive, active planets suggests someone with a need to make an impact on the world (see pages 146–7), no matter where the sun-sign is placed.

Example chart: 4 positive, 6 negative, supports the receptive sun-sign polarity.

4 Qualities An emphasis on a particular quality can overcome the quality of the sun-sign (see pages 136–45).

Example chart: 5 fixed planets overcomes the mutable sun-sign.

5 Sun-sign This is the incarnating Self becoming individuated through life experience. Unless the Moon is strongly placed, with powerful aspects, the sun-sign is usually the more obvious influence (see pages 154–9).

Example chart: Virgo Sun is hidden in the twelfth house behind the Ascendant.

6 Moon sign The Moon indicates the emotional approach to life, shining light on ingrained patterns and habits that lie beneath the surface. It can be a potent force in the personality (see pages 160–65).

Example chart: Strong Taurus Moon with difficult aspects.

7 Do the Sun and Moon harmonize or conflict? If the

Sun and Moon are in the same element, polarity or quality, they harmonize and blend. Placed in different elements, they may conflict, producing a surface appearance of one type of personality and a very different inner-self.

Example chart: The Sun and the Moon are both in earth signs.

8 Does Mercury support or change self-expression?

If Mercury is in a positive sign and the Sun is in a negative one, Mercury increases self-expression, making it more extroverted. If Mercury is in a negative sign and the Sun in a positive one, self-expression is slowed down, making it more introverted. If the Sun and Mercury are in the same sign, the qualities of the sign are enhanced. Rulership can also have an effect.

Example chart: With Sun in Virgo, ruled by Mercury, and Mercury in Libra the criticalness of the Virgo mind is emphasized as is the desire for justice and perfection.

9 Ascendant

The Ascendant can mask or enhance a sun-sign depending on how much camouflage the rising sign offers to the Sun and how willingly the Sun accepts the opportunity to disguise itself. Positive Ascendants tend to be more active than negative ones.

Example chart: The positive, cardinal Libra Ascendant disguises the twelfth house Virgo Sun, further hidden behind the veil of Neptune in the first house. The Ascendant encourages bringing together self and others, a major theme in the chart.

10 Emphasis on houses

Houses that contain a planet are energized, but houses that contain two or more planets make a definite impact on life (see pages 228–63). Strong placements of planets in houses that have the same element as the Sun strengthen the element's slant.

Example chart: Strong emphasis on the twelfth and eleventh houses.

11 Aspects

List the major aspects. Powerful aspects create themes in the chart and may encourage or retard expression of the personal planets (see pages 264–85).

Example chart: Sun conjunct Mercury and North Node square Saturn; Uranus opposite Chiron T-square the Moon; Venus conjunct Pluto opposite Chiron, T-square Jupiter; Venus conjunct Pluto trine Saturn, sextile Neptune; virtually unaspected twelfth house Mars in Libra.

12 Aspect patterns Major aspect patterns strongly colour a chart, and may overtake a sun-sign (see pages 270–71).
Example chart: The chart opens into two T-square 'angels wings', which are trying to rise above the mundane level of the chart.

13 Emotional needs Consider the Moon and its aspects, then Venus and the parental houses.
Example chart: Powerful instinctual need for security and stability (Moon in Taurus) offset by square to Uranus, trying to shift entrenched patterns into emotional freedom. Needs to heal the emotional wounds indicated by Chiron. Venus conjunct Pluto and trine Saturn has powerful need for love but feels unlovable.

14 Mental approach Consider Mercury and its aspects, Uranus, and the third and ninth houses.
Example chart: Intellectually orientated with potential for acute perception and analysis (Mercury in Virgo) but a struggle to make this visible (twelfth house). Acuteness of mind is restrained by Saturn in Capricorn in third house.

15 Health Examine the planets in the sixth house, the house ruler and aspects to the ruler.
Example chart: With the South Node in the sixth house and Pisces on the cusp, Neptune (ruler of the sixth) in the first house, and the Virgo Sun in the twelfth, vitality may be lowered. Diseases arise out of the past.

16 Wealth Examine the second and eighth houses, their rulers and aspects to the rulers.

Example chart: Second house Jupiter suggests the ability to manifest abundance or at the least sufficient for needs. Taurus Moon wants to hold on to all it has.

17 Career Examine the tenth and sixth houses.

Example chart: Cancer MC and Virgo Sun would suggest a caring profession, emphasis on the twelfth house a career in institutions.

18 Partnership Examine the seventh and eighth houses, their rulers and aspects, and Venus.

Example chart: The desire to be an individual (Aries on the cusp and a slant towards the Ascendant) is balanced by the Libra Ascendant need to be in partnership. Two individuals need to unite in equal relationship with a space for individual expression.

19 Family Examine the fourth and tenth houses.

Example chart: Whilst security is craved (Capricorn IC and Taurus Moon), Uranus in the tenth house suggests that change and instability in the family environment is experienced, with the possibility of one parent leaving – may be a one-parent family centred around the father (Uranus/Chiron T-square Moon: separation from the mother).

20 Emerging themes The element balance, emphasis on a particular planet or certain signs or an element; several aspects with the same feel, such as a preponderance of squares or trines; or house placements with the same theme, leads to the emergence of one or two major themes in the chart. They may, for example, centre around attitudes to love (aspects to Venus, the fifth, seventh and eighth houses,

and several planets in Libra or Libra on the seventh house cusp); will
or power (Mars or Pluto aspects, Leo and Aquarius) or communication
(Mercury aspects, Gemini and the third or ninth houses).
Example chart: Emotional pain but change is difficult (Moon),
including pain around relationships (aspects to Venus). Need to
integrate self and others (chart in two halves, Libra Ascendant).
Tendency to 'people please' rather than be authentic; assertion and
vitality weakened.

21 Integration and synthesis All sides of the chart need to be
brought together to see which energies are strong and the ways in
which they contrast with and complement each other.
Example chart: This chart is strongly split between the past and how
others have been related to, and the need to develop and express the
self more clearly when in relationship. Assertion has to be integrated
and the self made more visible.

22 Personality Bring together sun-sign, Moon, Ascendant and
major aspects.
Example chart: Essentially practical, repressed and quiet, hard-working
and service-orientated, ignoring the needs of the self in favour of
service to others. Moon highlights a tendency to be a square peg in a
round hole and there is a distinct aversion to change, and a need to be
approved of by others. The essential self is hidden behind the 'niceness'
of the Libra Ascendant and the illusion spun by Neptune, a difficult
person to know. Isolated Mars in twelfth house Libra may suggest
passive aggression.

CHART INTERPRETATION CHECKLIST

1 General shape

2 Elemental balance

3 Polarities

4 Qualities

5 Sun-sign

6 Moon sign

7 Do the Sun and Moon harmonize or conflict?

8 Does Mercury support or change self-expression?

9 Ascendant

10 Emphasis on houses

11 Aspects

12 Aspect patterns

13 Emotional needs (Moon, Venus, fourth and tenth houses)

14 Mental approach (Mercury, Uranus, third and ninth houses)

15 Health (sixth house, ruler and aspects to ruler)

16 Wealth (second and eighth houses, rulers and aspects to rulers)

17 Career (sixth and tenth houses)

18 Partnership (seventh and eighth houses, rulers and aspects)

19 Family (fourth and tenth houses)

20 Emerging themes

21 Integration and synthesis

22 Personality

The unfolding

The natal chart is not a static event, it continually unfolds. The day-to-day movements of the planets kickstart or block the energies present in the chart, bringing about activation and change. Planets do not cause anything to happen, *but it feels as though they do.* When planets move through a sun-sign, land on an Ascendant or activate another planet, an effect is felt. Transits may pinpoint periods of change, such as a new home, a career move or a fresh relationship. However, many transits occur 'internally', heralding a period

chart

of inner growth. Little is visible on the surface, but the pressures subtly press for an inner shift or new understanding. Movements of the personal planets have an effect for a short time, but the outer planet transits are active for much longer, and the effect is sensed for up to six months before the transit becomes 'exact'. It can take another six months to integrate the effects. The chart can also be unfolded through progressions, and solar and lunar charts give an indication of the year ahead.

TRANSITS

Transits release potential, blending together ingrained drives and transitory stimuli. Easily calculated by computer, transits signal a period of change and activation, representing an opportunity to cooperate more closely with the planetary combination involved and to make necessary adjustments in the way the energies are used.

Transits sometimes bring together complementary planets, which boost each other's energies. At other times, the energies conflict, exactly as in a natal chart. Notwithstanding, people react to transits differently according to their level of self-awareness. If someone is strongly attuned to a planet, either because it is the ruler of the sun-sign or is placed prominently in the natal chart, cooperation willingly takes place with that planet's transits. If not, buffeted by the transits, it feels as though 'something out there' was forcing changes.

Transit timing

As planets move at different speeds, the period during which transits are active varies. Moon transits last a few hours, whereas Mars takes a few days. Saturn covers long, slow months, and it can take up to two years for the effects of Pluto to work through.

ORBS

The traditional orb given to a transiting planet is 2°, but wider orbs can make themselves felt.

With the outer planets, the effect of the combined energies is felt for some time before and after the actual transit. When an outer planet passes through a house, it can

TRANSITING ASPECTS

Aspects between the transiting planets and positions within a natal chart are calculated in exactly the same way as aspects within the natal chart itself, except that a smaller orb is used. 'Difficult' aspects usually indicate pressure, but can lead to favourable resolution, whilst 'easy' aspects can take longer to work through. The type of aspect made has the same relevance as natal aspects: a conjunction, trine or sextile allows an easier flow of the energies than does an opposition or square. Certain transits occur at a fixed age and have a major impact (see page 304).

TRANSITS TO NATAL
from 1st to 23rd January 2004

Computer programs are used to calculate transits and show aspects to the natal planet and the house being transited, and pinpoint the date of ingress to each house. These transits are for the example birthchart on page 291.

Date	Planet	House	Aspect	Transiting planet	House
1, 1, 04	♂	11	△	⚷	6
2, 1, 04	♄r	1	⊼	⚷	6
8, 1, 04	♂	11	⊻	♀	10
9, 1, 04	♂	11	☍	♆	5
9, 1, 04	♂	11	△	♇	3
22, 1, 04	♂	11	⊻	☉	10
23, 1, 04	♂	11	⊻	♂	10

have a long-term effect on the affairs of the house concerned. This is particularly noticeable when a natal planet or aspect is involved or if the house 'completes' a natal aspect, such as a T-square.

The retrograde effect

Retrograde motion slows things down. This type of motion can mean that a planet transits the same point up to three times, so intensifying the on-going process connected with that planet. There are three opportunities to grasp the challenge or gift of the transit. At the first pass, the initial crisis is experienced; at the second pass, as the transiting planet 'moves back' across the transited planet, more insight is gained and action begins; as the planet moves forward once again, the crisis is resolved and resolution found.

As a planet turns retrograde or direct, it 'makes a station' over a degree, that is, it apparently comes to a standstill for a short time. If that degree is sensitive in the natal chart, the effect of the stationary transit is powerfully intensified.

THE NATURE OF PLANETARY TRANSITS

The planets take varying times to transit other planets or angles, and can have a range of effects.

Planet/Period	Stimulates
Sun (3 days)	Physical energy, libido, health and vigour; the need to stand up for oneself and conflict with authority figures.
Moon (3 hours)	Mood swings, habits, emotions, transient feelings and people from the past.

Mercury
(1 day to a
month or more)

Mental clarity and communication, which is blocked or
problematic when Mercury is retrograde; mental shifts and
new information.

Venus
(1 day to a
month or more)

Amorous feelings, brief attractions and spending sprees.

Mars
(1 week to a
month or more)

An energizing effect on other planets, physical energy,
vigorous activity, angry outbursts, burns, stabbing, cuts,
shooting; activates the affairs of a house.

Jupiter
(5 months
to 1 year)

Growth, expansion or excess; prosperity, opportunity or
inflation; loss, travel, law and problems with the law.

Chiron
(up to
18 months)

Wounds or healing processes, integration or disintegration.

Saturn
(up to 1 year)

Structure and restructuring, lessons, restrictions,
responsibilities, consolidation, blockages, delays, losses, falls,
blows, collisions, crushing, depression.

Uranus
(1–2 years)

Change, catalytic or cataclysmic events, the unexpected,
transformation, a different viewpoint, chaos, explosions,
electrocution, accidents with machinery, terrorism and
revolution.

Neptune
(1–2 years)

Illumination, illusion, deception, confusion, breakdown and
disintegration, flooding, drowning, self-sacrifice, martyrdom.

Pluto
(1–2 years)

Inevitable change, transformation, psychological pressure,
regeneration, disintegration, breakdown, control and power
struggles, compulsions and obsessions, problems with sewers
and drains, death and endings, deception, huge upsurges of
intense emotion.

North Node
(a few weeks)

New expression of the planetary energy concerned.

South Node
(a few weeks)

A new presentation of old planetary energy, so that it can be
reworked or lessons revisited.

THE MAJOR AGE-RELATED TRANSITS

Certain major transits made by the outer planets in respect to their positions on the natal chart occur at a specific age, marking staging posts in a person's life, indicating periods of opportunity or challenge.

Transit	Effect
Nodal return (Every 18 and a half years)	Reiterates and reactivates purpose.
Jupiter return (Every 12 years)	The commencement of a fresh cycle of opportunity and expansion.
Saturn return (Every 28–29 years)	Major period of reassessment. This is when people ask themselves questions such as whether they are following their life plan, what they need to do in order to grow and what they must let go in order to move forward.
Uranus opposition (Age 38–44)	Catalytic mid-life crisis, involving drastic change and endings; all that is outgrown must be let go so that something new can emerge.
Uranus return (Age 84)	Reassessment and an opportunity to shift to a higher state of awareness.

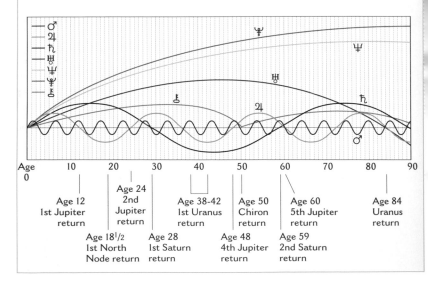

TRANSITS TO THE HOUSES

When a planet transits a house, the affairs of that house are stirred up and coloured by the energy of that planet for the period of the transit, particularly if a natal planet in the house is aspected by the transiting planet.

Transits to the first house are immediately apparent as they stimulate interaction between the unfolding Self and the external environment.

Transits to the second house stimulate issues pertaining to personal values, money and possessions.

Transits to the third house affect communication, contractual obligations and siblings, but may be reflected in education and travel involving short journeys.

Transits to the fourth house may indicate a physical move or bring parenting issues to the fore, but also focus on inner, psychological events.

Transits to the fifth house stimulate questions of creativity and love affairs, but also affect children and leisure time. Under this transit, a new activity may be taken on.

Transits to the sixth house reflect issues around health and wellbeing.

Transits to the seventh house stimulate relationships of all kinds and may indicate marriage or divorce. This transit can also signify the existence of hidden enemies.

Transits to the eighth house are reflected in inheritances and questions around shared resources and higher consciousness, and may involve death and endings.

Transits to the ninth house may profoundly affect your belief system or perhaps take you into higher education or on a long journey.

Transits to the tenth house stimulate career and ambition, particularly what is striven for.

Transits to the eleventh house involve social interaction and group responsibilities and may indicate the start of a new friendship.

Transits to the twelfth house may bring hidden secrets to light or bring about contact with institutions of all kinds.

The transiting Moon cycle

The transiting Moon has a powerful universal effect during its monthly and yearly cycles, but also has a personal effect for a short time each month. For two and a half days, the Moon moves through your sun-sign, bringing any underlying emotional issues to the surface. At this time, you will be more sensitive than usual, and may need to withdraw into your inner-self to process and release your feelings.

Twice a year, a new or full Moon occurs in each sun-sign. At these times you have an opportunity to let go of the past and make a new start. Seeds are planted; ideas are sown; and with the next full moon projects come to fruition. The full Moon in your sun-sign may also activate a crisis in your personal life. You may appear to behave irrationally, but in actuality, you can no longer repress the emotional urges that need to be released or fulfilled.

The Moon transiting a natal or progressed planet has a fleeting effect, but it can bring to the surface the irrational or ingrained habitual expression of that planet's energy and may invoke depression or elation. Eclipses also have an especially powerful effect (see pages 382–89), particularly when falling on natal planets or the angles.

Returns

Age	
Crown Chakra	60
Brow Chakra	
Throat Chakra	40
Heart Chakra	
Solar plexus Chakra	29
Sacral Chakra	
Base Chakra	birth

TRANSITS AND THE CHAKRAS

Life can be divided into age-spans, relating to the flow of subtle energy through the physical, emotional, mental and spiritual bodies. Initiated by major outer planet transits, planetary energy is transmitted through the chakras (energy centres in the body), via the endocrine system, activating the subtle bodies.

Body	Effect
Physical (0 to age 29)	The lower chakras, allied to the sexual organs, are activated and attuned to the life-force at the physically creative level.
Emotional (Saturn return, age 29 to 38–44)	The solar plexus and heart chakras are activated with the emotional body. Feelings about self and others are examined. The challenge is to master the emotions, remaining centred, with a calm heart, unaffected by the extremes of pain or joy.
Mental (Uranus opposition, age 38–44 to 50)	Maturity sets in and energies move up to the throat chakra and brow, activating the higher mind and mental creation, and moving into the mental body. Awareness of self expands. Failure to achieve full experience of the self at this age can result in heart attacks in men and a blocked throat chakra in women, who feel they are 'unheard and cannot speak'.
Spiritual (Chiron return, age 50–51 to 58)	The soul finds a new form, the Self solidifies, the brow and crown chakras are activated and there is a connection to wider consciousness.
Spiritual (second Saturn return age 58–59 onwards)	The past must be released or lessons reiterated, leading to re-visioning. If the transition is successful, karmic rewards are reaped and the individual comes into his or her own wisdom.

CYCLE OF OPPORTUNITY: JUPITER

Jupiter takes 12 years to travel around the chart, making a challenging aspect to its natal position every three years. Hence, every 12 years (at ages 12, 24, 36, and so on) a new cycle of opportunity commences. Different 12-year cycles of opportunity also operate between Jupiter and the natal Sun or Ascendant, which are similarly activated when transiting Jupiter reaches these points in the natal chart. At the beginning of a Jupiter cycle, opportunity is grasped, seeds are sown, and then cultivated for three years. The benefits are reaped for six years. At the nine-year point, the cycle starts to wind down, ready to begin once more.

Chiron transits

A Chiron transit brings out the nature of the transited planet and raises issues about how that planetary energy is being used. Chiron transits to Mars, for example, highlight issues around will and self-assertion, and may involve experiences of aggression if assertion skills have not been honed.

Chiron experiences often entail separation from the physical in order to experience other dimensions, be those emotional, mental or spiritual. A balance has to be struck between existing form and the new energy systems that are struggling to raise their vibrations. During these transits, the grip on the past has to be loosened, so that the pain of the past can be lanced and healing can take place.

To find the first Chiron square, locate the natal placement of Chiron on the left-hand row, and read up to find the age in the top column.

CHIRON–CHIRON TRANSITS

Chiron transits to itself are turning points. Due to an erratic, elliptical orbit, they occur at different ages according to natal placement–it takes eight and a half years for Chiron to pass through Aries but less than two to go through Libra.

First Chiron square Separates from what comforts most, and can be a time of profound spiritual crisis and recognition that the soul inhabits a body. Past-life memories can be triggered and the karmic wound emerges.

Chiron opposition At this point, the individual gets a 'handle' on the inner wound and how it arose. Initially, such awareness may be projected, leading to a crisis of meaning.

Second Chiron square The wound re-emerges, or is reiterated, and the need for healing is acknowledged, although awareness may remain limited. Healing may not come until Chiron's return.

Chiron return (age 50–51) The wound returns, bringing with it all its pain, and demanding recognition, healing and integration. The situation in the outer world often mirrors that which created the wound, or the internal pain. If this crisis is successfully negotiated, there is a move into wider consciousness, uniting heart, mind and spirit, and facilitating creative living. If not, the cycle begins again.

Age

PROGRESSIONS

Progressions illustrate how a chart evolves and pinpoint significant ages at which changes or developments occur, based on configurations within the 'progressed' chart or aspects to the natal chart. Whereas the natal chart indicates life-long tendencies or traits, a progressed chart, showing subsequent planetary movement, can highlight a phase that lasts for a year or two or – in the case of the progressed Sun or Ascendant changing signs – can usher in a psychological change lasting for up to 30 years.

Outer planet progressions are not as significant as personal ones, unless the outer planet changes sign or direction, so heralding a change

EPHEMERIS EXTRACT
AUGUST 1982

Progressions can be counted forward in an Ephemeris or, more easily, be calculated on a computer.

AUGUST 1982 — LONGITUDE

Day	Sid.Time	⊙	0 hr ☽	Noon ☽	True ☊	☿	♀	♂	♃	♄	♅	♆	♇
2 M	8 43 1	9 ♌ 51 59	7♊ 4 42	12 59 25	13R 16.8	18 40.0	15 27.7	29 26.2	2 16.3	17 7.5	0R 35.7	24R 34.8	24 21.0
3 Tu	8 46 57	10 49 23	18 55 13	24 52 28	13 16.4	20 40.3	16 40.3	0♏ 0.3	2 22.3	17 11.7	0 35.4	24 33.8	24 22.0
4 W	8 50 54	11 46 49	0♋ 51 28	6♋52 29	13 14.5	22 29.8	17 53.0	0 34.6	2 28.5	17 16.0	0 35.1	24 32.8	24 23.0
5 Th	8 54 51	12 44 15	12 55 44	19 1 27	13 11.3	24 22.4	19 5.8	1 9.1	2 34.8	17 20.3	0 34.9	24 31.9	24 24.1
6 F	8 58 47	13 41 42	25 9 48	1♍ 20 56	13 6.9	26 13.4	20 18.6	1 43.7	2 41.2	17 24.8	0 34.7	24 30.9	24 25.1
7 Sa	9 2 44	14 39 10	7♍ 35 0	13 52 7	13 1.7	28 2.8	21 31.4	2 18.5	2 47.8	17 29.3	0 34.6	24 30.0	24 26.3
8 Su	9 6 40	15 36 39	20 12 23	26 35 55	12 56.4	29 50.6	22 44.3	2 53.5	2 54.5	17 33.8	0 34.6	24 29.2	24 27.4
9 M	9 10 37	16 34 10	3♎ 2 50	9♎ 33 13	12 51.6	1 36.9	23 57.2	3 28.6	3 1.4	17 38.5	0D 34.5	24 28.3	24 28.6
10 Tu	9 14 33	17 31 42	16 7 11	22 44 52	12 47.9	3 21.6	25 10.2	4 3.9	3 8.4	17 43.2	0 34.6	24 27.5	24 29.8
11 W	9 18 30	18 29 15	29 26 20	6♏ 11 43	12 45.7	5 4.8	26 23.2	4 39.4	3 15.5	17 48.0	0 34.6	24 26.7	24 31.0
12 Th	9 22 26	19 26 50	13♏ 1 5	19 54 30	12D 45.0	6 46.4	27 36.3	5 15.0	3 22.7	17 52.8	0 34.8	24 25.9	24 32.2
13 F	9 26 23	20 24 26	26 52 1	3♐ 53 35	12 45.7	8 26.6	28 49.4	5 50.9	3 30.1	17 57.8	0 35.0	24 25.2	24 33.5
14 Sa	9 30 19	21 22 4	10♐ 59 8	18 8 30	12 47.1	10 5.2	0♐ 2.6	6 26.8	3 37.6	18 2.8	0 35.2	24 24.5	24 34.9
15 Su	9 34 16	22 19 43	25 21 25	2♑ 37 34	12 48.3	11 42.4	1 15.8	7 3.0	3 45.2	18 7.8	0 35.5	24 23.8	24 36.2
16 M	9 38 13	23 17 24	9♑56 26	17 17 29	12R 48.5	13 18.0	2 29.0	7 39.3	3 53.0	18 13.0	0 35.8	24 23.2	24 37.6
17 Tu	9 42 9	24 15 6	24 39 59	2♒ 3 11	12 47.2	14 52.2	3 42.3	8 15.8	4 0.9	18 18.2	0 36.2	24 22.5	24 39.0
18 W	9 46 6	25 12 50	9♒26 11	16 48 6	12 43.8	16 24.9	4 55.7	8 52.4	4 8.9	18 23.4	0 36.7	24 21.9	24 40.4
19 Th	9 50 2	26 10 35	1♓ 7 59	1♓24 55	12 38.7	17 56.1	6 9.0	9 29.2	4 17.0	18 28.8	0 37.2	24 21.4	24 41.9
20 F	9 53 59	27 8 21	8♓38 3	16 46 36	12 32.1	19 25.8	7 22.4	10 6.1	4 25.3	18 34.2	0 37.7	24 20.8	24 43.4
21 Sa	9 57 55	28 6 8	22 49 54	29 47 28	12 24.9	20 54.0	8 35.9	10 43.2	4 33.7	18 39.6	0 38.3	24 20.3	24 44.9
22 Su	10 1 52	29 3 57	6♈ 38 53	13♈23 58	12 18.0	22 20.7	9 49.4	11 20.4	4 42.2	18 45.1	0 39.0	24 19.9	24 46.4
23 M	10 5 48	0♍ 1 47	20 2 40	26 35 2	12 12.1	23 45.8	11 2.9	11 57.8	4 50.8	18 50.7	0 39.7	24 19.4	24 48.0
24 Tu	10 9 45	0 59 39	3♉ 1 18	9♉ 21 48	12 7.9	25 9.4	12 16.5	12 35.4	4 59.5	18 56.3	0 40.4	24 19.0	24 49.6
25 W	10 13 42	1 57 31	15 36 57	21 47 16	12 5.6	26 31.4	13 30.1	13 13.0	5 8.3	19 2.0	0 41.2	24 18.6	24 51.2

of focus. If a planet was retrograde at birth, the age at which it turns direct harnesses its energy, rendering it more visible in the life experience at that time.

Day-for-a-year progressions

Secondary progressions, or the 'day-for-a-year' method, equate one day in the ephemeris with one year of life. Take the date of birth and add to it the age in years, making allowance for change of month, to give the progressed birth date. A 24-year-old Leo, for example, born on 2 August 1982 would look at a chart for 25 August 1982 to view the current year's progressions, that is the 25th year of life. In this example, the progressed Sun has just moved into Virgo, ushering in a new vibration. (See Ephemeris extract, opposite.)

Solar arc progressions

In solar arc progressions, all the planets and angles move the same distance as the progressed Sun each year. Solar arc progressions are calculated by ascertaining how far the Sun has moved and then each planet and angle in the chart is moved by the same number of degrees. So, for instance, if the Sun has moved 22° as in the example above, all the planets move forward 22° and Pluto changes position from 24° Libra to 16° Scorpio.

Progressed personal planets

Progressed personal planets, being faster moving than outer planets, tend to make the most aspects to natal planets (planets in the birthchart). The significance of these aspects is read according to the nature of the planets involved and the time–corresponding to a person's age — at which the contact is made. The earlier the aspect occurs, the more significant but unconscious the change may be. The later it occurs, the more opportunity there is to make conscious use of the change of energy. If the effect of a natal aspect between an inner and outer planet is tightened by the progressed personal planet moving closer, the tension or flow embodied in that aspect is felt more acutely.

PROGRESSED PLANETS IN ASPECT TO THE NATAL CHART

The personal planets have a significant effect when they move into aspect to the planets in a natal chart, according to the nature of the planet aspected.

Progressed Planet

Sun	Major adjustments and integrations are called for, the lifeplan unfolds in accordance with planetary characteristics.
Moon	Emotional adjustments are activated by external circumstances and inner drives coloured by the aspected planet.
Mercury	Increased mental activity is stimulated and may occur through travel or reading material.
Venus	Affairs of the heart are stimulated or may be curtailed according to the nature of the aspected planet; creative pursuits and values are emphasized.
Mars	Activity and initiative are increased, conflict may arise and impulsive action should be avoided.

THE PROGRESSED MOON CYCLE

By secondary progression, the Moon spends two and a half years in each sign or equal house (in quadrant house systems the time varies). The cycle indicates new ways in which instinctual energy is expressed. Attracting people and situations that mirror the energy of the sign, the progressed Moon stimulates questions focussed through the lens of the house it occupies.

Progressed Moon in

Aries	Induces centering around the eternal Self or the ego, and brings up issues for resolution.
Taurus	Tests inner security and asks what the Self, rather than the ego, values.
Gemini	Concerned with self-expression especially in social encounters.
Cancer	A challenge to begin the process of self-nurturing – and to let go of emotional patterns from the past.
Leo	Stimulates development of self-confidence and asks how a person will shine.
Virgo	Leads into exploration of psychosomatic conditions and turns the Self towards service to others.
Libra	Brings relationship issues to the fore and asks what adjustments are required to live in harmony.
Scorpio	Triggers issues around control and manipulation. Facing the shadow may involve a trip into the depths.
Sagittarius	Explores the world in an effort to find meaning.
Capricorn	Asks how inner discipline and authority can be developed, and may well indicate more responsibility in the community.
Aquarius	Moves into the wider world, seeking to find new ways to fit into society – or to adapt society to a new vibration.
Pisces	Brings the challenge of outgrowing outworn emotions and letting go illusions, to find wholeness.

SOLAR AND LUNAR RETURNS

A solar return chart is calculated for the precise moment when the Sun returns to its natal degree, giving a picture of the year to come. (This return won't necessarily coincide with a person's birthday.)

Solar returns can be used in several ways. The chart itself can be read in the same way that a natal chart is read, to glean a characteristic flavour for the coming year. Houses that are emphasized thereby indicate which areas of life are prominent, and planets identify drives or challenges that will be coming more sharply into play or which are fading away. To see the year ahead more precisely, the data may be used to plot the transit of the Sun or Ascendant around the solar return chart – 1 degree taken as roughly equal to one day. Fairly accurate timings for events or inner shifts can be ascertained by establishing when planets will be 'set off' by the Sun or Ascendant transit. Alternatively, the solar return may also be read in terms of aspects made to the natal chart. Solar returns can be relocated to the current place of residence, which changes the Ascendant and house positions.

A lunar return chart describes the moment when the Moon returns to its natal position. (This may be different to the birthday.) Lunar returns tend to pinpoint emotional changes or resurgences taking place during the year.

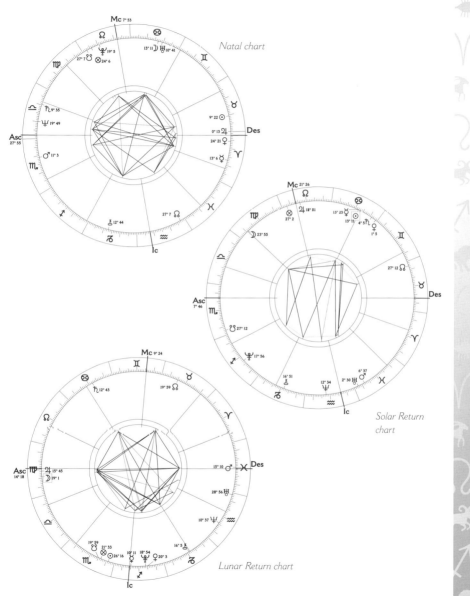

Natal chart

Solar Return chart

Lunar Return chart

Relationship

Astrology can tell you a great deal about your attitudes to relationships and the type of relationship you attract. Whilst your partner's sun-sign indicates how he or she will behave in love, the placement of Venus and Mars in your own chart, and the planets that inhabit your seventh house, give you an understanding of your own needs and what you expect from a partner.

Attraction can be an instant thing between opposing signs. Two Suns in the same element suggest a harmonious

astrology

relationship, whereas squares tend to be difficult as they attempt to bring together disparate elements.

You can discover significant facts about your interaction with a partner from the geometric relationships your charts make to each other, known as interaspects. The art of synastry (chart comparison), and the grids and interaspects associated with it, may look complex at first glance but is easily learned.

WHAT A SUN-SIGN CAN TELL YOU ABOUT A PARTNER

Simply knowing someone's sun-sign can tell you a great deal about that person and how they will function in a relationship. Each sign sends out characteristic sexual signals, and each behaves in its own unique way when in love or lust. With a little help from the zodiac, you can learn to understand the deeper dynamics of your partner's relationship needs and how best to please or support that person. When you realize that some signs simply have to flirt, but do not necessarily mean anything by it, your fears will be allayed about flirtatious behaviour. On the other hand, your partner's sun-sign may suggest that suspicions you have of infidelity are well founded.

Relationship style

A sun-sign can also tell whether you have a partner for life or are involved, at best, in serial monogamy. You can discover whether your partner is prepared to work to make the relationship better, or whether a 'grass is greener elsewhere' attitude prevails. Your partner's sun-sign illuminates sexual style, goals, expectations, sexual fantasies and turn-ons. It reveals whether your partner is passionate or romantic, faithful or otherwise; and whether he or she is looking for lust or friendship.

When you know what your partner really means or wants, and when you recognize what your partner needs in order to feel safe and comfortable, it can completely change the way you experience relationships, as it helps you to adapt and adjust, and to take advantage of the potential within a partnership.

Compatibility

Use the chart on pages 320–321 to establish your compatibility rating with the other signs of the zodiac. The hearts represent a sliding scale, with five hearts indicating optimum compatibility.

Synastry can help you to adapt and adjust to the demands of a relationship and take advantage of its potential.

COMPATIBILITY CHART

	Aries	Taurus	Gemini	Cancer	Leo	Virgo
Aries	♥♥♥	♥	♥♥♥	♥♥♥	♥♥♥♥	♥
Taurus	♥	♥♥♥♥♥	♥	♥♥	♥♥♥	♥♥♥♥
Gemini	♥♥♥♥	♥♥♥	♥♥♥♥♥	♥	♥♥♥	♥
Cancer	♥♥	♥	♥	♥♥♥♥♥	♥	♥♥♥♥
Leo	♥♥♥♥♥	♥♥♥	♥♥♥	♥	♥♥	♥
Virgo	♥♥♥	♥♥♥♥♥	♥♥♥♥	♥♥♥	♥♥	♥♥♥♥♥
Libra	♥♥♥♥♥	♥♥	♥♥♥♥	♥♥♥♥	♥♥♥♥♥	♥
Scorpio	♥♥♥	♥♥♥♥♥	♥	♥♥♥♥♥	♥♥♥♥	♥♥♥♥
Sagittarius	♥♥♥♥♥	♥♥	♥♥♥♥♥	♥	♥♥♥♥♥	♥♥♥
Capricorn	♥♥♥	♥♥♥♥♥	♥♥	♥♥♥	♥♥	♥♥♥♥♥
Aquarius	♥♥	♥♥♥	♥♥♥♥	♥♥♥	♥♥♥♥♥	♥♥♥
Pisces	♥	♥♥♥♥	♥	♥♥♥♥♥	♥♥	♥♥♥♥♥

	♎︎ Libra	♏︎ Scorpio	♐︎ Sagittarius	♑︎ Capricorn	♒︎ Aquarius	♓︎ Pisces
♈︎ Aries	♥♥♥♥♥	♥♥♥♥	♥♥♥♥♥	♥♥♥♥	♥♥♥♥♥	♥
♉︎ Taurus	♥♥♥	♥♥♥♥♥	♥♥	♥♥♥♥♥	♥♥♥	♥♥♥♥
♊︎ Gemini	♥♥	♥♥	♥♥♥♥♥	♥	♥♥♥♥	♥♥
♋︎ Cancer	♥	♥♥♥♥	♥	♥♥♥♥♥	♥♥♥	♥♥♥♥♥
♌︎ Leo	♥♥♥♥♥	♥♥♥♥	♥♥♥♥♥	♥	♥♥♥♥♥	♥♥♥
♍︎ Virgo	♥♥	♥♥	♥♥	♥♥♥♥	♥♥♥	♥♥♥♥♥
♎︎ Libra	♥♥♥♥♥	♥♥	♥♥♥♥♥	♥♥♥♥	♥♥♥♥	♥♥♥♥
♏︎ Scorpio	♥♥	♥♥♥	♥	♥♥	♥♥♥	♥♥♥♥
♐︎ Sagittarius	♥♥♥♥♥	♥	♥♥♥♥♥	♥	♥♥♥	♥
♑︎ Capricorn	♥♥♥	♥♥♥	♥	♥♥♥♥♥	♥	♥
♒︎ Aquarius	♥♥♥	♥♥♥♥	♥♥♥♥	♥	♥♥♥♥♥	♥
♓︎ Pisces	♥♥♥	♥♥♥♥♥	♥	♥♥	♥	♥♥♥♥♥

ARIES
The ardent lover

Erogenous zones	Ears, hair and nape of the neck, tongue
Turn-ons	A smouldering look, anything red, sexy underwear
Aphrodisiacs	A single red rose, ginger, tomatoes, leather
Fantasies	Romantic, fast and furious, Aries comes to the rescue
Make it work	Let Aries be the boss; act defenceless

Brash and pushy, Aries is a passionate lover who enjoys conquest. There is little finesse involved when this sign goes on the sexual rampage. Once committed, Aries usually remains faithful but, lacking the patience to work problems through, has a tendency towards serial relationships.

Aries has to be in charge. This is not a partner who settles happily for a quiet night in. At home, expect passionate seduction. Aries people love to act out their fantasies and are often too impatient to wait for the bedroom. This sign cannot tolerate frustration or delay.

Your Arien lover has no difficulty saying I love you and meaning it. A generous partner who showers you with unexpected gifts, this sign acts in the moment and lacks the subtlety to carry on a long-term affair. But, surprisingly for such a confident sign, your Aries partner does need admiration and reassurance that he or she is loved. This can lead to a great deal of innocuous flirting and the occasional fling. This me-orientated sign demands total attention and, if you do not provide it, he or she looks elsewhere. No matter how often Aries might stray, you are expected to wait patiently, showing unswerving loyalty. The straying may not necessarily involve sexual partners, either. Aries has much to occupy him or herself and being tied down is anathema to this freedom-loving sign. Your partner expects to see friends and pursue activities without you constantly by his or her side.

To live happily with an Aries you need to accept that the sign is self-orientated and is, for most of the time, insensitive to your needs. This is the Arien nature, and it can't be helped. To maintain harmony, it is important to remember that Aries knows best. The Arien catchphrase is 'I think you'll find I'm right', and woe betide a partner who argues or reminds Aries of times when this was not so. This is a highly competitive person who hates to be humiliated. When Aries is defeated, it is best to pretend it never happened.

Arguments flare quickly with this tempestuous sign, but are over just as fast. As partner, you are expected to forget anything said in the heat of the moment. Occasionally, Aries sulks, but flattery always brings him or her round in the end.

Aries is one of the most passionate and romantic signs in the zodiac.

TAURUS
The sensual lover

Erogenous zones	Neck, taste buds and the senses
Turn-ons	Massage, sensual silk on skin, food, perfume, money, silken sheets
Aphrodisiacs	Chocolates, musk, scented oils, truffles
Fantasies	Sybaritic surroundings, exotic food, utterly willing partners
Make it work	Never push or hurry; introduce change gradually

Sensual Taurus is an indolent lover, but a tenacious one. Once committed, Taurus gives and demands absolute loyalty. Divorce is highly unlikely, although Taurus is not averse to a long-term affair, which wouldn't be deemed disloyal because it wouldn't involve 'love', only sex. If *you* are tempted to stray, however, you should know that Taurus is one of the most possessive and jealous signs of the zodiac.

Taurus likes to be the breadwinner and to be in charge of joint finances, but otherwise is happy in an equal partnership. This sociable sign enjoys entertaining, but is also content with a quiet night in. One thing Taurus does demand is a comfortable home.

Since this sign is concerned primarily with solid, tangible matters, Taurean lovers tend to suffer from a lack of imagination and a certain insensitivity. Your partner is unlikely to be tuned into what you feel or what you need emotionally. While Taurus has no problem saying I love you, he or she will show few spontaneous gestures of affection, and the subtleties of emotion pass this pragmatic sign by. Flowery expressions of sentiment are not deemed necessary by this sensual sign, who saves up all physical expression of love for the bedroom.

The quiet confidence of Taurus means that little is required in the way of emotional reassurance, provided your lover remains inside their comfort zone. What a Taurean does need is a deep sense of security. Taurus gains this sense of security not only from a solid relationship but also from material goods. House and car are both status symbols and anchors. This is the person who, when asked why he or she stays in unrewarding relationship, answers 'Well, there is the house'. Endings are terribly difficult for Taurus, who does everything possible to keep the relationship going. Divorce is particularly painful because it means dividing up the spoils.

When pushed outside the bounds of what is known and comfortable, Taurus becomes extremely obstinate. This sign has a terrible temper. Slow to rouse, when Taurus does finally blow the result is awesome. The bull snorts and bellows and paws the ground. Do not, under any circumstances, laugh at this display. Taurus has the longest memory in the zodiac and finds it almost impossible to forgive or forget.

Taurus is one of the most sensual and faithful signs of the zodiac.

GEMINI
The eloquent lover

Erogenous zones	Between the ears, fingers and toes
Turn-ons	Erotica, light touch, soft porn, phone or computer sex
Aphrodisiacs	Gin, talking dirty, uniforms
Fantasies	Virtual sex, orgies, making a porn movie
Make it work	Listen well, be interesting, improvize, buy the Kama Sutra

Gemini can talk anyone into anything. This loquacious sign delights in innuendo and animated discussion, little of which is aimed towards sexual conquest, although it may slide into a quick fling. This sociable sign needs other people to bounce ideas off and has a circle of platonic friends with whom he or she flirts outrageously but has no intention of taking things further. Many Geminis spend more time fantasizing about sex than participating.

Faithfulness is not something this sign does well, and Gemini doesn't expect it of a partner, either. Airy Gemini basically has a problem with commitment to a long-term partnership and needs plenty of space. This sign goes reluctantly into marriage and may quickly divorce.

More important than sexual compatibility is intellectual companionship. You need to know that this sign hates to be bored. Innate mischievousness can easily turn to spite. Gemini stirs up an argument simply to make things happen. You can choose not to be drawn in, but will need to provide a

Gemini is the most vocal lover in the zodiac.

distraction. Debates are something Gemini enjoys, so you might as well get used to them. This two-faced sign argues black is white one minute and black is black the next. You need to be mentally agile to keep up, and to bear in mind that promises and firm decisions are not this sign's forte. Try not to take it personally.

Gemini is not a good listener, especially to emotional angst or everyday practicalities, finding it impossible to keep a secret. If you crave emotional intimacy, you will not find it here, Gemini simply does not know how to make a deep emotional connection. Rather than unburden to Gemini, who will dissect your feelings out of existence, it is better to have a close friend with whom you can share such matters.

A Gemini partner is full of surprises. Just when you feel you have finally got to know this complex character, you see yet another side. It is as though several personalities were inhabiting one body. Some of these are prone to sudden black moods of deepest depression. At such times, retreat is the best course of action. It shouldn't take long for your partner to return to his or her charming self.

CANCER
The caring lover

Erogenous zones	Nipples, breasts and stomach
Turn-ons	Cuddles and being needed, oral sex
Aphrodisiacs	Moonlight, water, avocado, sea-food, grapes
Fantasies	Intensely private and romantic, often featuring water
Make it work	Share feelings, provide cuddles and reassurance, and remember anniversaries

There is nothing your Cancerian partner likes more than looking after you. Whether male or female, Cancer tends to mother a partner. Once this sign has sidled up and committed to relationship, there is no turning back. Possessive and clinging, Cancer will not consider separation or affairs, and flirtations are rare. This sign demands total emotional melding, which can be suffocating, but you can count on loyalty and faithfulness.

Understanding Cancer in a relationship can be challenging. Tough and confident on the outside, the inner-self is anything but. This is a complex and vulnerable sign, acutely sensitive and soft-hearted, underneath the hard shell of the crab. Cancer needs, above all else, to be needed. Acutely tuned to every nuance of your moods, Cancer needs to feel safe to reveal his or herself. You may be surprised at the moodiness and depth of self-pity your partner can show, especially when feeling misunderstood or overlooked. You need to be extra demonstrative to satisfy the unspoken craving for affection. But there are times when your partner needs to withdraw to process deep emotions, particularly during the dark of the moon. Allowing your partner space, without withdrawing love, or giving extra reassurance as required can be extremely beneficial.

With Cancer, everything is bound up in emotion and homemaking. This sign shows feelings through nurturing. If you a reject Cancer's food-offering, you reject them. As this sign is sensitive to the slightest rebuff, such things tend to be taken personally, as does any refusal on your part to share your feelings. If Cancer sulks, which this sign certainly will, first check the phase of the moon, and then that it is not something you said. Cancer can sense an insult even when one is not intended, and expects a sincere apology even if you did not mean anything by your remark.

If your partner sometimes appears to be stingy, this is because, for Cancer, security is closely bound up with money in the bank. No Cancer likes even the best-loved partner to spend money without careful consideration, and household accounts are closely scrutinized. On the plus side, this is a shrewd sign and your partner is ambitious so material prospects are good.

Cancer is a sentimental sign so if you want to spice up your relationship, give a surprise party to celebrate the first time you met. Cancer also appreciates time spent together cuddling up and watching an old film as the most satisfying moments occur in the home.

LEO
The proud lover

Erogenous zones	Lower back
Turn-ons	Admiration and flattery; stroking or clawing like a cat
Aphrodisiacs	Gold, bananas, the sun
Fantasies	Dominatrix
Make it work	Admire, adore and flatter; Leo needs to feel special

Sex and romance are essential ingredients for a happy life as far as flamboyant Leo is concerned. Your hot-blooded Leo partner has a strong sex drive and looks for regular satisfaction. What Leo craves, however, is protestations of undying love and fidelity – there is a surprisingly unconfident interior behind the confident, sunny self that is shown to the world. Once committed to a relationship, Leo continues to hold court with an admiring circle of friends but is rarely unfaithful, preferring instead life as a serial monogamist.

Leo is not a subscriber to equal partnership. Needing to be dominant, your partner demands to be the centre of your attention and organizes your life around what Leo wants to do. This involves being seen at all the best places. Dramatic Leo has a natural inclination to show off and partners tend to be viewed as possessions, so you might well find yourself being put on show. Appearances are important to Leo, who is extremely vain. Your partner wants you to look good because Leo sees you as a reflection of him or herself. After all, your Leo reasons, he or she is special, so a beloved partner must be too.

Leo is a fixed sign and likes routine, so introduce changes gradually. Give plenty of notice if you are planning an outing because Leo takes an inordinate amount of time to prepare. This dislike of change also keeps Leo faithful, even when a relationship is not going well, but Leo is too proud to admit this. Pride is one of Leo's most intractable qualities. Sunny and playful most of the time, if you inadvertently ruffle your partner's dignity, or, worse still, poke fun, you will need to do a lot of coaxing to return Leo to his or her usual sunny self.

It takes Leo some time to unburden him or herself. After all, the lion does not want to seem weak or inadequate. Trust is important for this sign and if you betray that trust, you never get it back. Your Leo partner has an almost naïve faith in people, and is all too often let down.

Leo is an extremely faithful and loving sign.

VIRGO
The discerning lover

Erogenous zones	The mind, skin and extremities
Turn-ons	Massage, erotica, nibbling fingers or toes, nurses' uniforms
Aphrodisiacs	Soap and water, ginseng, celery, rubber
Fantasies	Orgies, porn movies, bathrooms
Make it work	Try to be perfect

Although Virgo may appear cool and a touch prim on the outside, a strong libido runs beneath the surface. This sensual sign enjoys the security of a long-term relationship and an active sex life. Nevertheless, discreet and witty flirtation can takes place outside the relationship. Sociable Virgo enjoys the mental stimulation this offers, and the occasional one-night stand is not out of the question. On balance, however, this is an extremely trustworthy sign.

Virgo is a curious mix of fastidious and inquisitive as far as sex goes. Your partner is happy to think about sex and to discuss it at length, and even to experiment, but for many Virgos the actual business of sex is rather too messy. Most of the time, Virgo prefers quiet affection.

Virgo sets high standards in all things. As a partner, you must be pleasing to the eye and your behaviour must accord with Virgo's notions of correctness and desirability. There will undoubtedly be times when you feel unjustly criticized, but remember that your Virgo partner is equally self-critical. It comes out of the sign's urge for perfection. An extremely picky partner, every little detail is subject to stringent quality control. If your partner seems introspective, it is probably because he or she is attempting to work out how they could have handled something more efficiently. In order to boost your partner's somewhat fragile ego, it's a good idea to combat Virgo's nagging inner voice with praise, especially regarding sexual performance.

Ruled by talkative Mercury, Virgo is into communication in a big way but you may find your partner strangely reticent about his or her own feelings, as befits an earth sign. You may also find that what you learned about your partner initially is never expanded upon. Behind an apparently open façade, Virgo is actually quite shy and has difficulty with emotional intimacy.

What you most need to know about your Virgo partner is that this sign wants to be appreciated for all those little services that are performed for you on a daily basis. It is also worth remembering that most Virgos cannot stand dirt or untidiness. This partner expects you to pay scrupulous attention to personal hygiene and to maintain impeccable surroundings.

Most Virgos are workaholics who push themselves hard and, as a result, suffer from nervous stress. The best thing you can offer your partner is the opportunity to relax and take life easy.

LIBRA
The winsome lover

Erogenous zones	Buttocks, eyes, ears, mouth, lips, skin
Turn-ons	Being in love, sensuality, sophistication, harmonious surroundings
Aphrodisiacs	Perfume, candles, strawberries, champagne, patchouli oil
Fantasies	The ideal lover, giving or receiving forbidden pleasure
Make it work	Never, ever, argue

Libra was made for love. This charming partner takes the trouble to woo even after years of marriage. There is nothing Libra likes more than to be half of a couple and, if your partner believes that you are a soul mate, your relationship will last forever. Not that this stops Libra flirting, but you needn't be concerned. For Libra, flirting is as natural as breathing. Keep cool and your partner will return to you, refreshed by the mental stimulation of new ideas.

Libra works extremely hard to keep a relationship hassle-free. On the surface, this sign is a paragon of virtue, indulging your every whim and putting your pleasure first. This sign learns early on to be a people-pleaser. There is nothing Libra dislikes more than arguments or disharmony, so your partner adapts and adjusts and compromises to keep the peace. If there are problems in a relationship, a Libran partner apologises for what is seen as a personal failing. You will not be blamed. You might wonder sometimes if there is something insincere beneath such a pleasant exterior. There is, but it takes a great deal to bring it out. On occasion, all those personal needs that have been submerged and suppressed break through, surprising Libra as much as you. However, it doesn't take long before harmony is restored and the mask of perfect niceness is donned once more.

Libra has a reputation for being lazy and indecisive, and can drive other people to distraction as this sign debates and vacillates. The problem is, Libra sees all possibilities and wants to make the perfect choice – and to be fair to everyone. Justice is an important Libra concept, as is being perfect. Your partner wants to look good and to behave in the right way, always. The drive for perfection means that Libra has a critical streak buried beneath all that niceness, although the desire for relationship at all costs may mean that your partner does not speak out. If you can encourage a mutual sharing in your relationship, it would benefit you both.

Libra enjoys the trappings and the pleasure of seduction.

SCORPIO
The jealous lover

Erogenous zones	Genitals, groin, anus
Turn-ons	Massage, power, pain, bondage, erotica, sexy underwear
Aphrodisiacs	Pomegranates, asparagus, leather, lobster
Fantasies	Darkly erotic and forbidden
Make it work	Don't pry into Scorpio secrets

Scorpio is a sexually intense sign but, in public at least, the depths of passion are hidden behind an enigmatic exterior. Cautious Scorpio has a compulsion to be secretive, which precludes intimacy and makes this a difficult partner to get to know. Your Scorpio would prefer to be emotionally self-sufficient, and yet needs an outlet for that powerful libido. However, needing a partner makes Scorpio feel vulnerable.

Immensely private and self-protective, a Scorpio partner does not disclose him or herself lightly, which stems from a great fear of being controlled. Something is always held back. Scorpio is itself a controlling sign, driven to dominate and master. As Scorpio's partner, you are expected to be utterly loyal and faithful, as Scorpio is to you, for the most part. For Scorpio, love and lust are firmly separated so a discreet fling isn't out of the quesion. But if *you* stray, the legendary Scorpio jealousy comes into play. This sign neither forgives nor forgets. Once trust is lost, it takes forever, if then, for Scorpio to trust again.

Scorpio is not content with the surface of life, but inclines towards all that is hidden and taboo. Sometimes seeming to have a death wish, a Scorpio lover is fascinated by forbidden knowledge. Sexually and spiritually, Scorpio needs to come face to face with the blackest part of him or herself. It helps if you are a compassionate and accepting partner in the meantime.

The Scorpio sting is legendary – and lethal. For Scorpio, attack is the best form of defence. This sign has a caustic tongue that can reduce you to tears. It is Scorpio's nature to sting first without provocation. It might help to know that, regardless of how it feels, the sting is not personally directed. Behind the inscrutable interior, your partner harbours doubts about his or her competence. When emotional tides threaten to sweep Scorpio away, he or she feels vulnerable and fears being out of control, and so lashes out.

Scorpio is a perceptive partner, who can see right into your heart. Your partner knows your strengths and your weaknesses, and does not hesitate to play on these for his or her own ends. Scorpio can be manipulative and insensitive and the next moment considerate and caring. Your charismatic partner can also be supportive, and will encourage you to make the best of your potential.

Scorpio enjoys what other signs may fantasize about.

SAGITTARIUS
The adventurous lover

Erogenous zones	Hips and inner thighs
Turn-ons	Shared ideas and an exotic location
Aphrodisiacs	Luggage, ice cream, yohimbe
Fantasies	Travel and escape from dull routine; horses may play a part
Make it work	Allow plenty of space and freedom

Romantic Sagittarius is a free spirit who finds it difficult to commit to a one-to-one relationship. If your Sagittarian partner shows signs of straying, there is cause for concern, although light-hearted flirtation is not unusual. But you're not likely to receive notice: if Sagittarius is planning to leave, this sign usually ups and goes.

Sagitarrius has an enormous need for personal space and freedom. If you try to tie this lover down, the relationship will fail. But if Sagittarius is given plenty of space, and positively encouraged to explore, you could well have a lasting and equal partnership. This is particularly true if you can accompany Sagittarius on those spontaneous adventures. Your partner dislikes long-term, carefully made plans, preferring to throw a few clothes into a suitcase and take

Sagittarius can be a romantic, if inconstant, lover.

off for the sun, naturally assuming you'll be free too, or to buy a house on impulse. Whilst the wilder Sagittarian impulses may need cautious restraint, on the whole this way of life works well. Sagittarius has an innate trust in the universe that attracts luck.

This is an uncomplicated sign. Usually truthful, although sometimes given to exaggeration, Sagittarius prefers things to be out in the open. Unsubtle and never devious, this sign genuinely dislikes pretence and is repelled by the emotional games more complicated signs can play.

Along with the honesty, comes a reputation for being tactless. It is rare that your partner sets out to hurt you, but the verbal blunders can be painful because Sagittarius has an unhappy knack of hitting on the truth. Don't ask Sagittarius if you look fat in something unless you are prepared for a straight answer. And never expect your partner to apologize: Sagittarius barely knows the meaning of the word nor sees a need to explain.

Sagittarian partners have a tendency to promise more than they can deliver. Not liking to say no or simply not stopping to think of what's involved, this sign takes on far too much and inevitably has to disappoint someone, but does so with insouciance.

CAPRICORN
The consistent lover

Erogenous zones	Back of the knees, skin
Turn-ons	Power, massage, fur, music
Aphrodisiacs	Money, classical fragrances, uniforms, caviar, fine wines
Fantasies	Earthy and erotic, punishment or submission
Make it work	Submit gracefully

Capricorn is one of the most reliable signs, possessing enormous strength of character. Most people refer to their Capricorn partner as their rock. Relationships last with this sign and, although there may be minor affairs, home and family ultimately take precedence. Capricorn places great emphasis on duty and takes responsibility seriously. In fact, a Capricorn partner is somewhat serious in general, although this is enlivened by a wicked sense of humour. With Saturn as the sign's ruler, frivolity is discouraged and emotional expression reined in – despite a powerful libido. As with all the earth signs, there exists a split between body and emotions. On many occasions Capricorn genuinely does not know what he or she is feeling.

To understand your partner you need to consider both age and sex. Capricorn women more easily overcome the restraints of Saturn, making them more emotionally open and in touch with their sensual nature than Capricorn men. Maturity suits Capricorn better than youth. A young Capricorn is old beyond his or her years, and often feels weighed down by life. An older Capricorn, who is no longer driven by a need for security and achievement, almost seems to grow younger. In these later years, Capricorn can reach beyond the trappings of material success to find a deeper satisfaction from life, making for a more rounded relationship.

Once committed to you, Capricorn will want to spend leisure time with you, following a routine. Whilst this is not an equal partnership, because Capricorn remains in control, you play an important part. The hardworking nature of your partner, particularly in youth, may mean that business takes precedence over pleasure. You could end up spending time alone while your partner pursues an ambition.

Conventional Capricorn is prone to 'oughts and shoulds' and your partner gives him or herself a hard time trying to live up to some high

standards. Your partner constantly seeks approval from the outside world and that includes you. The desire for 'success' in the world's eyes is based on deep feelings of inadequacy. Anything you can do to encourage your partner to lighten up is beneficial. What this sign most needs to learn is the art of live and let live.

Capricorn partnerships usually last a lifetime, and often improve with age.

AQUARIUS
The dispassionate lover

Erogenous zones	Calves and ankles
Turn-ons	What goes on inside the head, light touch, body paint
Aphrodisiacs	Marijuana, incense, candles
Fantasies	Anything goes, the weirder the better
Make it work	Be prepared for the unexpected

Aquarius is an extremely independent and unpredictable sign. Getting to know this partner is something of a challenge. However, if you can get over the first hurdle – getting Aquarius to commit to relationship at all – you have come a long way, even though it may not feel like it. The fact is that your partner finds a settled partnership surprisingly reassuring. Nevertheless, Aquarius likes to make statements about personal freedom by flirting when opportunity arises, usually by engaging in deep and meaningful discussion. You can pretty much discount this kind of behaviour.

If Aquarius does have an affair, this sign will be utterly nonplussed by any jealously you express. This sign does not have a jealous bone in his or her body, and offers everyone equal freedom. You get an equal partnership too. Aquarius upholds and celebrates everyone's unique individuality and encourages expression of this. Hence Aquarius can be part of some fairly unconventional arrangements when it comes to partnership and romance.

Aquarius is known as the most unemotional sign in the zodiac, and yet this rational sign has strong passions. It is simply that Aquarius is not in touch with them. Although content to intellectualize and discuss abstract feelings this self-sufficient sign has enormous problems with intimacy, preferring a meeting of minds. Sometimes it's as though Aquarius is wearing a sign warning others to keep off. The need for space means a partner has to be particularly understanding. Many people can feel rejected by this free-spirit and their quest for freedom, but should not take it personally.

One of the most important things to recognize about an Aquarian partner is the deep need to be *different*. This may be expressed through clothes, beliefs, outlook or lifestyle, and is a reflection of Uranus, co-ruler and catalyst. Saturn, this sign's other planetary ruler, can create a conflict inside your partner, as though an irresistible force were meeting an immovable object. If you can encourage your highly-strung partner to channel this force into something other than confrontation, life will be a lot less stressful for both of you. If not, expect sudden explosions of pressure.

Most Aquarians feel alien on earth, as though home is a long way away, or in a future where humankind is in a better place. This is a misunderstood sign, by themselves as well as others, and they spend time trying to work out what makes themselves tick.

PISCES
The romantic lover

Erogenous zones	Feet, the imagination
Turn-ons	Being in love, being by water, satin sheets, love songs
Aphrodisiacs	Red roses, oysters, champagne, nutmeg
Fantasies	Life itself is a fantasy
Make it work	Romance, romance and more romance

Pisces is an incurable romantic. With rose-coloured spectacles firmly in place, this lover has a tendency to lose him or herself in another person, but another side of this dual sign is surprisingly shrewd yet terribly impractical. It's an emotionally complex sign that is difficult to understand. Once committed, Pisces wants to merge with you as a soul mate, professing eternal fidelity. But then again, Pisces swims off to flirt with other possibilities and is seldom properly separated from previous partners, so unification doesn't quite ring true. This is one of the most unfaithful signs but also one of the most forgiving.

Pisces rarely knows where he or she ends and the outside world begins. With a soft heart and trusting naivety, Pisces always falls for a sob story, and past partners and friends tend to take advantage of this.

Beneath a placid surface, your partner is pulled this way and that as Pisces is pulled between powerful internal emotions and external demands. With little understanding of self, Pisces relies on the outside world to reflect back what is going on inside. You can assist this process by gently sharing your perceptions and helping Pisces respond thoughtfully rather than automatically.

Pisces lives for love and loves to live.

As a deeply empathetic and perceptive water sign, Pisces knows exactly what you are thinking or feeling, and responds intuitively to any unspoken desires on your part. Indeed, your partner may know how you feel before you know yourself – and hopes that you will reciprocate in the same way, which is problematic if you belong to one of the less intuitive signs. Pisces is adept at emotional communication, but not so adept at the verbal communication that would ensure a harmonious relationship. Pisces cares deeply about you and, in an effort to express this, may engulf you. If you can understand that this comes out of a deep insecurity, it may help you to give the love and assurance that your partner needs whilst at the same time retaining a firm sense of your own self.

This sensitive sign often finds the world too harsh and longs for escape. The flight may be into fantasy and may entail addiction and delusion. This sign's desire to save the world often takes Pisces into a role as victim. At such times, practicality and some rational good sense is the best thing you can offer.

THE SEVENTH HOUSE AND RELATIONSHIPS

The seventh house gives you a general picture of what you can expect in relationships. It shows what someone needs from a partner and whether it is easy to adapt to partnership – indicated by the flexibility of the sign on the cusp. This sign may match a partner's sun-sign as it represents an inner picture of an ideal partner. Planets placed in the seventh house highlight expectations and needs, and heighten or restrict adaptability. (A partner's planets falling in this house when the signs are placed together has the same effect, see Bi-wheels, pages 364–5.)

PLANETS IN THE SEVENTH HOUSE

Sun	Non-adaptive. The self grows and is expressed through relationship and this placement needs a partner. The partner may take on or reflect the role or qualities of the father; or the person concerned may take a paternal role in the relationship. The partner may have been the father in a previous life.
Moon	Adaptive. Close emotional ties with a partner are essential for this security-orientated placement. The partner may take on or reflect the role or qualities of the mother; or the person concerned may take a maternal role in the relationship. The partner may have been the mother in a previous life.
Mercury	Adaptive. Mental rapport with a partner is essential and companionship may be more important than sex. The partner may have been a sibling in a previous life.

Venus	Adaptive. Venus needs to be in a relationship and can be somewhat demanding or dependent on a partner, especially for approval. A charming, sociable partner is sought. In past life astrology there is karma around relationships of all kinds.
Mars	Non-adaptive. Relationships are active and outward-looking, but may end abruptly after disagreements. An assertive partner is sought but aggression may mar the relationship.
Jupiter	Adaptive. The self expands through relationships and attracts helpful partners and mentors. As always with Jupiter, this placement indicates a tendency to go over the top. A confident partner is sought.
Saturn	Non-adaptive. This placement indicates a deep desire for stability in relationships although the resulting restrictions may become onerous. A dependable partner is sought, who may be older. In karmic terms, all kinds of unfinished business may surface.
Chiron	Adaptive. The partner may be wounded or wounding, although a healing relationship is sought. In karmic terms, wounds colour relationships.
Uranus	Non-adaptive. This placement indicates that freedom is all-important, making this the traditional divorce placement. The self grows and evolves, leaving the partner behind, unless arrangements can be made to provide space for growth. A partner almost inevitably is unusual or different. In karmic astrology, there have been sudden endings and lack of intimacy.
Neptune	Adaptive. This is the placement of illusion, delusion and fantasy. The idealized and idolized partner appears to be perfect – until the flaws are revealed. A sensitive and romantic partner is sought.
Pluto	Non-adaptive. This is an emotionally demanding placement. It indicates that power plays are common and hints at abuse. A powerful partner is sought.

LOVE AND LUST: VENUS

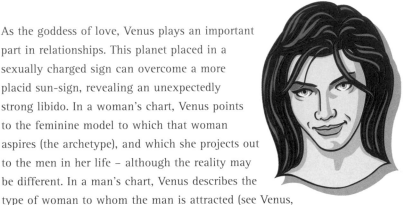

As the goddess of love, Venus plays an important part in relationships. This planet placed in a sexually charged sign can overcome a more placid sun-sign, revealing an unexpectedly strong libido. In a woman's chart, Venus points to the feminine model to which that woman aspires (the archetype), and which she projects out to the men in her life – although the reality may be different. In a man's chart, Venus describes the type of woman to whom the man is attracted (see Venus, pages 172–7), as well as his inner anima, the feminine qualities of his nature that he projects on to his 'ideal woman'.

Compatibility

If Venus harmonizes with a partner's Sun, Moon or Mars, both parties share similar sexual desires and values, and lust is expressed in compatible ways. If other factors support it, this can make for a comfortable, long-term relationship. If Venus clashes with a partner's personal planets, the relationship won't be a cosy one, but it could be exciting. This kind of conflict is commonly found in short-term, passionate affairs. However, if other factors support it, it could also indicate a sexually stimulating, lifelong relationship.

THROUGH THE SIGNS

Venus in Aries (the predatory female) A rapacious, sexually active placement that goes all out for what it wants. With this feisty combination, there is no holding back.

Venus in Taurus (the voluptuous female) An indolent, sensuous placement that prefers to take things slowly and yet has a strong libido hidden beneath the apparently calm surface.

Venus in Gemini (the skillful seductress) A seductive placement that is skilled in subtle manipulation and persuasion. Variety is most certainly the spice of life for this engaging companion.

Venus in Cancer (the mother goddess) This placement is sentimental and clinging, preferring romance to lust. Very strong emotional attachments are formed.

Venus in Leo (the drama queen) Proud, boisterous and playful, this glamorous placement gives off intense sexual heat. It is impossible to ignore.

Venus in Virgo (the chaste maiden or fecund female) This placement is torn between two extremes: coolly critical until roused, there is underlying powerful sensuality and strong libido.

Venus in Libra (the love goddess) This erotically pleasing combination was made for love but settles for sybaritic, sensual gratification or gentle companionship.

Venus in Scorpio (the sultry seductress) A siren call, this placement has unstoppable lust and magnetic attraction. Intensely jealous, it will kill to get what it wants.

Venus in Sagittarius (the courtesan) This flighty combination enjoys lusty sexual adventures but needs engaging companionship to keep the relationship on track.

Venus in Capricorn (the foxy lady) Venus is at her most controlling in Capricorn and a strong libido is blocked by difficulty in showing feelings.

Venus in Aquarius (the wacky woman) Unpredictable and dispassionate, this placement is somewhat baffled by the force of lust and love, but enjoys kinky sex.

Venus in Pisces (the fantasy princess) Drifty and dreamy, this gullible combination so wants to be in love it often finds itself a victim to love.

LOVE AND LUST: MARS

Virile Mars is the god of passionate lust. Where Mars resides, potent desire is translated into unstoppable action or into active fantasy and dreams if Mars is in a passive sign. Mars placed in an active sign can overcome a more placid sun-sign, heightening libido and demanding immediate gratification.

In a man's chart, Mars points to the archetype to which that man aspires, and which he projects out to the women in his life – although the reality may be different. In a woman's chart, Mars describes the type of man to whom she is attracted (see Mars, pages 178–83) and her inner animus, the masculine qualities of her nature that she projects on to her 'ideal man'.

Compatibility

If Mars contacts the Sun, Moon or Venus across a couple's charts, the indication is that sexual attraction is intense but not always harmonious. Lust can run high, but deeper sexual incompatibilities soon make themselves felt in the absence of supportive interaspects.

THROUGH THE SIGNS

Mars in Aries (the macho man) Selfish and highly competitive, this pushy placement goes for instant sexual conquest. The chase stimulates, libido runs high and gratification is demanded, instantly.

Mars in Taurus (the caveman) Sex equates to ownership in this case. It indicates a powerful sex drive, but one that may be reigned in for increased gratification at a later date.

Mars in Gemini (the toy boy) Verbal persuasion works for this placement and sex may be seen as a way of starting a new friendship, although flirtation is considered an acceptable sex substitute.

Mars in Cancer (the househusband) This romantic placement approaches the object of its desire circuitously and then homes in. Sexual gratification is closely bound up with security.

Mars in Leo (the passionate performer) A serial monogamist, this passionate placement has a strong appetite for life, love and sex.

Mars in Virgo (the virgin lover) The libido is repressed until earthy sexuality breaks through; hang-ups are common.

Mars in Libra (the romantic charmer) Weak-willed and pleasure-loving, this placement falls easily into flirtation and prefers being in a relationship to sexual gratification.

Mars in Scorpio (the demon lover) With a magnetic aura of power, this highly sexed placement is attractive, but extremely intense.

Mars in Sagittarius (the devil-may-care adventurer) This sexual philander seeks meaning through sex but finds close relationships restricting.

Mars in Capricorn (the father-figure) This calculating placement weighs up the rewards of sex before indulging its horny nature.

Mars in Aquarius (the 'new man') This coolly impersonal placement fights to the death for a cause, but has immense difficulty with intimate relationships. The libido is ignored.

Mars in Pisces (the dream lover) Lust is confused with passion in a heady romance, or sexual desire may be transcended in favour of spiritual union or promiscuity.

ELEMENTAL ATTRACTION

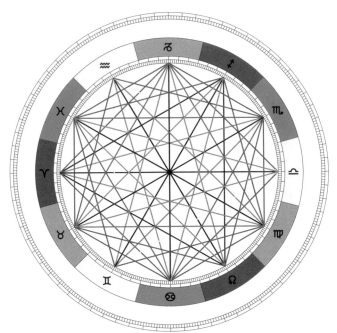

KEY

harmonious and lasting	strong attraction
empathetic and lasting	personality conflicts despite shared goals
intense attraction but may be too fiery	harmonious but unexciting
attracted but uncommitted	inharmonious despite initial attraction

If the Sun, Moon, Mars, Venus, or the Moon's Nodes in two people's charts fall in compatible elements, attraction is quick to develop and the relationship immediately feels comfortable. Serious differences may emerge later, but on the surface at least, the relationship appears to have everything going for it.

ELEMENTAL PAIRINGS

Fire and Fire A passionate pairing but lust may burn out as fast as it ignites.

Fire and Earth Carnal desire burns hot, at least until the routines of earth threatens to put out the flame. Earth finds it difficult to adapt.

Fire and Air Lust ignites quickly, but air might ruin it by talking too much or passion burns out equally fast. Long-term commitment is difficult.

Fire and Water Scalding steam or a damp squib. Water finds it hard to cope with fire's independent ways; hurt feelings abound.

Earth and Earth Long, slow and sensual – when they eventually get it together. These two are totally loyal and would find it difficult to part.

Earth and Air Air thinks earth is too serious and earth is exasperated by air's frivolity, but this may be the rock that air need.

Earth and Water A sensual pairing, these two either engender an enduring partnership or a muddy mess. Both are too placid to argue.

Air and Air This relationship is all talk. The sex would be inventive, if they ever stopped talking. Telephone sex may be the answer.

Air and Water A problematic combination, since air spends hours explaining what it thinks, while water tries to show how it feels.

Water and Water Lifelong empathy. Emotions run deep and bind these two together – even after physical parting, the emotional tie remains.

SYNASTRY: GRIDS AND INTERASPECTS

In synastry, the charts of two people are compared to ascertain how their relationship functions and what themes or potentials will emerge. Both natal charts are prepared and then the interaspects (the geometric relationships between planets in the charts) are calculated. The significance of the planets falling into a partner's houses is also considered (see pages 364–5).

Orbs

In traditional astrology, 2° orbs are used in synastry, but allowing wider margins can pinpoint karmic themes and issues that potentially unfold as the relationship progresses. On the example charts on pages 356–7, the following orbs have been used:

- 8°: conjunctions, trines, squares, oppositions and quincunxes
- 6°: sextile
- 2°: minor aspects (rarely used for synastry)

These orbs may be expanded, particularly for outer planet to inner planet interaspects, if the natal charts map the issues strongly and if, by doing so, an interaspect repeats both ways across the charts (a 'double whammy'). An interaspect opposition of 10° between personal and outer planets could be considered if it accompanied a 6° trine and reflected a 4° conjunction in one of the natal charts, for example.

COMPARING TWO CHARTS

The aspects across charts (interaspects) show different kinds of interaction:

• Aspects between the Sun, Moon and Angles of one chart to those in another are immediately noticeable in the relationship as they attract and feel harmonious. Conjunctions play an enormous part in instant attraction, particularly between the Sun and the Moon, and aspects to the Angles can indicate a long-lasting partnership. These aspects are felt at an especially personal level.

• Easy aspects between Mercury, Venus and Mars tend to be harmonious and can lead to instant attraction and on-going companionship, especially if supported by other factors. Difficult aspects between these planets can indicate initial attraction that often leads to irritation. These aspects are felt at a personal level in everyday life.

• Aspects between Mercury, Venus or Mars in one chart to the Sun, Moon or the angles in the other can lend support to mutual harmony but are not in themselves as significant. These aspects make themselves known in everyday life.

• Aspects between the personal planets in one chart and the outer planets in the other, especially if they are a 'double whammy', are of great significance as they delineate karma, issues and attitudes that have been brought forward for resolution. These aspects are felt at the soul level. If the aspects are one-way only, they may indicate karma-in-the-making: karma that arises from the present interaction or issues that are not personal to the couple but which one, or both, needs to address.

• Aspects between the outer planets tend to have little personal impact as they are felt at a generational level.

• Aspects to the Nodes are highly significant as they help or hinder the expression of karmic and soul purpose. If a personal planet conjuncts the Nodes it feels like a soulmate relationship, although South Nodes conjunctions may signify a time to move on. Any planet that conjuncts the South Node is stultifying, leaning back into the dead end of the past. A planet that conjuncts the North Node propels into a new way of being, and a planet that squares the Nodes either brings about resolution or tears the partnership apart.

HOW TO IDENTIFY INTERASPECTS

Pinpointing interaspects is like finding aspects on a natal chart, only there are two charts to consider. Try working through the following steps using the example charts.

• Note the degree in which the Sun falls on one chart.

• Note the degrees in which planets fall on the other chart.

• If any of these planets fall within 8° either side of the Sun-degree and make a major aspect, write them down.

• Repeat for the remaining planets in the first natal chart.

• Repeat for the second natal chart.

• Working down the lists, put an asterisk where aspects are made between the same pairs of planets across the charts. These are two-way interaspects ('double whammies').

• Finally, note whether any planets aspect the nodes across the charts.

Most computer programs quickly calculate interaspects as a grid or as a list (see examples). The easiest way to work with these is to put a red box around two-way interaspects and underline important one-way interaspects (see list, right).

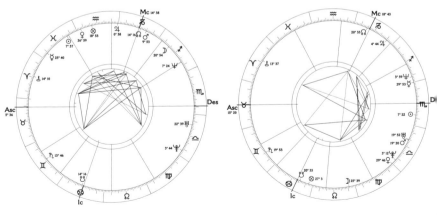

Example chart A   Example chart B

EXAMPLE INTERASPECT LIST

	☉	△	☉	0.3
	☉	□	☿	7.7
	☉	⚻	♀	7.9
*	☉	⚹	♃	2.9
	☉	□	♆	3.6
	☉	⚻	♇	4.4
	☽	△	☽	4.7
	☽	⚹	♂	1.6
	☽	☍	♄	1.0
*	☽	⚹	♅	1.0
	☽	⚻	As	5.6
	☽	△	⚷	7.3
	☿	⚻	☽	0.0
	☿	△	☿	4.2
*	☿	☍	♀	4.1
	☿	⚻	♂	6.3
	☿	□	♄	5.8
	☿	⚻	♅	5.8
*	☿	☍	♇	7.5
	☿	⚹	☊	5.1
	♀	☍	☽	1.3
*	♀	□	☿	2.9
	♀	⚻	♀	2.8
	♀	△	♂	7.7
	♀	△	♄	7.1
	♀	△	♅	7.1
	♀	□	♆	7.0
*	♀	⚻	♇	6.2
	♂	⚹	☉	2.5
	♂	☌	♃	5.1
	♂	□	♇	6.7
	♂	△	As	5.5
	♂	□	⚷	3.7
*	♃	⚻	☉	6.7
	♃	△	☽	5.0
	♃	☍	☿	0.8
	♃	⚻	♀	0.9
	♃	□	♆	3.4
	♃	⚻	♇	2.6
	♄	⚻	☉	6.4
	♄	△	♂	5.6
	♄	☌	♄	6.1
	♄	△	♅	6.1
	♄	⚻	Mc	4.9
	♄	⚻	☊	6.8
	♄	⚹	⚷	0.2
*	♅	⚹	☽	3.0
	♅	☌	♂	3.3
	♅	△	♄	2.8
	♅	☌	♅	2.8
	♅	⚻	As	7.3
	♅	□	Mc	3.9
*	♅	□	☊	2.1
	♆	☌	☿	2.5
	♆	☌	♆	5.1
	♆	⚹	♇	6.7
	♆	⚻	As	5.5
	♆	△	⚷	3.7
*	♇	⚹	☿	3.9
*	♇	☌	♀	4.0
	♇	□	♃	1.0
	♇	⚹	♆	0.2
	♇	☌	♇	0.5
	As	☍	☉	1.8
	As	⚻	☿	5.7
	As	⚻	♀	5.8
	As	△	♃	0.9
	As	⚻	♆	1.6
	As	⚻	♇	2.4
*	☊	□	♅	5.4

* = double whammy

The planets in the left-hand column relate to chart A. The planets in the right-hand column relate to chart B. Aspects have been identified between the two.

EXAMPLE INTERASPECT GRID

	☉	☽	☿	♀	♂	♃	♄	♅	♆	♇	As	Mc	☊	⚷
☉	+△ 0°15	•	+□ 7°45	+⚻ 7°51	•	+⚹ 2°54	•	•	+□ 3°39	+⚻ 4°26	•	•	•	•
☽	•	△ 4°45	•	•	+⚹ 1°35	•	+☍ 1°02	+⚹ 1°02	•	•	+⚻ 5°34	•	•	+△ 7°17
☿	•	+⚻ 0°01	△ 4°12	☍ 4°06	+⚻ 6°21	•	+□ 5°48	+⚻ 5°48	•	☍ 7°32	•	•	+⚹ 7°07	•
♀	•	+☍ 1°20	□ 2°53	⚻ 2°47	+△ 7°40	•	+△ 7°07	+△ 7°07	□ 6°60	⚻ 6°13	•	•	•	•
♂	+⚹ 2°30	•	•	•	•	+☌ 5°09	•	•	•	+□ 6°41	△ 5°28	•	•	□ 3°45
♃	□ 6°45	+⚻ 4°59	+⚹ 0°45	+△ 0°52	•	•	•	•	⚹ 3°21	△ 2°34	•	•	•	•
♄	+⚻ 6°21	•	•	•	△ 5°33	•	☌ 6°06	△ 6°06	•	•	•	⚻ 4°56	⚻ 6°47	+⚹ 0°09
♅	•	⚹ 3°00	•	•	+☌ 3°19	•	+△ 2°46	+☌ 2°46	•	•	+⚻ 7°19	+□ 3°56	+□ 2°06	•
♆	•	•	+☌ 7°31	•	•	•	•	•	+☌ 3°25	+⚹ 4°12	⚻ 7°56	•	•	△ 6°13
♇	•	•	+⚹ 3°51	+☌ 3°58	•	□ 0°60	•	•	⚹ 0°15	+☌ 0°32	•	•	•	•
As	☍ 1°46	•	+⚻ 5°43	+⚻ 5°50	•	+△ 0°52	•	•	+⚻ 1°37	+⚻ 2°24	•	•	•	•
Mc	•	•	•	•	□ 4°42	•	⚻ 5°15	□ 5°15	•	•	△ 0°42	☌ 4°05	☌ 5°55	+□ 1°01
☊	•	•	•	•	□ 5°04	•	⚻ 5°37	□ 5°36	•	•	△ 1°04	☌ 4°27	☌ 6°17	+□ 0°39
⚷	+⚻ 6°48	•	•	•	☍ 5°09	•	⚹ 5°42	☍ 5°42	•	•	•	□ 4°32	□ 6°23	+☌ 0°33

This chart shows the same information in a different format. The planets along the top relate to chart B and the planets down the side relate to chart A.

PLANETS IN INTERASPECT

Note that the terms 'easy' and 'difficult' relate to how the energy is experienced, rather than the type of the aspect. Only significant relationship interaspects have been included.

☉ INTERASPECTS TO THE SUN

Sun to Sun
Easy Harmonious with immediate rapport, lasting relationship.
Difficult Fundamentally different approaches to life result in inharmonious partnership.

Sun to Moon
Easy Strong emotional rapport, good understanding and powerful attraction; common in marriage.
Difficult Attraction may be powerful but fundamental differences may cause problems.

Sun to Mercury
Easy Mental rapport and shared interests.
Difficult Impossible to understand each other.

Sun to Venus
Easy Strong attraction and shared values and desires.
Difficult Fundamentally different values and desires.

Sun to Mars
Easy Instant attraction, but relationship may be volatile.
Difficult Arguments likely.

Sun to Jupiter
Easy Expansive relationship, beneficial to both partners; may involve travel.
Difficult May involve recklessness, exaggeration and over-spending.

Sun to Saturn
Easy Anchored and stable relationship.
Difficult Inhibition and restriction.
Karmic Debts, duties, lessons and obligations between the parties.

Sun to Chiron
Easy Mutual commitment to healing and integrating the past.
Difficult May be a deeply wounding interaction, especially if 'double whammy'.
Karmic Emotional and karmic wounds to heal.

Sun to Uranus
Easy A stimulating but unpredictable partnership that needs space.
Difficult Disruptive and volatile.
Karmic A freedom/commitment dilemma.

Sun to Neptune
Easy Idealized, idyllic and romantic.
Difficult Delusion, illusion and deception.
Karmic Difficulty in distinguishing between two individuals; shared selves.

Sun to Pluto
Easy Powerful and empowering.
Difficult Overpowering and symbiotic.
Karmic Symbiosis – one person had power over or owned the other.

Sun to the Nodes
Soulmates, but may still need to separate.
North Node One person helps the other to grow and evolve.
South Node: One person is pulled back into what they used to be instead of growing.

☽ INTERASPECTS TO THE MOON

Moon to Moon
Easy Harmonious emotions and mutual understanding.
Difficult Emotional conflict; domestic problems likely.

Moon to Mercury
Easy Good emotional communication.
Difficult Emotional misunderstandings.

Moon to Venus
Easy Affectionate, easy emotional expression.
Difficult Emotional misunderstandings.

Moon to Mars
Easy Strong attraction.
Difficult Strong physical attraction but potential emotional conflicts.

Moon to Saturn
Easy Emotional commitment.
Difficult Emotional repression and inhibition.
Karmic A commitment to be together but one person may feel inadequate.

Moon to Chiron
Easy Potential to heal emotional wounds.
Difficult Potential for emotional wounding.
Karmic The need to heal old wounds.

Moon to Uranus
Unstable, unpredictable and volatile.
Karmic Freedom-commitment dilemma.

Moon to Neptune
Easy Romantic and idealized.
Difficult Deceptive and delusionary.
Karmic 'Old soulmates' with difficulty distinguishing between each partner's feelings; may need to separate.

Moon to Pluto
Symbiotic, smothering, mothering issues repeated with abandonment, rejection and emotional pain. Partner becomes a 'mother'.
Karmic Working out mothering issues and emotional abuse. Mother/son.

Moon to the Nodes
Soulmate aspect, but may need to separate.
North Node One person is what the other is striving to be.
South Node Pulled back into old emotional patterns and karmic interactions.

☿ INTERASPECTS TO MERCURY

Mercury to Venus
Easy Mutual understanding.
Difficult Mutual disagreement.

Mercury to Mars
Easy Mental stimulation.
Difficult Stimulating but can have intellectual disagreements.

Mercury to Jupiter Assists with learning and mental growth.

Mercury to Saturn
Easy One partner helps to structure the ideas of the other
Difficult One mind is inhibited by the other.
Karmic One partner controlled the mind of the other.

Mercury to Chiron Words can wound.
Karmic Need to heal wounds inflicted by words.

Mercury to Uranus
Stimulating ideas and intuitive understanding.

Mercury to Neptune
Easy One person totally understands the other.
Difficult Confusion and delusion.
Karmic Old telepathic contact needs to be broken; difficulty in distinguishing own thoughts.

Mercury to Pluto
Easy Profound insights are possible.
Difficult Mind control and coercion likely.
Karmic One person has control over the mind of the other.

♀ INTERASPECTS TO VENUS

Venus to Mars
Strong sexual attraction

Venus to Saturn
Easy Emotionally stable relationship.
Difficult Emotionally repressive relationship.
Karmic Debts or duties owed to each other; one has agreed to support the other.

Venus to Chiron
The potential to heal emotional wounds or the prospect of emotional wounding.
Karmic Wounding love affair from the past.

Venus to Uranus
Emotionally volatile.
Karmic An old freedom-commitment dilemma or friendship.

Venus to Neptune
A soulmate aspect with the potential for unconditional loving.
Karmic Old soulmates, no boundaries, may need to separate; 'madonna-whore dichotomy'.

Venus to Pluto
Easy Strong emotional attraction.
Difficult Emotional symbiosis or power struggles.
Karmic A symbiotic relationship in which one person was owned by the other.

Venus to the Nodes
A soulmate aspect.
To the South Node Can be pulled back into an old relationship that needs to be let go.

♂ INTERASPECTS TO MARS

Mars to Jupiter
Mutual encouragement.

Mars to Saturn
May bring stability or obstruction.
Karmic A 'master-slave' situation where one person had total control over the other.

Mars to Chiron
Karmic Wounding of the will or assertion has to be healed.

Mars to Uranus
Highly disruptive but stimulating.

Mars to Neptune
Physical harmony or confusion.

Mars to Pluto
The possibility of abuse and misuse of power and aggression, usually karmic.

CONJUNCTIONS TO THE ANGLES

Sun conjunct an Angle
Powerful contact that encourages or inhibits self-expression within the partnership.

Moon conjunct an Angle
Powerful emotional contact that may pull back into the past.

Mercury conjunct an Angle
Communication is extremely important in the partnership.

Venus conjunct an Angle
Focuses on intimate relationship.

Mars conjunct an Angle
Energizes the partnership but may create disagreements.

Jupiter conjunct an Angle
Indicates an expansive and profitable partnership with much travel involved.

Saturn conjunct an Angle
Can either bring stability or restriction to the partnership.

Uranus conjunct an Angle
Acts as a catalyst for change or creates chaos.

Neptune conjunct an Angle
Romantic illusions may make it impossible to see the partner and create confusion and deception.

Pluto conjunct an Angle
May signal a compulsive physical and emotional attraction but one person has power over the other.

BI-WHEELS

Understanding of a relationship, as revealed by bringing two charts together, can be deepened still further by superimposing one chart on another and ascertaining which planets fall into which houses. This form of synastry, which can be facilitated using a computer program (see bi-wheel illustration below), indicates the areas of life that are stimulated by a partner and through which a partner is most immediately experienced.

The table opposite is a general reference. The nature of the planets involved and the aspects and interaspects to them affect the nature of the interaction.

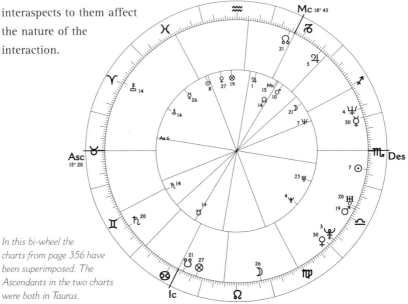

In this bi-wheel the charts from page 356 have been superimposed. The Ascendants in the two charts were both in Taurus.

PLANETS IN A PARTNER'S HOUSES

First house
Stimulate self-expression and interaction with the outer world. The partner may make an impact on appearance or personality.

Second house
Signify a partner who is closely involved in joint finances and security.

Third house
Signify that communication with the partner is particularly important, and constant short journeys may well feature in the relationship.

Fourth house
Bring up issues of home and of raising children.

Fifth house
Enliven life, pointing to joint leisure activities and attitudes to children and love affairs.

Sixth house
May indicate that partners work together, or may point to illness affecting the relationship.

Seventh house
Have a profound effect on the relationship (see pages 252–3).

Eighth house
Point to shared resources and sexual experiences.

Ninth house
Bring a philosophical focus to the relationship and shared religious beliefs may be important.

Tenth house
Impact on the social and work aspects of the relationship.

Eleventh house
May point to joint work for the good of society or to membership of a particular social grouping.

Twelfth house
Point to the hidden dynamics underlying the relationship, which may be of a karmic nature.

COMPOSITE AND RELATIONSHIP CHARTS

A composite chart is derived from the midpoints of the planetary and angle placements in two charts, whereas a relationship chart is derived from the midpoint in time between two births. Both are read in exactly the same way as a natal chart and reveal the areas of life in which the relationship is prominent, its challenges, the purpose behind the relationship and how it functions (see pages 352–7).

Using the charts

Highlighting essential factors, these charts can throw deeper light on the interaspects formed between two charts, identifying the relationship's strengths and weaknesses, and bringing issues more strongly into focus (see Interaspects, pages 350–57).

Composite and relationship charts can also be read in conjunction with the natal charts. Planets in composite charts falling on planetary aspects or in houses in the natal chart activate the issues of the aspect or house, rendering the dynamics more apparent in the relationship (see page 365).

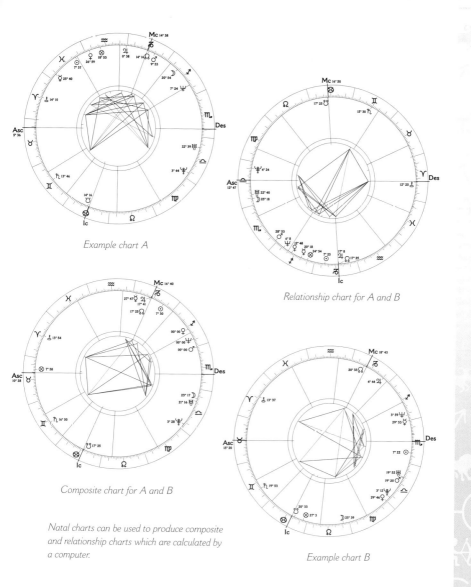

Example chart A

Relationship chart for A and B

Composite chart for A and B

Natal charts can be used to produce composite and relationship charts which are calculated by a computer.

Example chart B

Astrology

Astrology can point to imbalances created by the lack or excess of an element. Each sign responds to stress in a specific way, and the tissue salts and flower remedies associated with that sign can dramatically readjust the body's response. In a birth chart, the Sun shows the level of vitality a person has and indicates possible physical weakness. The Moon indicates emotions and their psychosomatic effect on health, and governs physiological processes. Planets in the first house indicate vitality and stamina, whereas the sixth house pertains to health and, in

and health

particular, chronic conditions. Psychological problems show up in the twelfth house. Traditionally, cardinal signs and dynamic planets, such as Mars, require pacification whilst fixed signs and placid planets, like Neptune, require more activity; mutable signs and neutral planets, such as Mercury, need improved coordination, alignment and rhythm. Planets in certain signs or the sign on cusp of the sixth house can indicate a predisposition to certain conditions, and require appropriate remedies.

MEDICAL ASTROLOGY

The humours

Traditionally, astrologers believed that a person could be characterized
by one of four humours as indicated by the sun-sign and planetary
ruler. These humours contributed to personality and to dis-ease.

Choleric people were considered emotionally volatile, given to anger
and associated conditions. Illnesses tended to the hot and dry kind,
such as fevers. Melancholic people were, as the name suggests, given to
sadness and had weak constitutions. Illnesses were of the cold and dry
type, such as metabolic imbalances. Sanguine people were pleasant and
optimistic, but essentially pliable and given to sudden change. The hot
and moist nature of the humour was reflected in conditions such as
viral infections. Phlegmatic people, whilst lacking vitality, were
nevertheless quietly strong. However, the cold and moist nature of the
humour could be reflected in conditions such as ulcers.

Physiological correlations

The signs and planets have always been associated with different parts
of the body and with the organs within it. Modern astrology has
attributed astrological associations to the more subtle organs, such as
the endocrine system. Specific dis-eases of the body may be related to
astrological polarity. The Arien tendency towards headaches, for
example, may have at its core a deficit of kidney energy, which is ruled
by Libra, the opposite sign.

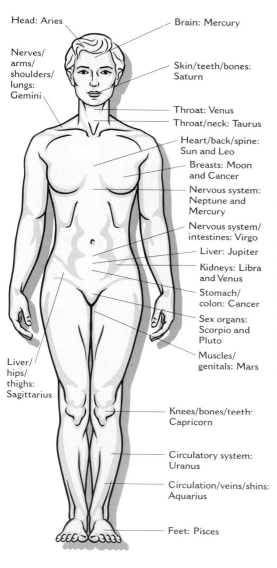

Head: Aries

Brain: Mercury

Nerves/arms/shoulders/lungs: Gemini

Skin/teeth/bones: Saturn

Throat: Venus
Throat/neck: Taurus

Heart/back/spine: Sun and Leo

Breasts: Moon and Cancer

Nervous system: Neptune and Mercury

Nervous system/intestines: Virgo

Liver: Jupiter

Kidneys: Libra and Venus

Stomach/colon: Cancer

Sex organs: Scorpio and Pluto

Muscles/genitals: Mars

Liver/hips/thighs: Sagittarius

Knees/bones/teeth: Capricorn

Circulatory system: Uranus

Circulation/veins/shins: Aquarius

Feet: Pisces

Health and the sun-signs

Each sun-sign has a specific correlation to a part of the body, leading to particular illnesses and a distinctive response to stress. These characteristic illnesses can be treated with the sign's tissue salt, associated Bach flower remedy, healing foods and herbs. Recognizing how you build up physical tension and stress, and changing your behaviour to combat this, will also help to protect and enhance your health.

ARIES

Humour: choleric

Temperament: hot and dry

Physiology: head and face, adrenal and suprarenal glands

Illnesses: severe headaches and migraines, neuralgia, inflammation, fevers, sunstroke, head injuries, haemorrhages, skin eruptions, ringworm, smallpox, harelip, polyps, epilepsy, apoplexy or stroke, toothache, baldness, giddiness and psychiatric disturbances

Stress: this strong constitution thrives on stress but too much tension leads to headaches, fevers and digestive disorders

Herbsl/healing foods: briony, nettles, crowsfoot, honesuckle, rhubarb, tomatoes

Tissue salt: kali phos. (potassium phosphate)

Bach flower remedy: impatiens

Acupuncture meridian: kidney

For optimum health: eat a balanced, nutritious diet and rest regularly; control temper as irritation drains energy.

TAURUS

Humour: melancholic

Temperament: cold and moist

Physiology: throat, vocal cords, neck, thyroid gland, ears

Illnesses: sore throats, diphtheria, thyroid problems and goitre, bronchitis, obesity, earache, genital or uterine problems, metabolic imbalances, a stiff neck

Stress: this sign has a strong constitution but reacts badly to stress, which goes to the throat. An inability to give up and rest, and a tendency to take too much on can result in a stiff neck or other psychosomatic problems

Herbs/healing foods: mint, arrack, beans, elder, celery

Tissue salt: nat. sulph. (sodium sulphate)

Bach flower remedy: gentian

Acupuncture meridian: triple warmer

For optimum health: exercise to let off steam, relax through massage and do not over-eat. Wear a scarf during cold, wet or windy weather.

GEMINI

Humour: sanguine

Temperament: cold and dry

Physiology: nervous and respiratory systems, hands and arms, thymus

Illnesses: nervous diseases, coughs, viral infections, exhaustion, eye strain, rheumatism, sprains or broken bones, infirmities or muscular pain in the arms, shoulders and hands; pulmonary afflictions such as asthma, bronchitis, pneumonia, pleurisy

Stress: this resilient constitution thrives on stress – until total nervous collapse occurs.

Herbs/healing foods: caraway, carrot, fern, haresfoot, lavender, lettuce, cauliflower

Tissue salt: kali mur. (potassium chloride)

Bach flower remedy: cerato

Acupuncture meridian: liver

For optimum health: concentrate on one thing at a time, take regular exercise, relax and sleep well; supplement the diet with vitamins and minerals, especially vitamin C.

CANCER

Humour: phlegmatic

Temperament: cold and moist

Physiology: breasts, lymphatic system, female reproductive organs, alimentary canal.

Illnesses: gastric and digestive disturbances, ulcers, fluid retention, uterine and breast disorders and immune system deficiency

Stress: this sign responds badly to stress, which leads to stomach problems, but recovers quickly. The immune system is strongly affected by emotion

Herbs/healing foods: lemon balm, flax, saxifrage, watercress, milk

Tissue salt: calc. fluor. (calcium fluoride)

Bach flower remedy: clematis

Acupuncture meridian: stomach

For optimum health: maintain emotional balance, avoid worry, eat regularly and let go of resentment and the past.

LEO

Humour: choleric
Temperament: hot and dry
Physiology: heart, spine, lower back
Illnesses: pleurisy, cardiac problems, lower back pain, fevers, jaundice, high blood pressure
Stress: although this sign has a strong constitution, Leo dislikes stress, which quickly affects the back or heart
Herbs/healing foods: bay, celandine, walnuts, plums, peas, oranges
Tissue salt: mag phos. (magnesium phosphate)
Bach flower remedy: vervain
Acupuncture meridian: heart
For optimum health: avoid frustration, exercise regularly, maintain sexual activity and avoid over-indulgence, anger and stress.

VIRGO

Humour: melancholic
Temperament: cold and dry
Physiology: abdomen, intestines, spleen, central nervous system, digestive enzymes, diaphragm
Illnesses: intestinal and nervous disorders including parasites and colic, ulcers, appendicitis, irritable bowel syndrome, eczema and gallstones, hypochondria
Stress: Virgo has a somewhat delicate constitution and tends to run on nervous energy. Stress goes straight to the gut. This sign is prone to psychosomatic ailments
Herbs/healing foods: lavender, caraway, horehound, myrtle, lemons
Tissue salt: kali. sulph. (potassium sulphate)
Bach flower remedy: centaury
Acupuncture meridian: large intestine
For optimum health: stop worrying, relax, try to avoid self-criticism.

LIBRA

Humour: sanguine

Temperament: cold and moist

Physiology: veins, kidneys, liver, lumbar region, endocrine system

Illnesses: kidney complaints including stones; lumbago, sluggish metabolism, chronic fatigue

Stress: stress does not suit this delicate constitution, which reacts with headaches, fatigue and toxic conditions

Herbs/healing foods: aloe, asparagus, chestnuts, daisy, garden mint, strawberries

Tissue salt: nat. phos. (sodium phosphate)

Bach flower remedy: scleranthus

Acupuncture meridian: circulation, sexuality

For optimum health: pamper the body, avoid late nights and over-rich food, detox regularly, and drink plenty of water.

SCORPIO

Humour: phlegmatic

Temperament: cold and moist

Physiology: genitals, male reproductive organs, bladder, urethra, rectum

Illnesses: genital and reproductive disorders, venereal disease, renal stones, ruptures, nasal catarrh, ulcers, adenoids, polyps, constipation, fistulas

Stress: this resilient constitution can use stress to its advantage, but too much causes a decline in libido and can cause chronic constipation. Nervous tension causes shoulder and neck pain

Herbs/healing foods: witch hazel, broom, furze, hops, tobacco, prunes

Tissue salt: calc. sulph. (calcium sulphate)

Bach flower remedy: scleranthus

Acupuncture meridian: bladder

For optimum health: stop pushing too hard, let go, talk things over, eat plenty of roughage and detox.

SAGITTARIUS

Humour: choleric
Temperament: hot and moist
Physiology: sciatic nerve, hips and thighs, pituitary gland
Illnesses: hip disorders, sciatica, rheumatism, pulmonary and liver complaints, fevers, sports injuries, sprains and broken bones
Stress: this sign tends to go all out and then crash, but recovery is swift. Stress can lead to chest infections
Herbs/healing foods: borage, betony, dandelion, moss, asparagus, horsetail, cucumber
Tissue salt: silica (silica oxide)
Bach flower remedy: agrimony
Acupuncture meridian: pancreas, spleen
For optimum health: exercise the body and mind and avoid over-indulgence of any kind.

CAPRICORN

Humour: melancholic
Temperament: cold and dry
Physiology: knees, skin and skeleton, gall bladder, calcium metabolism
Illnesses: skin and digestive disorders, knee and joint problems, tooth decay, depression, chronic fatigue, falling hair, leprosy
Stress: this sign thrives on pressure but doesn't know when to slow down, which can weaken the immune system. Stress often shows in the skin or skeleton, or may result in depression
Herbs/healing foods: comfrey, amaranthus, beet, hemlock, onion, cabbage, kale
Tissue salt: calc. phos (calcium phosphate)
Bach flower remedy: mimulus
Acupuncture meridian: gall-bladder
For optimum health: let go, relax and stop worrying about old age, take long walks, and look after teeth and gums; ensure a good intake of calcium and fresh vegetables.

AQUARIUS
Humour: sanguine
Temperament: cold and dry
Physiology: shins and ankles, circulatory system, pineal gland
Illnesses: varicose veins, sprained ankles, cardiac and circulatory disorders, depression, headaches, cramps, clots, sudden ailments that do not last
Stress: with Uranus as a co-ruler, Aquarius often finds stress stimulating but may rely too heavily on the endurance of Saturn and collapse into exhaustion
Herbs/healing foods: mandrake, heartsease, hemp, medlar, quince, pomegranate
Tissue salt: nat. mur (sodium chloride)
Bach flower remedy: water violet
Acupuncture meridian: lung
For optimum health: slow down, play well, exercise, drink plenty of water and use complementary medicine or have a massage; take personal time out.

PISCES
Humour: melancholic
Temperament: cold and moist
Physiology: the feet, circulatory system, pineal gland, lymphatics
Illnesses: bunions, gout, foot rashes, psychosomatic disorders, especially in the abdomen; liver or renal problems, addictions of all kinds, anaemia, boils
Stress: this adaptive sign responds to stress by flowing this way and that, but eventually succumbs. A sensitive constitution combines badly with a tendency to emotional excess
Herbs/healing foods: evening primrose, dock, fig, sage, dates, raisins, cereals
Tissue salt: ferr. phos (iron phosphate)
Bach flower remedy: rock rose
Acupuncture meridian: small intestine
For optimum health: live near water; do not become over-emotional; avoid drink and drugs, either prescribed or recreational; look after feet and consult a reflexologist or podiatrist.

DIS-EASE

The balance of the elements within a chart can indicate subtle dis-ease, depletion or excess. Imbalances may be innate (the natal chart) or temporary (progressed charts, solar returns and strong transits).

WATER

Depleted water results in thirst, dehydration, cramps, insomnia, poor memory, inability to show feelings

Antidotes to weak water drinking plenty of water, vegetable juices and herb teas; living near water, salt baths or sea bathing; eating moist, juicy foods and garlic; taking up art, wearing tourmaline, pearl, opal or smoky quartz

Excess water creates mucus; causes pneumonia, fluid retention, obesity, clogged arteries, lymphatic retention

Antidotes to excess water exercise; avoiding raw, salty and sweet foods, meat and snacks; drinking diuretic herb teas such as elderflower and nettle; enjoying flute music and social interaction; using rose quartz, pink tourmaline, kunzite, green aventurine or fluorite.

EARTH

Depleted earth results in weakness, incohesion, fractures that fail to heal

Antidotes to weak earth exercise, gardening, working with clay, eating root vegetables

Excess earth creates obesity, blockages, depression, ossification, calcification, loss of sensory sensations

Antidotes to excess earth exercise, less sleep, eating light spicy food, cultivating responsiveness.

AIR

Weakened air results in poor circulation, lack of self-confidence, despondency, nightmares, nausea, toxicity, oxygen deficiency, shortness of breath, fatigue

Antidotes to weak air deep breathing exercises, desert climates, shaking the duvet each morning, eating leafy vegetables, taking long walks or dancing and social activities

Excess air creates nervous disorders, restlessness, hypersensitivity to pollutants, harsh sounds and odours; rough skin, brittle hair, bones and nails, flatulence, asthma, coughs, constipation, insomnia, schizophrenia, arthritis

Antidotes to excess air drinking more fluids, especially chamomile tea, eating wholegrains and leafy vegetables, taking vitamin B complex, magnesium and manganese; hot or steam baths; increasing consumption of edible oil; massaging with hot oil, wearing warm clothes and taking moderate outdoor exercise; humid climates; eating dairy products, wearing deep blue and violet colours; using lapis lazuli, sapphire, aquamarine, blue tourmaline, chrysocola, green calcite; white chestnut remedy.

FIRE

Depleted fire results in low vitality, despondency, loss of appetite, pallor, cold, slow and inadequate digestion, migraine, phobias, low immunity, poor circulation and muscle tone, possible diabetes

Antidotes to weak fire sunshine, aerobic exercise, hot and spicy food and drink including cayenne, cardamon, cinnamon; ginger or peppermint tea; wearing red and orange; applying crystals such as ruby, bloodstone, carnelian, topaz

Excess fire creates anger and aggression, heartburn, liver and gallbladder problems, digestive complaints, ulcers, excess bile, fever, skin eruptions, a tendency to body odour, blurred vision, hypoglycaemia

Antidotes to excess fire applying wet towels to the body, increasing fluid intake, eating sweet foods, drinking chamomile tea, wearing blue and green, applying crystals such as emerald, green garnet, aventurine, malachite, aquamarine, green calcite.

PLANETS, HEALTH AND THE SIXTH HOUSE

The sixth house is the house of health and wellbeing. The sign on the cusp of this house (see pages 250–51) and the planets placed here indicate the type of dis-ease that may arise. As this house is also linked to vocations, placements such as Saturn may indicate that a chronic condition could be experienced through, for instance, a nursing career. If there are no planets in the sixth house, look to the house ruler.

PLANETS AND HEALTH

The planets have long been regarded as indicators of health, or lack of it. They indicate a propensity towards a particular type of dis-ease, especially when placed in the sixth house.

Sun
Vitality and growth. The Sun indicates a propensity to conditions associated with its sign's physiological correlations, being linked to hot, feverish conditions and to the heart. In the sixth house, the Sun indicates a strong constitution.

Moon
Fluid balance within the body, physiological processes, pregnancy and gynaecological conditions, especially those that pass through the matriarchal line. In the sixth house, the Moon suggests that an illness may be psychosomatic.

Mercury
The nervous system and problems arising from excessive mental stimulation or worry.

Venus The kidneys and fluid retention. Its placement in a sign may indicate illnesses caused by self-indulgence or from venereal disease or miasms (subtle influences) passed through the family line.

Mars Connected with all hot, feverish and eruptive conditions, and with stings and bites, and ruling surgery. Mars may indicate lack of coordination and a propensity to accidents caused by impatience or to overwork.

Jupiter The liver and problems arising from over-indulgence and conditions of excessive growth, such as tumours. In the sixth house, Jupiter points to conditions arising out of abuse or misuse of the body in a former life.

Chiron Karmic wounds, hereditary dis-ease and conditions that require integration.

Saturn The connective principle concerned with the bones and skin. Associated with chronic conditions, this depressive planet has the effect of slowing things down, producing blockages, poor functioning and crystallization. In the sixth house, Saturn may indicate a chronic worrier about health and illnesses arising from ingrained attitudes and emotions.

Uranus Accidents, nervous tension and erratic functioning. Uranus can indicate that the electrical circuits of the body are misfiring. Sudden events such as rupture or haemorrhage are likely.

Neptune Implicated in addictions of all kinds and connected to wasting diseases, allergies, lack of energy and psychiatric disturbance and delusions. Neptune conditions are rarely straightforward. Many arise out of over-sensitivity and are best treated with homoeopathy.

Pluto The reproductive and excretory systems or may point to phobias and karmic dis-ease carried forward. Underlying stress may be a cause of dis-ease.

Eclipses

Eclipses – some total, others partial – occur twice a year at new and full moons, with 14 days in between. On rare occasions, there are three eclipses, which in ancient times was deemed a signal of doom and catastrophic events.

During eclipses, the light of consciousness (the Sun) is blocked out, and subconscious and collective forces (the Moon) are able to surface, or rational consciousness (the Sun) overcomes the irrational (the Moon). As such, an eclipse can be the moment that repressed energies burst through with great force, and ingrained attitudes and karma, whether personal or collective, are released.

Eclipses that conjunct planets in an individual's natal chart trigger questions and events around those planets. The house in which the eclipse occurs is also significant, as is any planet which it aspects and any incidence of the eclipse falling on the mid-point between two planets. Due to the way that eclipses are distributed around the heavens, some people never experience the powerful effects on the natal chart, and others are regularly touched by them, but the collective effect is felt by everyone.

THE ECLIPSE EFFECT

An eclipse is like the lunar tide: it draws to the surface all that has been hidden and makes manifest shadow energies. As a time when intuitions and insights can emerge, it can also be extremely positive. Eclipse effects are either personal or collective. The personal occurs when something in the natal chart is triggered, giving rise to unexpected situations that have a personal effect. The collective effect is seen through events in the outside world.

Eclipses and the natal chart

The effect of an eclipse is at its height in the month leading up to the event itself, although there are intimations for up to six months before. If the eclipse aspects a planet in the natal chart, the effect goes on working itself out for six months after the event, and if a transit

A solar eclipse occurs when the Moon is placed between the earth and the Sun.

re-activates the degree of the eclipse within six months, it reiterates the effect. An eclipse is, in effect, a transit to the natal chart. As such, the usual orb allowed is 2°, although transits within 3 to 4 degrees can have a visible effect, particularly when several planets or sensitive points are concerned. The influence wanes as the orb widens.

If an eclipse triggers a sensitive point in a natal chart, it compels that person to let go of whatever is stuck in the past. It is often a time in which inner demons – and angels – are faced. Lunar eclipses in particular can be periods of great inner conflict, when people challenge deeply rooted beliefs about themselves.

Eclipses and the elements

An eclipse is affected by the element in which it falls, producing a challenge in the part of life represented by the element. In fire signs, the eclipse challenges energy flow and activity; in earth signs, physical and material existence; in air signs, mental and communication processes; and in water signs, emotions and security issues.

Eclipses and the houses

The house in which an eclipse falls indicates the area of life in which a cleansing process is required. It may be that you need to shed old attitudes, change your behaviour, let go of the past and accept an ending. If the process is not entered into willingly a crisis may be precipitated, especially if a transiting planet also occupies that house and moves over the degree of the eclipse. This crisis clears the way for a rebirth and for new possibilities to emerge, according to the nature of the house.

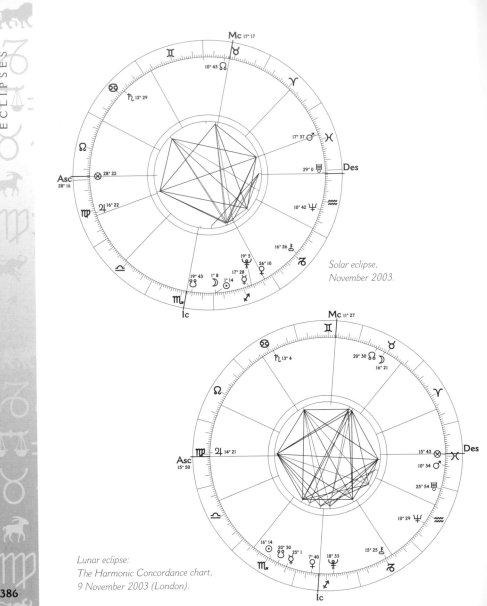

Mc 17° 17

10° 43 ☊

17° 37 ♂ ♓

29° 0 ♅ ——— Des

☊ 12° 29

10° 42 ♆ ♒

Asc
28° 16

⊗ 28° 22

♃ 16° 22

16° 26 ⚷ ♐

19° 5 ♇

19° 43   1° 8   17° 28   26° 10
☋   ☽   ☿   ♀

Ic

*Solar eclipse,
November 2003.*

Mc 11° 27

20° 30 ☊ ☽
16° 21

♄ 13° 4

15° 43 ⊗
10° 34 ♂ ♓ ——— Des
25° 54 ♅

Asc   ♃ 14° 21
15° 50

10° 29 ♆ ♒

16° 14 ⊙   15° 25 ⚷ ♐
20° 30 ☋
25° 1 ☿
7° 40 ♀   18° 33 ♇

Ic

*Lunar eclipse:
The Harmonic Concordance chart,
9 November 2003 (London).*

THE HARMONIC CONCORDANCE

On 9 November 2003 a lunar eclipse conjunct the nodes of the Moon in Scorpio and Taurus formed part of a grand sextile, set around a door to higher consciousness, the Star of David. Many astrologers referred to this formation as the Harmonic Concordance and hoped it would presage world peace and a massive earth healing. In the chart of 9 November, Uranus, the Great Awakener, was isolated at the end of Aquarius with only a square to Mercury connecting it with the rest of the chart. The solar eclipse that followed on 23 November was isolated at the bottom of the chart in Sagittarius, its only aspect an almost exact square to revolutionary Uranus, which had just entered Pisces.

In the weeks between the eclipses, car bombs exploded throughout the world as acts of Uranian terrorism multiplied. Following the eclipses the world began to question the basis of the 'war on terror'. By the time the Nodes reached the exact degree of the lunar eclipse, a new Moon in Leo, on 6 February 2004, squared the lunar eclipse. Enquiries were set in motion on both sides of the Atlantic as to the validity of the intelligence information on which the decision to go to war had been based, but terrorism (Uranus and Pluto) continued. Fundamental changes were called for at all levels and what had been hidden had to be brought into the light.

ECLIPSE QUESTIONS

Eclipses that conjunct planets in an individual's natal chart trigger events and fundamental questions around those planets. The house in which the eclipse occurs is also significant, as is any planet which it aspects and any incidence of the eclipse falling on the mid-point between two planets.

FUNDAMENTAL QUESTIONS

Eclipse conjunct natal Sun How can I shine? How might I be more myself and manifest more of my creativity and potential? How can I parent myself?

Eclipse conjunct natal Moon How can I be more in touch with my feelings? What emotional patterns do I have that are no longer appropriate and what unconscious desires are driving me? How can I release these and find better ways to nurture and parent myself?

Eclipse conjunct Mercury What do I need to communicate? How can I let my old beliefs go and find new ways to think and to communicate?

Eclipse conjunct Venus What do I value? What do I need to change or let go of in my relationships? How can I be more in touch with and express my feminine energy?

Eclipse conjunct Mars How well do I assert myself? What action do I need to take? How could I be more in touch with and express my masculine energy?

Eclipse conjunct Jupiter How can I expand? How can my beliefs grow in truth? What opportunities am I overlooking?

Eclipse conjunct Saturn What responsibilities do I need to shed and what new ones should I take on? What karmic lessons am I learning? What boundaries must I transcend?

Eclipse conjunct Chiron Where do I need to be healed? How can I let go my wounds and integrate new energies?

Eclipse conjunct Uranus What have I been ignoring and what will be the catharsis? What is my inner terrorist doing? How can I find liberation and a catalyst for my growth? How can I change and transform this part of my experience? What must I let go of?

Eclipse conjunct Neptune How do I atone for the past? How can I find at-onement? How can I remove illusion from my life? How can I be more in touch with and express my sources of inspiration and spiritual sustenance?

Eclipse conjunct Pluto What must I eliminate from my life? What must I transform? What secrets am I hiding and what are being hidden from me? How can I use my will and power more constructively?

Eclipse conjunct natal North Node What skills, talents and behaviours might I develop and express in order to become the person I am capable of becoming? How can I fulfil my soul's purpose?

Eclipse conjunct the Ascendant How can I make my mark? How do people perceive me? What lies behind the face I present to the world?

Eclipse conjunct the Descendant How can I find true relatedness? What changes do I need to make in my partnerships?

Eclipse conjunct the Midheaven What can I contribute to society? What should I be striving for? What can I do to be on top of the world?

Eclipse conjunct the IC How can I reach my core? What do I need to put down roots and feel secure?

GLOSSARY

ANGULAR: a house is said to be angular when it commences with the Ascendant, Descendant, IC or MC.

APPLYING: when two planets are not yet in conjunction but the faster of the two will soon 'catch up' the other, they are said to be applying.

AT-ONEMENT: the state of being in harmony with self and the universal spirit energies.

BENEFIC: in traditional astrology, certain planets were designated as particularly beneficial. These benefic planets are Venus (the lesser benefic), Jupiter (the greater benefic), the Sun, the Moon and North Node.

CADENT: a house that precedes the Ascendant, Descendant, IC or MC.

CHART RULER: the ruler of the sign on the Ascendant. In medieval astrology, the ruler was known as the Lord of the Horoscope and was said to be the deity who presided over birth and who guided the individual on his or her path.

COMBUST: a conjunction with an orb of less than 5°.

CUSP: the division between two houses.

DECUMBITURE CHART: the chart drawn up by a medical astrologer to coincide with the onset of illness, used for diagnosis and treatment.

DESPOSITOR: the planet that rules the sign in which the planet is placed. If Mercury is in Leo, for example, the despositor is the Sun.

DETRIMENT: a planet is said to be in detriment, and therefore exerts least influence, when in the sign or house opposite to that which it rules.

DIRECT: the forward motion of the planets, as viewed from earth.

DIS-EASE: a sense of not being at ease within one's physical body or the environment, which may manifest as an illness or emotional or psychiatric disturbance. An individual suffers from dis-ease when the body, mind and emotions are not in harmony.

DOUBLE-WHAMMY: an interaspect between two planets that repeats both ways across the charts. Particularly significant if it reflects an aspect in one or both natal charts.

DUAL SIGNS: extremely adaptable signs that have two distinct sides to their nature. Gemini, Sagittarius and Pisces are included in this category, and Libra may also be considered a dual sign because of its strong need for relationship between two things.

DYNAMIC PLANETS: planets that are active and reactive, that initiate change and have a masculine quality, namely the Sun, Mars, Saturn, Uranus and Pluto.

ECLIPTIC: the apparent path of the Sun around the earth.

EGRESS: the moment a planet moves out of a sign.

ELEVATION: in traditional astrology, the planet closest to the Ascendant or MC was said to be extremely powerful, and as such was able to overcome otherwise malefic or beneficent planets above which it was elevated.

EXALTATION: a planet is said to be in exaltation in the sign where it exerts its most characteristic and powerful influence.

FALL: a planet is said to be in fall when placed in the sign opposite the one in which it exerts its most powerful influence.

FLAT CHART: a chart that uses the Sun as an Ascendant and the Equal House method, constructed to examine an untimed event or if time of birth is unknown.

INGRESS: the moment a planet moves into a new sign.

INTERCEPTED SIGN: a sign that falls wholly within a house, with a partial sign on either side.

LUMINARIES: the Sun and the Moon.

MALEFIC: in traditional astrology, certain planets were felt to have unhelpful intent. These malefic planets are Mars, Saturn and Pluto.

MIDPOINT: the point exactly halfway between two planets, which brings the energies together. Midpoints are significant in natal charts if they coincide with another planetary position, and in transits when a transiting planet activates the midpoint, bringing the two planets into close relationship. Transits to midpoints can often explain events that have no obvious transit link.

MUTUAL RECEPTION: two planets are in mutual reception if each is in the sign of the other's rulership or exaltation.

NEUTRAL PLANETS: planets without significant energy that can be either passive or dynamic according to the planets with which they associate; Mercury and Chiron.

PARALLEL: two planets sharing the same declination north or south of the celestial equator are said to be in parallel. The astrological effect is similar to a conjunction.

PART OF FORTUNE: symbolically, the position of the Moon at sunrise. It is calculated as the same distance away from the Ascendant as the Moon is from the Sun.

PLACID PLANETS: passive planets, namely the Moon, Venus, Jupiter, Neptune.

RECTIFICATION: a process whereby significant events are examined through transits or progressions and their correlation with significant points in the chart such as the Ascendant or Descendant in order to establish the birth time or precise start of an enterprise.

REVERSED NODAL PLACEMENT: the sign of the Node falls in the opposite house to its natural placement. Pisces in the sixth, for example, and Virgo in the twelfth.

RISING SIGN: the sign of the zodiac rising over the eastern horizon at the moment of birth or when a question is asked.

RULERSHIP: planets with particular affinity to a sign were designated as that sign's ruler. The Sun and Moon each rule one sign, and each of the five planets that can be seen by the naked eye rule two signs.

RULERSHIP OF A HOUSE: rulership of a house is assigned to the ruler of the sign on its cusp.

SEPARATING: when two planets, having been in conjunction, move away from each other, they are said to be separating.

SIDEREAL ZODIAC: a zodiac that rotates with the stars.

SIGNS OF LONG AND SHORT ASCENSION: signs of long ascension are slow to rise and those of short ascension rise quickly.

SINGLETON: an unaspected planet. The energy of a singleton is difficult to express but makes itself felt suddenly and unexpectedly, with great force.

STATIONERY: a planet that apparently comes to a standstill before turning retrograde or direct.

STELLIUM: five or more planets in one sign or house are known as a stellium, giving great emphasis to that area of the chart.

SUCCEDENT: a house that falls between an angular and a cadent house.

SYNASTRY: the comparison of two charts to understand the relationship.

TROPICAL ZODIAC: a zodiac that is fixed by the seasons.

BIBLIOGRAPHY

Hall, Judy, *The Crystal Bible*, Godsfield Press, 2003

Hall, Judy, *The Hades Moon: Pluto in aspect to the Moon*, Samuel Weiser, 1998

Hall, Judy, *Karmic Connections*, Wessex Astrologer, 2001

Hall, Judy, *Illustrated Guide to Astrology*, Godsfield Press, 1999

Hall, Judy, *Past Life Astrology*, Godsfield Press, 2002

Hall, Judy, *Patterns of the Past*, Wessex Astrologer, 2000

Hall, Judy, *Sun Signs for Lovers*, Godsfield Press, 2005

Hand, Robert, *Planets in Transit*, Para Research, Rockport MA, 1976

Marks, Tracy, *The Astrology of Self Discovery*, CRCS Publications, 1985

Michelsen, Neil, *The American Ephemerides for the 20th and 21st Centuries*, ASC Publications, San Diego, CA, 1996

Starck, M., *Earth Mother Astrology*, Llewellyn, St Paul, MN, 1990

INDEX

ACKNOWLEDGMENTS

AKG, London/Bibliotheque Nationale 11. **Corbis UK Ltd.**/34, 49, 72, 87, 90 main, 93, 101, 102, 104, 105, 345; /James L. Amos 71 main; /Craig Aurness 58; /Bettmann 181, 204; /Leland Bobbe 39; /Roy Botterell 243; /Andrew Brookes 109; /Christie's Images 209; /Geoffrey Clements 174; /Richard Cummins 46; /Randy Faris 98 main; /Charles Gupton 175; /Richard Hamilton Smith 122; /Martin Harvey/Gallo Images 118; /Herrmann/Starke 80; /Matthias Kulka 12; /Danny Lehman 185; /Araldo de Luca 169, 187, 192, 198; /Francis G. Mayer 179; /Tim Page; /Jose Luis Pelaez 61; /Carmen Redondo 86; /Roger Ressmeyer 8; /Bill Ross 106; /Joseph Sohm/ChromoSohm Inc. 121; /Hubert Stadler 216; /David Turnley 203; /William Whitehurst 157; /Tim Wright 113; /Mike Zens 70. **Creatas**/341/Image Source 15, 319. **Eyewire Images**/253. **Getty Images**/29, 63, 66. 95, 160, 163, 199, 247, 249, 255, 259; /Philippe Poulet/Mission 88. **Octopus Publishing Group Limited**/30, 32, 40, 44, 48, 50 top, 64 top right, 64 bottom left, 71 bottom right, 73, 78, 82, 90 bottom right, 92, 98, 103, 156, 166, 173, 205, 211, 263; /Mark Bolton/Design: Yvonne Mathews & Don Appleby, RHS Chelsea Flower Show 2001 37; /Colin Bowling 94; /Jean Cazals 335; /Steve Hathaway 339; /Alistair Hughes 85, 119, 331; /David Jordan 81; /Andy Komorowski 55 bottom, 111; /David Loftus 114; /Peter Myers 42, 215; /Ian Parsons 65, 180, 323; /Peter Pugh-Cook 245, 325, 337; /William Reavell 45, 69, 241, 261; /Russell Sadur 167; /Debi Treloar 47; /Ian Wallace 74; /Paul White 50 bottom. **Nasa**/152, 172, 178, 184, 190, 196, 202, 208. **Rubberball Productions**/Dreamscapes 79, 161. **Science Photo Library**/Rev. Ronald Royer 384.

Executive Editor Brenda Rosen
Managing Editor Clare Churly
Executive Art Editor Sally Bond
Designer James Lawrence
Illustrator Colin Elgie, Kuo Kang Chen
Production Controller Aileen O'Reilly